Governing Idaho
Politics, People and Power

Governing Idaho
Politics, People and Power

James B. Weatherby
and Randy Stapilus

CAXTON PRESS
Caldwell, Idaho
2005

© 2005 by James B. Weatherby
and Randy Stapilus

Library of Congress Cataloging-in-Publication Data

Weatherby, James Benjamin.
 Governing Idaho : politics, people and power / by James B. Weatherby and Randy Stapilus.-- 1st ed.
 p. cm.
 Includes bibliographical references.
 ISBN 0-87004-447-8 (trade pbk.)
 1. Idaho--Politics and government. 2. Local government--Idaho. 3. Central-local government relations--Idaho. I. Stapilus, Randy. II. Title.

JK7516.W43 2005
320.4796--dc22
    2004029645

Lithographed and bound in the United States of America
CAXTON PRESS
Caldwell, Idaho
172209

C. W. Cornell

CONTENTS

INTRODUCTION

When the United States was created near the end of the eighteenth century, it was fashioned out of whole cloth—invented from scratch. The founders had to make it up as they went along; there were no models.

Idaho was at the other end of the spectrum building off the national model. The physical symbol is the state's capitol building, modeled closely after the United States capitol, albeit on a substantially smaller scale. The legal symbol is the constitution, a document establishing a governmental structure containing a shadow of the federal model, with its three branches and partisan, bifurcated legislature.

The Idaho Constitution is not only based on the earlier federal model, but many state models as well. Some analysts consider it to be merely a modified California state constitution. That may be ungenerous, however, to the influences of the many other states where the Idaho constitution drafters had lived and worked before coming to Idaho. Some of them had helped draft other state constitutions, and apart from some local-specific elements, Idaho's constitution followed a model familiar to lawmakers in most other states.

Idaho lay at the far end of the road in other ways, too. It was not an initial destination for immigrants, and not until around the time of statehood did it even develop a substantial native population. Formed as a territory in 1863 and as a state in 1890, Idaho would not elect a native-born governor until 1930. Its first permanent community was formed by people under the misapprehension they were in another jurisdiction. At the time of statehood, the state's largest city was home to fewer than 2,400 people. It was a place people scurried through when on the Oregon Trail. It would be one of the last places in the contiguous United States to attract substantial numbers of permanent settlers. Eventually, immigrants did come. Idaho has become a growth state, with a substantial multi-generational population of locally-rooted people, and a big component of new arrivals. It is a new mix, and strain sometimes emerges between the new and the old, both operating under a governmental and social structure that did not anticipate such growth.

Idaho remains a divided state, with distinct regions and viewpoints. Neither the eastern nor the northern ends of the state look with particular favor on rapidly-growing Boise. Many concerns and interests remain distinct. Gradually, gently, however, those distinctions are fading. That is best reflected in Idaho politics, sharply competitive for many years, with distinct regional variations, but more recently of a nearly uniform one-party—Republican—hue.

In January 2005 Governor Dirk Kempthorne proposed an ambitious plan for mass upgrading of the state's highway system; one principal component involved improvements to the state's north-south route. (The fastest land route from Boise, the largest community in the south, to Coeur d'Alene, the largest in the north, still lies through Oregon and Washington.) Those distances, while still great, are less than they were just a generation earlier, with massive improvements on a number of highways and other roads. Telecommunications and the Internet revolution have cut distances and barriers, too. If the people of Bear Lake and Bonners Ferry want to attend a Boise City Council meeting, they merely have to dial it in on the Internet; no doubt many other government entities will soon develop their own distance technology.

If in times past a writer would be strained to tell of a single "Idaho," that is less true now. As the people of the North, the East, and the Southwest are ever more drawn together, as Idaho becomes more than ever before a single entity, its totality becomes a logical subject for review.

What follows in this book, in its discussion of politics and structures, interests and issues, is an overview of that totality and the pieces which comprise it. This discussion is not an end-all; no place containing almost a million and a half people, with a history running to a little over a century and a half, is that simple. But this discussion will provide, we hope, a useful starting point.

ACKNOWLEDGEMENTS

Few books are the sole production of its authors, and this one is less so than most. Its genesis stretches back well more than a decade, and its form and content reflects the ideas and insights of a small multitude.

We want to acknowledge with much appreciation the helpful comments and suggestions of those who have read one or more of the chapters of one or more of the many drafts of this book. The list of people helping us in one way or another is lengthy, but we want to offer special thanks to Steve Ahrens, Dan Chadwick, Lorna Jorgensen, John Kincaid, Michael C. Moore, Randy Nelson, Martin L. Peterson, Robert Sims, Alvin Sokolow, Jeff Youtz, Ben Ysursa, Linda Watkins, Dana Lynn Weatherby and John Weatherby.

And thanks go as well to the fine people at Caxton Press, especially Scott Gipson and Wayne Cornell, for their thoughtful editing and for so efficiently shepherding this long-running project into print.

Any errors that remain are, of course, ours.

James B. Weatherby, Ph.D.
Randy Stapilus
March 2005

The Last Place

M oses Alexander became part of Idaho in 1891. Born in Bavaria in a time and place of social and political unrest, he immigrated in 1867 to America, first to New York then—to join in a retail business opportunity—to Chillicothe, Missouri. He blossomed there, building a substantial business and winning election to the city council. Before long he felt the place was changing, crowding in, becoming a place of too little opportunity. He felt a need to move on. He considered Alaska, but en route paused in the new town of Boise, Idaho. He stayed, settled, built from scratch a new business, Alexander's men's clothing store. He helped found the first Jewish congregation in Idaho and eventually won election as mayor of Boise and governor of Idaho—America's first elected Jewish governor.[1]

Ron Rankin became part of Idaho in 1965. He had been a political activist in Orange County, California, a conservative Republican organizer and a local leader of the Barry Goldwater 1964 presidential campaign. But Rankin did not approve of California in the mid-sixties, of few of the political changes and almost none of the cultural changes. Rankin was strongly religious and dedicated to traditional, not new-form, styles of life. So Rankin, his wife and his five children moved north-northeast, to the pretty wooded lake country of Coeur d'Alene, Idaho, and settled there.[2] But he did not settle quietly. Rankin continued his political activism. In 1967, he sought (unsuccessfully) the recall of United States Senator Frank Church because of Church's liberalism and opposition to the conflict in Vietnam. Later Rankin became active in local Republican politics, running for office as an independent and finally, in 1996, winning election as a Kootenai County commissioner. Repeatedly, he rocked the boat of Idaho politics and kept on rocking until his death in October 2004.

For Alexander and for Rankin, Idaho was a place of escape both from unwanted changes and from limitations. Idaho was the last frontier where veteran miners went after most other western boom fields had played out (and before the Alaska fields would draw them north). It was where disaffected southerners came to farm and mine and cut timber, fleeing the destruction of the Civil War. It was where struggling Midwestern farmers came to start anew with—they hoped—fewer obstacles in their path. As the state opened its second century in the 1990s, Idaho was where suburbanites in fast-changing, cutting-edge places like southern California and Seattle fled, looking for a slower paced lifestyle and what they perceived as a more traditional American environment.

Idaho is the home of the last resort, the last frontier—the last place. For these people and for many others, Idaho has been and remains a place to escape to; the more extreme among them see it as the place where they'll make their last stand. Many who come see it as a movie title had it, "My Own Private Idaho."

OPPORTUNITIES: SOCIAL, ECONOMIC AND RESOURCE DRIVEN

For most of the state's history, economic opportunities attracted people to Idaho—a place to mine a fortune, to start a business or to find a new job. The early frontier provided opportunity and space for people to make a new way of life, and these people brought their values with them. The "tillers of the soil" were believers in opportunity but cautious and tight with a buck. The Mormons highly valued family, hierarchy, tradition,[3] and the Confederates cherished traditional values. The individualistic miners and lumbermen were more flexible in their beliefs but strong backers of the work ethic. The migrant waves of the 1990s and early 2000s were driven as much by culture as by economy, helping to make Idaho and the Intermountain West ever more conservative.

As more people arrive, as Idaho moves closer to the mainstream, as its few metro areas (where increasing segments of its population live) become ever more like the rest of the country, Idaho is becoming less "private"—and stands, over time, to become something very different.

Growth has become a challenge. In one survey "rapid growth" was perceived to be the state's "most important problem".[4] Idaho experienced a phenomenal growth rate from the late 1980s to the turn of the millennium, ranking third nationally in job growth for much of that time (up more than 53 percent), and third in population growth from 1990 to 1997. During those same years, manufacturing employment increased over 37 percent (fifth nationally), with high-tech employment increasing by 77 percent.[5]

While the urban areas have grown, rural communities have not. More than 60 percent of Idahoans live in the state's 201 incorporated cities, but 154 of these are under 2,500 in population. The hot spots such as Boise, the capital city, have boomed. *Money Magazine* and *Forbes* are two publications that repeatedly have selected Boise as one of the best cities for starting or operating a business.[6] But many smaller rural communities have slipped into stasis or decline, especially those in agricultural and mining areas where the local economies have stagnated.

Despite its explosive growth, Idaho's culture has changed only gently over the decades. Idahoans have always been slow to change, rarely making major changes in policies to either the left or right. Though Idahoans have flirted with populism and harbored extremists, the far left or right has never dominated Idaho politics, nor shaped its major institutions and attitudes.

The people of Idaho have plenty of room to roam and feel they are getting away from it all. They occupy the land at only 16 persons per square mile (a lower density than all but five other states). Some of Idaho's 44 counties still fit the 1890 census definition of a "frontier county", fewer than two people per square mile. A drive along an Idaho highway may include stretches of 30 and 40 miles without sighting anything that resembles a town.

EARLY MIGRATION PATTERNS

Idaho always has been more than—yet not fully—the frontier that so many other western states have been. Idaho and Nevada are the only states settled initially from the west not from the east. Settlers from California, Oregon, Washington and Utah originally passed over and passed by Idaho, only returning later when they had few options. Idaho was the last of the contiguous states to be seen by Europeans and its vast tracts were among the last to be settled by Euro-Americans.

When early explorers reached the shores of California, the Willamette Valley in Oregon, and the Puget Sound in Washington, they saw hospitable places that all but cried out for settlement. Idaho was part of the obstacle that kept people from easily reaching the Promised Land. When Meriwether Lewis and William Clark crossed northern Idaho, they reported high mountains, thick forests, whitewater rivers and other menaces. Most of the state is occupied by jagged ranges, anchored by the sharply spectacular Sawtooth Range in the center of the state. To this day, mountains make much of Idaho difficult to travel as just one narrow, winding road exists connecting northern and southern Idaho.

About 87 percent of Idaho (all but the northern Panhandle and the southeastern corner) is served by the massive Snake River system. Starting in Wyoming and exiting Idaho into Washington state at Lewiston, in the north-central part of the state, this system has provided much more useful water to the people of the state than ever seen by most other intermountain western states. Available water is one reason Idaho's population is relatively spread out rather than concentrated in bigger urban centers. Southwestern Idaho—with some of the state's fastest-growing cities—is served by the Snake River system, principally by the tributary Boise River. From the north to the southeast, most of the rest of the population of the state similarly is located on or near the Snake River. Tributaries of the Snake serve many of the state's other communities.

Four decades after Lewis and Clark, travelers heading to California, Oregon and Washington on the Oregon Trail, endured the southern Idaho deserts as one of the most hazardous and unpleasant parts of their journey, and gave no thought to stopping there. Southern Idaho is arid, and most of it is true sagebrush desert, mediated in places for human habitation by the technology of irrigation. The Snake River provides water for crops and cities. But few of those possibilities were evident to the earliest travelers.

That reality is a phenomenon stretching back hundreds of years. Idaho was not a traditional settled homeland to any major tribes. The Nez Perce Tribe, which today is located on a reservation in northern Idaho and often is identified with Idaho, was a scattered group of bands spread across parts of Idaho but with key ancestral homelands in the Wallowa area of northeast Oregon. There, not Idaho, is where Chief Joseph longed for his people to return, and where he wished to be buried; his father is buried just outside Joseph, Oregon. Most of the tribes identified with southern Idaho passed through the region, mainly as hunters. Idaho was no more an originally preferred homeland for many Native Americans than it would be for many of the travelers on the Oregon Trail.

The people who stayed in such country—after the boomtowns went bust—were of a special type. They were not only refugees from unwanted change or conditions in other places but, in many cases, many of them also spotted opportunity where others missed it.

Idahoans have this in common, to a point, with the people of Utah whose forebears found prosperity in Salt Lake Valley, a place even more forbidding than southern Idaho. Many places in eastern Idaho have a social and political culture much like Utah's. However, the strain of individualism Idahoans show is much stronger than in Utah; except for the Mormon pioneers in the east, most incoming Idahoans came to the state in small groups or one by one. The Utah pioneers and a few other isolated cases aside, Idahoans did not come to found idealized communities, but to fend for themselves.

POLITICAL CULTURE

A discussion of political culture is essential to a better appreciation of the complexities in Idaho politics. An understanding of this general orientation to politics gives insights into the importance given to political participation, deference to political authority, attitudes toward major social issues, and willingness to change the society.

Daniel Elazar, who has written about political culture as much perhaps as any scholar, points to at least three subcultures in the American political culture—traditionalistic, moralistic and individualistic.[7]

The southern plantation economy and politics shaped traditionalistic subculture, where well-defined social, political and economic elites predominated. This subculture places little emphasis on public participation; competition within society is among the elite rather than among the public in general. Government preserves the status quo, including perpetuation of the governing elite. Idaho was affected by the traditionalistic subculture in its early settlement days, when many southerners (confederate Democrats) migrated to the new territory during and after the Civil War. But generally, the traditionalistic subculture clashed with the individualism and equality of the frontier; it never really took hold in Idaho. The individualistic subculture is based on the "marketplace" model of politics where government is seen as promoting the interests of individuals rather than the common good. The focus is on the private interests of individuals rather than the general concerns of the community. In this view, government's role is viewed as minimal and as largely a threat to economic progress, and should allow individuals to freely pursue economic gains. This subculture is based upon the 19th century European immigration that spread to the mid-Atlantic states. Some of these immigrants moved to Idaho, particularly among the miners and lumbermen of northern Idaho. Individualism, unlike traditionalism, found fertile soil in the western frontier where the emphasis was upon rugged individualism.

The moralistic subculture is a sharp contrast to individualism. The concept of the commonwealth is emphasized in this subculture. General interests are more highly valued than individual interests. Government's role is to promote the public interest and there is a strong feeling that all have a duty to participate to further the public interest. Openness and ethics in government are extolled.

Government or community action is a positive force in the society and can be used for social and economic regulatory purposes. Elazar traced this subculture originally from the Puritans in New England and the Scandinavian and German Protestants who moved across the northern part of the country to settle in the West.

Within the framework of his analysis, Elazar classified Idaho as a mixed moralistic and individualistic state, much like each of its neighboring states except Oregon, where Elazar viewed a moralistic culture as being dominant. This mixed classification is no doubt based upon the fact that no one subculture has completely dominated another. Individualistic orientation has been more typical of northern Idaho attitudes while the moralistic subculture has been more reflective of southern Idahoans. Northern Idaho's loggers and miners took an individualistic approach: government's role was to provide minimal service and not to get in the way of making profits. Southern Idahoans, influenced by Midwestern farmers and Mormons, were more commonwealth-oriented: the needs of the community were paramount over the needs of an individual, especially when it came to irrigating southern Idaho.

Though Elazar's characterization of the Idaho political culture remains relevant, the culture is neither static over time, nor consistent from one geographic location to the next. As the country has become more mobile and mass communications have reached into virtually every home, the subcultures have become somewhat blurred as the country and its political cultures have become considerably nationalized.

Today, these traits continue to be important despite the rapid growth in the state.

Idaho's moralistic political climate is reflected in huge turnouts at statewide races. Idaho has been among the national leaders in voter turnout, validating Elazar's characterization of Idaho as having a significant moralist strain. Idahoans take seriously their duty to vote. Since 1948, Idaho has led the nation in turnout percentage in five general elections. In 20 elections, it has been in the top 10 in voter turnout.

It is the individualistic streak in Idaho that has led to some of the state's most unwanted notoriety. Said one observer, "As far as most of the world knows, northern Idaho is an uncivilized fragment of Northwest geography that is home to racists and fringe cult figures . . .northern Idaho has become a cruel national joke, a stereotypical haven for weirdos and racists." [8] Idaho is one of the least ethnically diverse states in the nation; as in most non-coastal western states, relatively few minorities live here. National news reports would suggest the state is a haven for neo-nazis, survivalists and conspiracy theorists; reality is that these residents are small in number and have little political or social impact on the larger society. Today, human rights activists far outnumber the extremists. There is another reason for the strong strain of individualism in Idaho. While many western and Midwestern states long were economic vassals of large faraway cities, Idaho has an unusually strong record of developing large homegrown businesses. The concept of the large corporation is often tied, in the minds of many Idahoans, with entrepreneurship—and with individualism.

Idahoans may believe in opportunity but they do not think it comes easy, and they respect people who seize it. Idaho's homegrown business leadership tends to be celebrated as much as envied and Idahoans understand the economic benefits of being the home to corporate headquarters. Though perhaps less true with the new millennium, analysts have said that "Nowhere in the Intermountain West, not even Denver, is this much corporate control to be found." [9] Few states look upon big business in quite the same way as Idaho.

CONSERVATISM AT THE POLITICAL CENTER

The center of the political spectrum in Idaho is much further to the right than that of its neighbors Oregon and Washington. That does not mean Idahoans are reactionary.

The 1994 election resulted in the first unified state government in 24 years—the same party controlled the executive and legislative branches and that has held true since. Despite this unification the next several sessions of "veto-proof" legislatures failed to result in major changes. The 1971–1994 tax policies and other major initiatives of the pre-unification Democratic administrations of Cecil Andrus and John Evans were left in place. These Democratic governors had successfully sponsored state funding for kindergartens, local land use planning, and increased support for economic development activities, but the single-party Republican legislature did not sharply cut taxes —a slice of the income tax in 2001 excepted—or slash budgets, nor pass major conservative social legislation.

Idaho legislators seem to reflect the sentiment of a majority of Idahoans; both are slow to accept change. Idahoans may be among the last to adopt new programs, but having adopted them they are reluctant to abandon them. There is in Idaho a healthy regard for existing policies and institutions. Two reactionary property tax ballot measures were defeated in the 1990s. A 1994 initiative proposition that would have discriminated against gays was defeated, while election of conservative Republicans swept the state.

The conservative attitude toward regulatory and tax policies and the role of government in general reveals an anti-government skepticism: government should support economic endeavors, not interfere, not intrude. Until 2005, Idaho was one of only nine states that did not regulate general contractor licensing. On either a per capita or income basis, Idaho ranks close to the bottom in many public spending categories. Like many other states, social welfare programs have not fared very well in Idaho nor are they enthusiasiastically supported by the general public.[10]

Idahoans' conservatism is also demonstrated in the concern for private property rights. Government is limited so that it does not encroach upon those rights even though a major land use planning bill was enacted in 1975 that included extraterritorial planning and zoning. "Takings" legislation of major significance has passed in other states but not in Idaho; a 2003 takings bill that did pass was notable more for its symbolism than substance. As in most other western states, water rights are considered an adjunct of property rights, and taken very seriously. Idahoans understand very well that the state is heavily dependent upon water, especially for irrigation of the vast arid spaces in southern Idaho. The politics of water resource development has been largely influenced by the need to protect water rights.

Idaho statehood in 1890 came just as irrigation was beginning to become an important economic and social factor in Idaho. An entire article in the state constitution is devoted to water; no other state constitution has such an article. Like most other western states, Idaho is considered a "prior appropriation" state; water is considered to be public property, and use of it is allowed through application for a water right to put it to beneficial use. Regulation of these rights – which are considered, in some respects, personal property even though tied to specific pieces of land—is undertaken by the state Department of Water Resources.

Idaho was among the states that adopted the Progressive Era reforms of initiative and referendum, but in contrast to its western coastal neighbors, those tools have been only modestly used in the Gem State. Reverence for tradition is a moderating, or limiting, force in Idaho. Only on unusual occasions does a voter initiative reach ballot status, win voter approval, and truly shake up the state. It has happened, but not often—and may happen less often in the future. Idahoans remain skeptical of radical change, despite their populist inclinations.

LAY OF THE LAND – "GEOGRAPHIC EXTREMISM"

Idaho's odd shape, the result of Congress carving out several other states from its original boundaries, has led to what journalist Neal Pierce has called "geographic extremism" and political scientist Martin has called a "sectional state".[11] One cannot understand its politics or people without understanding how divided Idaho is geographically.[12] **(See the map of Idaho in Figure 1)**

Idaho is said to have three state capitals. Boise is the capital in the southwest, the most populous and the major metropolitan region of the state. Salt Lake City is the capital of the southeast, with its connections to the religious and cultural origins of this region. Theological and social aspects of Mormonism have acted to separate Mormons from others in the state while strengthening their bond with neighboring Utah. Many residents in northern Idaho claim Spokane, Washington as their capital. Distance and topographical barriers separate the northern region from Idaho's political center in Boise, while Spokane serves the scattered communities of northern Idaho with many services including business services and headquarters, air transportation and media. Activists in the north have made attempts to separate from Idaho and join in the formation of a new state to be named Columbia or Lafayette that would unite northern Idaho, eastern Washington and western Montana. At the new millennium, federal and local officials considered the idea of uniting Spokane County, Washington, and Kootenai County, Idaho, in a single metropolitan statistical area, since they appeared to meet the requirements.

The frontier image of the rugged individualist has more currency in northern Idaho. Wilderness areas and forests are all around, and these seem most attractive to various types of "individuals" who can find somewhat safe harbor in the mountains of the region—such as Randy Weaver ("Ruby Ridge" recluse), Christopher Boyce (Soviet spy) and Richard Butler (neo-Nazi). These three may not be typical of the region, but they do suggest some of the lines of attraction. It is also, according to public opinion surveys, friendlier to minority groups even though the area is noted as the haven for "neo-Nazi activity".[13]

Population migration has impacted the partisan variations in the state, though it has not softened its regional cleavages. Many of the new residents came from the West—primarily Washington, Oregon and California—mostly to southwestern Idaho and in the Panhandle region. Unlike the gold miners and lumbermen before them, many came for cultural reasons—to find refuge, or to "seek out their own kind." This migration pattern has meant that the state has become more conservative, more Republican. Northern Idaho, traditionally a

Democratic stronghold, became mostly Republican in the 1990s reflecting the views of the newcomers. Several Intermountain West states once considered politically competitive have become virtually one-party states, and Idaho is foremost among these.[14]

Regionalism has impacted Idaho from the days of the earliest settlements. Regional interests promoted fights over the location of the capitol, and two years after Idaho was declared a territory, Boise interests literally stole the capitol (the seal and official papers) from Lewiston in northern Idaho. The "Mormon question" was addressed in 1884 by legislators from Boise and northern Idaho voting to officially prohibit Mormons (or, more precisely, anyone accepting the key tenets of that church) from holding office. Polygamy is still among the "pernicious practices" listed as prohibited in the state constitution.

Regional differences are apparent in voting patterns on statewide ballot measures in the 1990s. Rapid growth in northern Idaho brought out strong support for a major property tax limitation measure (one-percent initiative) with rising valuations virtually forcing higher property taxes. This region also is more likely to support development impact fees, whereas many southern Idahoans are more likely to oppose them. Northern Idahoans are more inclined to support term limits on state and local government officials, whereas southeastern Idahoans are generally opposed.[15]

Fighting over public facilities sites and funding continues even today. A major state university is located in each of the three regions of the state. Rivalries over funding issues have particularly been exacerbated by the rapid growth in southwestern Idaho, which has resulted in sharply increased enrollments at Boise State University.

Regional in-fighting has also been demonstrated by the conflicts over roles and missions at the three universities. The most dramatic example was raised when the state's largest private employer, Micron Technology, announced in the 1990s that its major expansion might occur outside Idaho. One of the reasons for out-of-state expansion was that southwestern Idaho (Boise State University) did not have an engineering school. That lead role and mission had been given to the University of Idaho in northern Idaho. Within a couple of years, and after considerable lobbying, the policy was changed and Boise State University was allowed to develop an engineering program.

Transportation funding is particularly important in the West where people often travel long distances between cities. The politics of highway funding reveals fierce regional conflict. Historically, northern Idahoans have believed that they do not get their fair share of state highway monies, and look with envy upon the safe southern four-lane interstate highways while they (excepting the short run through the area of Interstate 90) are forced to drive on treacherous two-lane roads. One statewide poll of driver satisfaction resulted in positive marks from southern Idahoans, but strong dissatisfaction by 47 percent of northern Idahoans.[16] U.S. Highway 95, which runs from Nevada to the Canadian border, is described by northern representatives as merely one of Idaho's roads in that part of the state, while southern Idaho legislators are more likely to regard it as "North Idaho's road."

The regions also split on liquor legislation. Northern Idaho legislators have historically fought to repeal liquor sales restrictions, while southern Idaho legislators, particularly in southeastern Idaho, have supported them.[17] Legislators have fought over the maintenance of the state monopoly liquor dispensary, which operates liquor stores across the state. Generally, legislators from northern Idaho have fought for privatization, while eastern Idahoans have backed the state monopoly. Lawmakers also have clashed over quotas on issuance of liquor licenses and distribution of liquor profits. Individualistic northern Idahoans prefer the market determining the number of licenses. Moralistic southern Idahoans prefer the more closed quota system. The distribution of profits for the liquor stores is yet another matter. "Dry" or light drinking southeastern Idahoans have preferred per capita distributions. Northern and southwestern Idahoans have preferred a point of sales distribution that allocates profits according to where the sales are actually made.

Because of all the differences, Idaho does have a distinctive political culture. Although conservative, Idaho politics has not been reactionary. Despite its strong conservative leanings, Idaho has a somewhat surprising history of voting for social reform. Idahoans have long felt uneasy about the big and the out-of-control. They supported William Borah's isolationism early in the 20th century, and in the 1960s this conservative state declined to oust Senator Frank Church for his calls to withdraw from Vietnam. Idahoans dislike the imposition of the world at large; they want the world at large to keep some distance.

Idahoans clearly care about their state, and identify with it. Since it is, after all, the "last place".

Chapter 1 notes

1 Robert Sims and Hope Benedict, eds., *Idaho's Governors: Historical Essays on their Administrations* (Boise, ID: Boise State University, 1992).
2 Jonathan Tilove, "The New Map of American Politics," The American Prospect (May 1999); and numerous other sources.
3 Neal R. Peirce and Jerry Hagstrom, *The Book of America: Inside Fifty States Today* (New York: Warner Books, 1984).
4 David R. Scudder, *Idaho Policy Survey, #8* (Boise, ID: Social Science Research Center, Boise State University), 1997.
5 Phillip M. Burgess and Richard F. O'Donnell, *Western Political Outlook* (Denver: Center for the New West), 1998.
6 Paul Beebe, "New West will be more than chips," *The Idaho Statesman*, October 1, 1995, p. B-1.
7 Elazar, Daniel, *American Federalism: A View from the States*, 2nd ed. (New York: Harper & Row, 1984).
8 Quoted in Stephen Shaw, "Harassment, Hate, and Human Rights in Idaho," in *Politics in the Postwar American West,* ed. Richard Lowitt (Norman, OK: University of Oklahoma Press, 1995), p. 94.
9 Peirce and Hagstrom, *Book of America*.
10 Scudder, *Policy Survey, #8.*
11 Boyd A. Martin, "The Sectional State," in *Politics in the American West*, ed., Frank Jonas (Salt Lake City: University of Utah Press, 1969).
12 Leslie R. Alm, Ross E. Burkhart, W. David Patton, and James B. Weatherby, "Intrastate Regional Differences in Political Culture: A Case Study of Idaho," State and Local Government Review 33, no. 2 (spring 2001): 109-119.
13 See Idaho Public Policy Surveys, 1989-1999
14 Michael Barone, "Divide and Rule," *National Journal*, no. 28 (July 12, 1997): 1411.
15 Alm, et. al.
16 Betsy Z. Russell, "Unlike others, North Idaho drivers pan roads," *Idaho Spokesman Review*, February 2, 2000, p. 1 (The Handle).
17 Betsy Z. Russell, "Bill would revise hard-liquor laws," *Idaho Spokesman Review*, February 26, 2000, p. 1 (The Handle).

CHAPTER 2
REGIONAL DIVERSITY

I n the late 1990s, it was an event that splashed photos and front page stories across the state: a deteriorating bridge on north-south U.S. Highway 95 just north of Riggins had to be replaced. The road north and south of the bridge hugged low mountains and ran next to the Salmon River. The bridge across the Salmon was to be moved about fifty feet to the side, and a new one built. Traffic would continue, for the short term, to use the old, moved bridge. There were no alternate routes—not for a hundred miles east or west.[1]

During the brief period when the old bridge was completely out of commission, traffic headed to northern or southern Idaho had to be routed hundreds of miles out of the way, deep into Washington and Oregon on the west, or through Montana on the east. Highway 95, often derided as a "goat trail" for its narrow and twisting character, is the only road connecting northern and southern Idaho. The Salmon River is often considered the dividing line between the region, partly because the North's Pacific Time Zone meets the South's Mountain Time Zone at the Riggins Bridge. And the bridge is significant for another reason: Idaho is one of the few states whose population is substantially split by time zone boundaries.

No alternate routes may ever be built. One reason is that much of the middle of Idaho is wilderness or wild country, congressionally designated as road-less. The only roads running through the remote backcountry are United States Forest Service or river resort roads best traversed with four-wheel drive vehicles during the summer. Idaho has the second-largest single wilderness area, in the lower 48 contiguous states, the Frank Church-River of No Return Wilderness; it includes parts of six national forests and four counties. But another reason—the reason no roads were built in the first place, even before the wilderness laws—is that this is extremely rugged country.

In most of Idaho you cannot go far without running into mountains; about 80 mountain ranges split people and watersheds.

To Idaho's east lie the Rocky Mountains, and the plains and deserts within and beyond them. Much of the eastern border with Montana is defined by the Continental Divide, from which all of Idaho's water flows west to the Pacific Ocean, while nearly all of Montana's goes the other way. To the south lie the Great Basin and the many mountain ranges of Utah and Nevada. To the north, the Canadian Rockies; and to the west, hundreds of miles of desert few people outside the area associate with the usual images of Washington and Oregon.

The mountains are a moderating influence. They affect the weather, for example. Most of Idaho's weather comes from the west, from the Pacific coast, and after a day or two most of Idaho gets some variation of what hits the Pacific coast in Oregon and northern California. But the variation is important, because the coastal and interior mountains wring most of the moisture from the cloud systems before they get to Idaho (though this is less true in northern Idaho); and the mountain ranges tend to slow winds and ease temperature fluctuations. The result is that Idaho is not nearly so temperate and moist as the Pacific coast, but much less windswept and extreme in temperature fluctuations than the Great Plains.

The mountains also have a moderating effect on people. They tend to slow immigration, or at least have through most of the state's history.

Boise's metropolitan area, with its communications, transportation and other services, is growing rapidly. Boise has the largest shopping center in the vast area between Denver, Portland and Seattle. Electronic and road links in Idaho were vastly improved in the 1980s and 1990s.

But settlement in Idaho is far flung. In most interior western states, population is overwhelmingly centered around one or two large metropolitan areas: Salt Lake City in Utah, Denver and Colorado Springs in Colorado, Phoenix and Tucson in Arizona, Albuquerque in New Mexico, Las Vegas and Reno in Nevada. People in Idaho are more spread out: about 60 percent live outside the Boise (Ada-Canyon County) area. That is changing gradually, however, as the Boise area is growing faster than the state overall.

Although Boise is clearly the dominant city, the many Idahoans who live far from it—the state reaches north 500 miles from Boise and east 300 miles—feel little connection to it. Anti-Boise feeling periodically waxes strong in the east and even stronger in the north.

But the whole situation is more complex: each region looks with suspicion at each of the others.

NORTHERN IDAHO

Regionalism is particularly important in northern Idaho, which nearly split off from southern Idaho a century ago. Secession movements periodically crop up, and half-baked discussion of the idea persists. As late as 1983, some local governments passed resolutions calling for secession. The north considers itself part of the Pacific Northwest, not the Intermountain Rockies, and it keeps any eye on Seattle. As many social observers have pointed out, Idahoans often refer to the Panhandle and the area just south of it—the northernmost ten counties—as "North Idaho," rather than north*ern* Idaho.

The distinction is significant. Secessionist movements in the northern part of the state, some fanciful and some serious, are grounded in a sense that southerners have little feeling for or understanding of the northern part of the state. An independent candidate for governor in 1962 campaigned on the platform of "northern Idaho the 51st State." One popular Panhandle bumper sticker of the 1980s read: "North Idaho: a state of mind." It was soon followed with: "South Idaho: a mindless state." Every two years since the early sixties, on the weekend following the general election, the North Idaho Chamber of Commerce invites all of the members of the Idaho Legislature to a northern Idaho tour, usually based either in the Coeur d'Alene or Lewiston area. It is, they suggest, the only way that the Idaho Legislature, which meets in the southern city of Boise and which is comprised mostly of southern members, will see or understand much of northern Idaho. Among the population, the feeling of separateness persists. In northern Idaho, people do see themselves as Idahoans, but as a different breed.

Northern Idaho's economy traditionally has been based on timber production and on mining. Labor unions have been strong in many of these natural resource-based communities, one reason so many of them have a Democratic heritage. Much of this is changing. The mining economy so critical to Shoshone and Kootenai counties, largely went bust in the early 1980s after a century of generally strong performance. Shoshone County is the only county in Idaho to lose population in both the 1980s and 1990s, and its population at the turn of the century was barely two-thirds of what it was in 1980.

The northernmost county of the state, Boundary, sits flat against the Canadian border and has United States Customs offices at Porthill and Eastport, and a substantial transportation hub at its small county seat, Bonners Ferry. But this county, where people are about nine hours away from their state's seat of government in Boise, is not where people go to be in the center of activity. People come here to get away from big cities, from modern life, from the complexities of society. It is a place of escape even now. This is where, in the 1990s, white separatist Randy Weaver chose to make his home at Ruby Ridge, several miles outside the small community of Naples. He set up a heavily-armed fortress on his hillside, and conflict was perhaps inevitable when federal authorities pursued weapons and other charges to his front door. The 1992 shootout brought Idaho back into the national spotlight and has been the subject of several books. Remarked one observer about Ruby Ridge, "Its details hum in Web sites on the Internet, scream from right-wing newsletters, fill government reports, and resonate in the minds of people who have no trouble imagining themselves in that besieged cabin."[2]

Northern Idaho—like rural eastern Washington to the west and rural Montana to the east—has attracted extremist and separatist elements in the last two decades. Sandpoint, the fast-growing community a half-hour's drive south of Bonners Ferry, entered the national consciousness in 1995 for related reasons. When Mark Fuhrman, the former Los Angeles city police detective involved in the O. J. Simpson investigation, found Los Angeles an uncomfortable place to be, he moved to Sandpoint. The national news media followed him there, and (to the irritation of many residents) pointed out that this was the community he now called home. In fact, a high number of retired southern California police officers have moved to the Sandpoint and Coeur d'Alene areas, describing it as a safer and more pleasant place to live than southern California. Some observers noted that the presence of only a small ethnic minority population in northern Idaho probably was not lost on them, either.

These factors—the remoteness, the ease of living, the homogenous white population, a sense that they were moving into what America once was—also were drawing cards for the white separatists and supremacists who moved into the area. Most of the attention went to the now-razed Aryan Nations compound near Hayden Lake, close to Coeur d'Alene. The compound was a fenced area patrolled by guard dogs, overseen by watch-towers and containing substantial amounts of firearms and ammunition. Most people living in the area considered it a blight on their community, and were not sad when the Aryans (about 40 members strong) lost a civil lawsuit to a woman who said she and her son were harassed while driving nearby. The compound was seized, sold at auction, and demolished in 2001; the land was later turned into a human rights center. After that, supremacist activity in the area diminished. A few supremacists have run for office in the area; all have been defeated overwhelmingly, even Aryan Nations leader Richard Butler who ran for Mayor of Hayden in 2003. Though this area may be better known for these neo-nazi groups than for anything else, in fact a large group of elected and civic leaders in Bonner and Kootenai counties have been national spokesmen on behalf of humanitarian and anti-racist activities.

Several effective counter groups have formed and far reaching anti-hate and harassment state laws, among the most comprehensive anti-discrimination laws in the nation, have been passed. "Even though we have the most comprehensive set of laws against hate crimes of any state in the nation, the racists continue to recruit on a message that this state will somehow welcome them," said Tony Stewart, head of the Kootenai County Task Force on Human Relations, in Coeur d'Alene. "It's a cloud that we've been under for a long time." [3]

The north has some of Idaho's finest recreation country. Lake Pend Oreille with the city of Sandpoint perched on its northern shore, is the largest lake in Idaho, and Lake Coeur d'Alene with the city of Coeur d'Alene on its northern shore, is Idaho's second-largest lake. Both are national tourism and resort draws, and the Hagadone Corporation has built an international-quality resort at Coeur d'Alene which draws meeting groups and tourists from around the globe. Along with Sun Valley, it is Idaho's leading tourist destination.

Tourism is increasingly becoming key to the Panhandle economy. Coeur d'Alene was once a timber town, but that activity decreased in the late twentieth century. The community has become more oriented toward tourism, toward serving the large number of retirees who have moved there since the 1960s, and some high-tech development also is underway.

Tourism is taking over Shoshone County as well. This is the cradle of the famous "Silver Valley," or more formally, the Coeur d'Alene Mining District. The area includes the cities of Kellogg, Osburn, Smelterville, Wallace and Mullan. It has produced more than $4 billion worth of silver, has been among the ten leading mining districts in the world, and employed thousands of people, many organized into strong labor unions. But the collapse in silver prices led to the shutdown of the Bunker Hill and most other mines in the district.[4] Community leaders have searched for economic alternatives and have heavily promoted the valley as a tourism site.

Tourism and other economic development has resulted in increased population in much of the Panhandle. The cities just outside Coeur d'Alene—Post Falls, Rathdrum, Hayden—have added new businesses and subdivisions at a startling rate. Kootenai County, the fifth most populous county in Idaho in 1980, ranked fourth in 1990, and third in 2000. It is now home to more than 100,000 people. It is part of the Spokane metropolitan area, and like most of the north, looks to Spokane as its regional center.

The rest of northern Idaho—the counties of Benewah, Latah, Nez Perce, Clearwater, Lewis and Idaho—are changing more slowly. Timber production remains important in all these places, and the largest single employer—Potlatch Corporation, with its large timber production facility at Lewiston—continues to be a very strong economic player. Timber employment, however, has gradually decreased as automation has replaced some jobs, as timber supplies from national forests and elsewhere have diminished, and as some timber production moved to other parts of the country or overseas. Dryland farming of wheat and some other crops also has been a mainstay of the local economy across the vast hill country, split by the Washington-Idaho border, called the Palouse.

Lewiston is home to a peculiarity—the state's only port, located about 300 miles inland from the Pacific Ocean. It is a working port used by many farmers and others from around Idaho. That fact has been central to a long-running debate over how best to save endangered salmon runs in the area. Some salmon advocates say the best approach involves breaching the four lower Snake River dams downstream in Washington state. If that happened, however, the Port of Lewiston might be lost, and with it a sizable chunk of the Lewiston economy. For that reason, "dam breaching" has been opposed by many Idaho politicians, who have suggested other approaches to helping the salmon runs.

Along with tourism, timber, and farming, higher education plays an important economic role in northern Idaho. Latah County is home to the University of Idaho at Moscow, the state's land grant higher education institution. With Lewis-Clark State College at Lewiston and Washington State University at nearby Pullman, north-central Idaho is unusually centered on higher education concerns.

SOUTHWESTERN IDAHO

The same kind of timber, tourism and farming economy continues south into southwestern Idaho, in the forested mountain country where most of the land is managed by the United States Forest Service, but the structure and the balance of the economy vary.

Reliance upon timber has continued to be an important part of the local economy south to Valley, Adams, Boise and Gem counties. Timber still is cut but the sawmills that were economic centerpieces in the smaller counties here through the twentieth century have diminished, and with the new millennium have almost disappeared. In the cases of Riggins and McCall, mills burned to the ground in the 1970s and were not rebuilt. Even so, both waterfront communities were booming in the 1990s with new tourism and resort development. Other towns, including Council (mill closed in 1995), Horseshoe Bend (mill closed in 1998), Cascade (mill closed in 2001), and Emmett (a large mill closed in 2001), face less certain futures. All hope for development of tourism or bedroom communities, and sometimes other businesses as well. For example, a large marketing research firm set up offices in Council in 1997 citing the low cost of doing business there (but moved back to Boise a few years later).

In the valleys and further south along the Payette, Weiser and Boise River basins, and in the desert lands east to Mountain Home, an intensive system of irrigation was developed around the turn of the 20th century and continues to sustain a usually prosperous irrigation-based farm economy. Almost all the valleys of southern Idaho are desert in nature, and creative use of water is a precondition for comfortable human habitation. The climate generally is dry in the lower elevations. Snowpack accumulating in the nearby mountains will dictate whether flood, drought, or moderate water levels dominate the spring, summer and fall to come.

Canyon County is the center of irrigation activity in southwestern Idaho. The state's largest man-made lake, Lake Lowell, was built specifically to provide a base for irrigation water. Canyon County, now Idaho's second most populous county, began as a farm county and much of its economic base is still farm-oriented.

The original development of southwestern Idaho, like much of northern Idaho, was prompted by mining. Boise County in the 1860s and 1870s was the site of the Boise Basin Mining District. In Owyhee County major mining developments also arose about the same time and prompted the need for supply towns. The role Coeur d'Alene and Lewiston filled for mining districts to the north, was played by Boise and later Nampa in the southwest.

Since 1865, when it became the capital of Idaho Territory, Boise has been the state's leading city and the undisputed center of southwest Idaho. While northern Idaho looks to Spokane and Washington state for much of its economic base and social life, and eastern Idaho looks south to Utah and Salt Lake City, southwest Idaho is simply too far from the nearest population centers of Portland or Reno to look to any place but itself. Southwest Idaho is the part of the state that most securely considers itself "Idaho," and that has, in some ways, the most clearly distinctive culture. More than elsewhere, it is where the libertarian and religious strains of Idaho conservatism meet and jostle, and attempt to bridge their differences—or go to war.

Boise had other advantages over other mining supply towns. It was located on the Oregon Trail—a major thoroughfare; a military fortress protected the town; it was the location of state government with many federal and other offices soon to come; and toward the end of the century, there was the rapid growth of agriculture. Within a decade of its founding in 1863, Boise became the largest city in Idaho and has been ever since, with a brief exception in 1962 when Pocatello surpassed it. Boise has grown, albeit slowly at times, almost continuously throughout its history. Since the late 1980s the Boise area of impact has nearly doubled in size, and the neighboring communities of Nampa, Meridian, Kuna and Eagle are the fastest-growing cities in the state. In the 2000 census, Nampa vaulted from fourth to second place among Idaho cities, Meridian from twelfth to fifth, and Eagle—which was not even incorporated until 1971—was the third-fastest growing city in Idaho. The Boise area anchors Idaho's population. Ada and Canyon counties together hold about 40 percent of the state's population, and the southwest region overall has about half.

Boise has been a corporate headquarters city for many years, but typically not heavily dependent on manufacturing as a centerpiece of its economy. That changed in the 1980s and 1990s as Micron Technology and Hewlett-Packard became the Boise area's two largest private employers. Both firms operate massive manufacturing plants around Boise: Micron on the east side, Hewlett-Packard on the west.

Idaho's farm communities are almost all Republican in orientation; in fact, southern Idaho is so generally Republican that exceptions can be considered as special cases. And there are special cases, from the small Democratic base at Emmett (because of unionized timber mill workers there when the sawmill was in operation) to the central and northern parts of Boise where the large number of government workers and Boise State University students and affiliates tend to vote Democratic.

THE MAGIC VALLEY

Apart from the high and often still remote mountains, most of southern Idaho is desert country. East of Boise most of the landscape away from the Snake River and its tributaries is desert-like, and vast tracts of it are simply uninhabitable. The Craters of the Moon National Monument is the most extreme variation on this theme, where black lava flows overrun thousands of square miles from the Blackfoot and Arco areas to the mountains north of Gooding and Mountain Home. This is an immense flat plain where almost no human activity of any kind takes place. In some areas, as in the Monument, the lava flows are still so sharp that no plants grow, no large animals live, and the rocks swiftly chew through the shoes of anyone foolish enough to try to hike across them. Detailed maps of Idaho still show a large oval area across the southern part of the state, north of the Snake River, bearing no indications of settlement or human activity or any other topographic details—because there are none, and may never be.

Little of southern Idaho would have appeared naturally inviting to travelers on the Oregon Trail. Then ingenuity was employed, based on the bisection of this vast desert by the Snake River. East of what is now Bliss, more than 100 miles past Burley and Rupert this area became a massive reclamation project. Private developers such as Ira Perrine, along with the federal Bureau of Reclamation, brought irrigation. This region, which runs from the Sun Valley area south to Nevada, and from Gooding County in the west through Minidoka County was named "Magic Valley". Life seemed to spring from presumably barren desert.

This region, which sees itself as distinct from southwestern and eastern parts of southern Idaho, owes much to the Carey Act, passed by Congress in 1894. The Carey Act allowed residents of each state up to a million acres of federal land, free, provided the land would be irrigated somehow. In 1902, Congress helped with the "how" by creating the Bureau of Reclamation. The impetus of free land provided the economic incentive for finding new ways to bring water to the land, and resulted in what amounted to farming boomtowns.

By way of comparison, the area west of Glenns Ferry all the way to Boise, which is similar high desert country also near the Snake River, never has been heavily irrigated. Except for the Air Force base community of Mountain Home, there are no substantial communities and agricultural activity mostly is confined to the banks of the Snake River or its tributaries.

Cattle-ranching is dominant in the dryer parts of this area, and in the 1990s massive dairy operations developed even near the Snake River, resulting in political controversy over the odor and pollution from some of the facilities. In 2002, Idaho became the fifth-largest milk-producing state in the nation. Agriculture, consisting of crop and cattle production, related food processing, and even massive trout production facilities, overwhelmingly remains the Magic Valley's economic mainstay. Like other agricultural areas of Idaho, the Magic Valley is overwhelmingly Republican.

The least populated of the distinct regions, with little more than a tenth of the state's people, the Magic Valley is anchored by the commercial center of Twin Falls. Twin Falls has become the regional shopping and service center, and grew rapidly in the 1990s. If forced to look to a larger metropolitan area for its economic and cultural leads, most people here would look toward Boise—though some would choose Salt Lake City instead.

The one substantial exception to the rule, in economics and politics, is the central Wood River Valley, an area in Blaine County from Bellevue to Ketchum. Sun Valley was founded in the 1930s as a destination for travelers of the Union Pacific Railroad. The resort community was created by Union Pacific Chairman Averell Harriman specifically as a promotion for the railroad which, ironically, has since been torn out. Although Twin Falls city grew rapidly as a commercial center in the 1990s, the Wood River Valley has grown even faster, and property prices there have exploded. Numerous celebrities own property in the area, and actor Bruce Willis has actually bought and redeveloped much of downtown Hailey and a ski resort in nearby Camas County. Willis notwithstanding, this area is overwhelmingly Democratic. Democratic Massachusetts Senator John Kerry has a vacation home and often visits the area, and had successful fundraisers there for his 2004 run for the presidency. Blaine County has become so Democratic that in 2002 U. S. Senator Larry Craig joked that he did not represent Blaine County—like it was another state.

In central Idaho, north of the Wood River Valley, a string of old Idaho communities abut the Frank Church-River of No Return Wilderness which occupies most of the very center of the state. With the future of the natural resource industry uncertain, several of these communities, such as Stanley and Salmon, are increasingly turning to tourism. Others, notably Challis, continue to rely on a variety of economic support mechanisms including timber production and mining. The economy of Custer County continues to boom and bust depending mostly on the current state of its large molybdenum mine at nearby Thompson Creek.

EASTERN IDAHO

In eastern Idaho, the basic economic pattern of an irrigation-based agricultural underlay continues as far as does the Snake River. Farms are clustered near the rivers, and crops become harder to raise farther away; cattle operations tend to appear in the more arid regions.

Farmers in the Mud Lake and Monteview area in western Jefferson County have drawn national attention by their strong reaction to infestations of non-farm animals. Many of the farms in that area are located near what was then called the Idaho National Engineering & Environmental Laboratory (INEEL) site, a vast area where hunting is prohibited. In the early 1980s, the jackrabbit population at INEEL exploded and swarms of the animals crossed nearby farms, destroying entire fields of crops in the process. That prompted the farmers to round up the animals and, in desperation, club them to death—an event referred to by national news media as the "bunny bop." (Needless to say, national outcry put an end to this activity.) Potential increases in the antelope population have raised the threat of a new drive against another species.

Beyond agriculture, there are several important economic and social wrinkles in the picture here. One is the dominating presence of the Mormon Church: the Church of Jesus Christ of Latter-day Saints commonly abbreviated as the LDS Church. The Mormon portion of the population is greater in Idaho than in any other state outside Utah, and while LDS congregations can be found in every county, the concentration of population is in the East where settlers a century and more ago ventured north from Utah to establish new farm settlements. The very first permanent Idaho town, Franklin in Franklin County, is so close to the Utah border that its first pioneers thought they were in Utah and had to be convinced by a census survey that they were not. Franklin remains heavily Mormon. In communities like Rexburg, Preston, Paris and Firth, the Mormon population generally has been estimated at upwards of 90 percent.

Most eastern Idaho communities were founded by Mormon farmers who swiftly brought their Utah irrigation skills to bear. In many of these communities, old and large families still dominate the landscape. In Rexburg, named for pioneer Thomas Ricks (through a latinization of the name), members of the Ricks family have been prominent in the community for more than a century. The LDS Church-owned university there, Brigham Young University-Idaho, was until 2001 known as Ricks College. In Malad, where members of the Evans, Jones and Williams families have all produced statewide elected officials, most people who grew up there can claim some shirt-tail relationship to most other people in town. Eastern Idaho as a whole is strongly Republican, but such family ties can prove more persuasive than political party affiliation, and a well-regarded member of a big local family can often sweep the local vote regardless of party. John Evans, a Democratic governor of Idaho from 1977 to 1987, did this repeatedly in his races for governor and earlier for the state Senate, even though his native Oneida County is generally Republican. In 1994, Democratic state Auditor J. D. Williams, a Malad-area native who practiced law in Franklin County, wound up the only statewide Democrat to keep his office in a Republican landslide, partly because his home region (albeit Republican) stayed loyal to him.

Because the Mormon Church is based in Salt Lake City, and because Salt Lake City is the closest large metropolitan area, much of this area takes its political, commercial and social cues from Salt Lake City. Local cable television in some communities carry the Salt Lake television stations, and same-day editions of the *Salt Lake Tribune* circulate in some communities. The *Tribune* once covered eastern Idaho thoroughly with full-time news and advertising staffs. In the border areas in Oneida, Bear Lake and Franklin Counties, most of the population is descended from Utah pioneers and still have many Utah relatives. Much of their trading is pointed south to Logan and Ogden rather than north into Idaho. The only LDS temple in eastern Idaho is located in Idaho Falls helping to make that city a regional center. (A second Idaho temple was built in Boise in the 1980s, and a third is planned for Rexburg.)

The other major forces in Eastern Idaho are nuclear energy and high-tech research.

Reaching back to a farm outside Rigby, early in the century a boy named Philo T. Farnsworth—looking at the rows of crops before him —conceived of how television broadcasting and reception could be made to work. He developed the basic idea there in Rigby, and later received funding for research and development in Los Angeles, San Francisco and Philadelphia. He is renowned today as the central figure in the invention of commercial television.

Today's technology centers in eastern Idaho, however, spring from different roots. The biggest single-institution employer in the east and the second-largest in the state is the Idaho National Laboratory (previously known as the INEEL). That impact is greatest at Idaho Falls, Idaho's fourth-largest city. Its economy is heavily reliant on both INL and on its role as a commercial center for the surrounding agricultural communities. Research at the site now ranges from new ways to clean up fish manure at the big fish farms near Hagerman, to development of more powerful batteries for electric cars. But in Idaho, and probably elsewhere, the INL remains best known for its nuclear activities. With a declining military investment in the site and an aging nuclear testing plant, some wonder whether INL will remain an active and substantial federal facility. Some Idaho leaders quietly predict that the Laboratory will be drastically scaled down or closed; others see a long-range broad-based nuclear and energy research future. Officials at the site have pushed for more diversified research activities.

Idaho Falls and other area officials also have pushed for increasing diversification of their economies. That is an approach that already has repaid some dividends at Pocatello, the state's third-largest city.

Pocatello, which in 1949 lost out to Idaho Falls in the contest for housing INL's administrative headquarters, had in the 1880s beaten out that other city, then called Eagle Rock, to become the regional rail hub. In those days, Pocatello instantly became a commercial center as well. For several decades Bannock County (Pocatello) ran a close second to Boise's Ada County for the most populous in the state. Like Lewiston to the north, Pocatello also became a substantial industrial center, especially after the J. R. Simplot Company and FMC Corporation built large phosphate-processing plants on the edge of town. Pocatello was also second in the state to obtain a substantial higher-education institution, what is now called Idaho State University. Pocatello political culture is influenced by a mix of merchant, labor union, university and farm service communities. This is the one large city in eastern Idaho, and one of the few, where Mormons are not clearly dominant in the population. They generally are estimated to make up about half of the Pocatello population.

Pocatello is also the "Democratic island in a Republican sea," to use an overworked description; but it is a swampy island. Republican wins at both the local level and at the top of the ticket are not rare, and the traditional Democratic advantage of labor union strength in this manufacturing city has diminished.

Pocatello has had mixed luck with attracting businesses and watching a number of them pack up and leave, or scale back. Union Pacific railroad employment levels have dropped drastically in recent years and the city's once-largest employer now employs only a few hundred workers. After the turn of the millennium, the city's largest employer became a high-tech company, AMI Semi-Conductor.

DIVERSITY'S STRENGTH

Does the whole add up to the sum of the pieces? Many northern Idahoans distressed by southern resistance to northern ideas, and vice versa., may not think so. Northern, Southwestern, Central and Eastern Idaho are all unique regions of the state in their geographic composition, economic base, social structure and political perspectives. This variety offers the potential for useful cross-fertilization and sets the stage for an examination of Idaho's broadly representative government in which different ideas compete and yield good and sometimes bad results.

Chapter 2 notes

1   Idaho Department of Transportation, press release file, 1998.
2   Jess Walter, *Every Knee Shall Bow* (New York: Regan Books, 1995) 3.
3   Stephen Shaw, "Harassment, Hate, and Human Rights in Idaho," in *Politics in the Postwar American West* (Norman, OK: University of Oklahoma Press, 1995).
4   Carlos Schwantes, *In Mountain Shadows* (Lincoln, NE: University of Nebraska Press, 1991), p. 226-7.

CHAPTER 3

POLITICAL CULTURE IN HISTORY

T hroughout its history, Idaho has rarely drawn people based on its own charms. Few Native Americans thought enough of it to call any part of it a homeland. Explorers trekked through it en route to somewhere else; it was not, as a general rule, one of the best fur trapping locales. The early Oregon Trail settlers considered it a Godforsaken piece of hell, the empty desert and sagebrush-covered mountains a horrid test to be endured before reaching the Promised Land of the rich Oregon country.[1]

Idaho has, in the last four decades, experienced a boom in population and economic growth with retirees and others coming to Idaho because of a perceived superiority in quality of life.[2] Many newcomers see Idaho as one of the last frontiers, as one of the last places to get away from it all in the lower 48 United States.

THE NATIVES

The first Idahoans, Native Americans, may not have considered themselves the owners of part of what is now Idaho. They had mobile societies, organized around hunting and gathering rather than crop farming. There were predominately two different groups, one in what is now the North American northwest, generally living in northern Idaho mostly north of the Salmon River and east of Montana, the other to the south, looking toward the great plains.[3]

The Great Basin tribes, prominent in Idaho for the last few hundred years before the coming of the Europeans, were Northern Paiute, and lived mainly in the southwestern part of the state. Two other Basin tribes, the Shoshones and Bannocks, were interspersed in the south-central and eastern parts of Idaho. They all were hunters and foragers, fishing for the salmon that spawned into what is now the Magic Valley, and hunting for the bison that were plentiful across southern Idaho in the early 1800s. The Bannocks and Shoshones (both phonetic corruptions of original descriptive names) had most of the best locations; the Northern Paiutes were later arrivals from Nevada who had to work harder to obtain the basics.[4] Conflicts sometimes arose, but every year until the 1860s the Great Basin tribes, sometimes along with the Umatilla and Nez Perce to the north, would meet in a month-long, peaceful celebration near what is now the city of Council.

The "Plateau Indians" to the north were also widely scattered. The Kutenai, Kalispel and Coeur d'Alene bands roamed across what is now the northern Idaho Panhandle, and west into Washington and east into Montana. Several distinct Nez Perce bands lived in the Clearwater and Salmon river drainage in north-central Idaho and in the Wallowa mountain and plain country on the west side of Hells Canyon in what is now Oregon.[5] These bands were somewhat less mobile than the bands to the south, and their settlements were more fixed, but only as a matter of degree. In large part they too were hunters and gatherers, and like the southern bands became expert horsemen after that animal was introduced by way of Mexico around 1700.

The Idaho of 1800 was unseen, so far as historical records can ascertain, by any European. The first to see it were those in the American expedition led by Meriwether Lewis and William Clark in 1805.[6] The Idaho-Montana line was where they crossed the Great Divide, and Idaho provided them little more than a series of obstacles. It may have been the only state they truly "discovered".

MOUNTAIN MEN, MISSIONARIES AND MINERS

After Lewis and Clark returned east, extolling the area's abundance of beaver and other fur bearing creatures, trappers from both the United States and from Great Britain's Hudson Bay Company moved into the area. Some early merchants built small, temporary trading centers. The first was Kullyspell House in 1809, not far from present-day Clark Fork; another early stopping-point was set up near what is now American Falls. Fur traders also met annually for several years at a big rendezvous at what is now Driggs, just west of Teton National Park. The 1832 event drew more than 200 trappers and more than 200 lodges of Native Americans.[7] But by the late 1840s, the land was largely trapped out and the sun had set on the day of the mountain man. In Idaho, remnants of the mountain man anti-culture can still be found in remote places of the state.[8]

The mountain men were followed by missionaries and later by settlers on the Washington and Oregon coasts. Idaho's mission era lasted from about 1836 to 1858, but left little lasting imprint on the state to come. A few of the missionaries did, however. The Spaldings at the

Lapwai Mission in north central Idaho developed Idaho's first irrigation system and planted the state's first potatoes. Further north, east of Coeur d'Alene, the oldest standing building in Idaho is the Cataldo Mission of the Sacred Heart , whose origins date to 1846; its mission succeeded on a human level as well, converting the Coeur d'Alene area natives.

These were exceptions. Idaho in general remained unchanged through the 1850s. Very little of Idaho was explored and none truly settled by Americans during this time. Not until 1859 was the first road built in what is now Idaho; it was John Mullan's military road which very roughly traces what is now Interstate 90 in the Idaho Panhandle.[9]

One reason for the late settlement is that, until mid-century, Idaho was a political no-man's land. It lay west of the Louisiana Purchase that stopped short of the Continental Divide. Under terms of an 1818 treaty, the United States and Great Britain were joint occupants of the vast area from there to the Pacific Ocean and north of California, but as time went on the two nations began contesting the region.

In 1846, the two nations agreed to a division at the 49th parallel (with a few exceptions), the United States receiving the southern portion including all of what is now Idaho. In those days, United States territories usually started as massive chunks of land that were subdivided, over and over, until eventually a piece matured to statehood. The area that would become Idaho formally became part of the United States in 1846 and part of the Oregon Territory in 1848. This was subdivided in 1853 into Washington Territory north of the 46th parallel, and Oregon Territory to the south; the areas now called northern and southern Idaho were split between the two. When Oregon became a state in 1859, its easternmost part—what is now Idaho plus parts of Montana and Wyoming—was annexed to Washington Territory.[10]

Interest in eventual settlement grew as many of the tribes in the area agreed or were coerced to settle on ever shrinking reservation lands. Washington Governor Isaac I. Stevens was well known for aggressively pursuing "a policy of forcing Indians into reservations and opening the land to white settlers." [11]

Washington Territory's capital was located at Olympia on the Pacific coast, hundreds of miles from much of the remote territory to the east. As long as few American citizens lived in that open expanse, Olympia officials were content to preside over it, and there was little objection.

That changed in the first four years of the 1860s, when precious metals discoveries drew sudden mobs of gold seekers to the eastern part of the territory. The first of these finds was located near Pierce in north-central Idaho, just off the Clearwater River. The discovery was made in August 1860 by Elias Davidson Pierce, namesake of the current city as well as the old camp town. By the next spring, thousands of miners swarmed into the area. Most of these early gold seekers were from other western communities. Whole cities were erected and demolished in a matter of months as the miners moved on to the next big discovery. No one knows for sure how many, but at least 2,000 miners took up residence, setting up the towns of Pierce and Oro Fino, complete with whiskey shops, gambling houses, saloons, hotels, restaurants, book shops, barbers and doctors.[12] Several entrepreneurs also established a supply camp settlement downstream at the mouth of the Clearwater River where it meets the Snake River, and dubbed it Lewiston (with a counterpart Clarkston across the Snake River). All of this activity was illegal since it was located on the Nez Perce Reservation. No federal officials tried to interfere, however, and tribal leaders did not raise any strong objections either. The miners, finding gold not so easy to obtain as they had hoped, moved on. Within a year of establishment, Oro Fino was gone and Pierce nearly vanished as well; Lewiston, however, survived as a jumping off point for area miners and a supply center for mining camps.

The swarm of miners moved due south to the next hot and trendy mining district. Gold was reported in the Florence and Elk City areas in what is now Idaho County, just north of the Salmon River. In the spring of 1862 an estimated 10,000 men overran the area. Nearly all were gone within a year, and very little of the settlement remains.

The next year, 1863, gold was discovered in the Boise Basin, about 40 miles northeast of Boise, which was founded as a supply base for the camp as well as a military headquarters. This and subsequent strikes lasted a little longer. Idaho City did not long retain its status as the largest city in the American Northwest[13] but the mines remained very productive for most of the decade and were worked on a smaller scale for several decades after that. Many of the workers were Chinese who had been brought in as cheap labor and then stayed to work on the claims "with great patience and accepting a small return for their efforts, whites universally regarded their presence in the diggings as a sure sign that a mining region had passed its peak."[13]

The same pattern followed in the Owyhee Mountains south of Boise, where major strikes were found at Silver City (which grew fast enough to support, for a while, Idaho's first daily newspaper) and Ruby City. A substantial portion of old Idaho City remains in place in that community, where most of one side of Main Street has been given over to a series of buildings which are in effect a large museum of the early mining days. Portions of old Silver City also remain in place, including the old hotel. Both are popular tourist attractions in southwestern Idaho.

Another big discovery came in the Wood River Valley, near present day Hailey. Hailey expanded so rapidly for a short time that it boasted the region's first electricity and vied to become the Idaho territorial capital.[14]

Finally, the biggest score of all came once again in northern Idaho, in what is now Shoshone County, part of the "Silver Valley." This 1884 discovery led to tremendous excavation of silver—eventually, more than $4 billion worth of it. These mines remained extremely active and profitable for most of a century, and major closures did not start until 1981, when the huge Bunker Hill and Sullivan Mines closed. Mining activity in the new millennium has continued on a drastically reduced scale.

IDAHO TERRITORY

The rapid influx of miners concerned officials at Olympia in Washington Territory. These remote mining territories were too far away to properly administer. This problem was exacerbated by fears that the interior city of Walla Walla, which was growing rapidly in response to demand from the mining communities, would bid to become the territorial capital. So in 1863, Washington Territory officials suggested that the interior area be split off to become a separate territory. Congress (where road-builder John Mullan had become an advocate of Idaho Territory) and President Abraham Lincoln were persuaded, and the new Idaho Territory came into being on March 4, 1863.

The strength of Republicans grew in western Washington Territory, especially in the Olympia area, as the Civil War progressed. This growing influence meant that chances for eventual admission to statehood by the Republican Congress and president were improving. The mining country in the interior, however, was ferociously Democratic. It was dominated by "Copperhead" Democrats, who did not favor the breakup of the United States but disapproved of Lincoln's insistence on pursuing the war against the Confederacy, and by refugees from southern states, especially Missouri and Arkansas. Many of the Idaho miners of the 1860s and 1870s apparently were Copperheads who wanted no role in the war. These people resented government control. In many cases they had fled to a land distant from conventional civilization to avoid the intrusions of the federal government.

One story from that era tells of a judge from Walla Walla who ventured to Florence, during that mining camp's 1862 heyday. He summoned a grand jury to consider criminal indictments. It did. It indicted Lincoln, his cabinet, various Union military officers, as well as the judge. The judge fled town and, as soon as he reached Walla Walla, resigned.[15]

The miners of the interior did not particularly favor creation of a separate territory since they already enjoyed a political balance of power at Olympia, even though there were only a little over 32,000 people in the territory. Their reaction to the new territorial governing officials at Lewiston in 1863 (all of course appointed by that hated Republican Lincoln) was predictably hostile. The local residents were, however, able to vote for a territorial delegate to Congress, and for the territorial legislature and county offices. The seeds of the anti-federal viewpoint that would dominate Idaho's territorial history, and recur after statehood, were planted early.

TERRITORIAL POLITICS

John Mullan had actually sought the governor's job, but he was too associated with interests at Walla Walla (one of the termini of his road). The appointment went to William Wallace, an old political crony of Lincoln's, who also had pushed the Idaho Territory Bill and had served as an official in Washington Territory. Wallace's first task was to declare Lewiston the territorial capital. It was still little more than a tent town and supply camp which he had not yet visited. He was also months late in arriving at the new capital. Once in Lewiston, Wallace installed Republicans in territorial offices, especially those in control of the first elections, and then hit the campaign trail to run for the office of Idaho's first delegate to Congress (the pay and living conditions in the nation's capital being a big improvement over those of the territorial governor). The territory was overwhelmingly Democratic (many of the Idaho miners were southerners) and Wallace first seemed to have little chance of being elected; but strict application of some of the registration laws blocked many Democrats from voting, and Wallace was narrowly elected along with many Republicans in other offices. Many Democrats considered that election corrupt and internal conflict accelerated.

In Congress, Wallace had the lasting impact on Idaho of splitting the huge territory apart, dividing it on the east at the Continental Divide. The eastern portion became Montana Territory with some of it later becoming part of the state of Wyoming. Little wonder that commentators have referred to Idaho as an historical accident or geographic mistake. Boundaries were drawn for purely political reasons without regard to the geography, economic or social structure of the state.

The Civil War had disrupted normal work in Congress, which was slow in making territorial appropriations. The territory ran on credit for two years before Idaho got its first federal money. Before it could even print its first law books, the state was $44,000 in debt. The tribes who had settled on reservations were, like the territory, getting little attention or aid from the federal government, and were threatening revolt. Many promises had been made and broken.

Wallace's successor, Caleb Lyon ("of Lyonsdale," as he described himself), was exactly the wrong choice to deal with all this. Lyon was one of the worst in a bad string of territorial governors. Unlike Wallace, who at least had substantial governmental experience, Lyon had only the desire to be a dandy and an orator, and was most notable as eccentric and erratic. At one point, flustered by political obstacles, he left the territory—leaving it without a governor for eleven months. When he left the governorship for good in 1866, he was suspected of having absconded with $46,000 earmarked for distribution to the tribes. Soon after, another territorial official, Horace Gilson, stole $41,000 from the treasury before fleeing to Paris and Hong Kong. Various county officials were busy embezzling funds as well. Other territorial governors barely made an appearance, leaving the territory, at times, to be governed by secondary officials.[16]

Confederate losses helped feed the growing number of Democrats in Idaho Territory, and in 1864 they swept the territorial elections. The voter base was concentrated in the mining districts and Democrats would remain dominant in the territory for nearly two decades. That also meant they were at odds with their governors and executive officials who were appointed almost without exception by Republican administrations in Washington. The new territorial legislature, both the council (upper house) and the house of representatives (lower house), controlled by miners from the Boise Basin area, voted to move the territorial capital south to Boise (away from Republican influences in Lewiston), effective December 1864.

Democrats continued to dominate local politics and delegates to Congress. The mining population fluctuated, but Democrats gained additional support from the farm country of eastern Idaho to where Mormon farmers from Utah were moving. These settlers built Idaho's first permanent town at Franklin in 1860, and over the rest of the decade expanded rapidly through what is now Franklin and Bear Lake Counties in southeastern Idaho. The Idaho Republican Party was strongly anti-Mormon, a popular position among many gentiles (non-Mormons). But factions split along many lines in Idaho in the

1870s as spoils and other squabbles around the "Boise Ring" (the federal officials in the capitol) kept the territorial government in turmoil.

TRIBAL CONFLICT

The turmoil within the state government did little to help relations with the Native American tribes. Interactions with the resident tribes had long been just friendly enough to avert war even though the tribal lands had been sharply diminished to one-tenth their original size to accommodate miners and land hungry farmers. (The main exception in the 1860s was the conflict at Bear River, when a California troop sent to protect Mormon settlers in Franklin County slaughtered an estimated 368 Indians, including women and children.).

In 1877 serious conflict arose between federal troops and the Nez Perce. Federal officials had agreed that the Wallowa Nez Perce band could stay in its ancestral home area in the Wallowa Mountains in eastern Oregon but then reneged when pressured by white settlers for more land. All the Nez Perce bands were ordered to a reservation in the Clearwater River area above Lewiston. Irritations grew, a group of young tribal members shot and killed several settlers near the Salmon River, and that escalated into a larger conflict. Chief Joseph was considered by the whites to be the tribe's leader (though internally he would have been regarded as one leader among several). The rebelling Nez Perce began a long march, fighting a rear-guard action, through Idaho and Montana. Their goal was to reach Canada. They were cornered and defeated in Montana and exiled to Oklahoma until 1885, when many were sent back, most to a reservation in Colville, Washington. Chief Joseph was not allowed to return to his beloved Wallowa Valley. He died at Colville in 1904.

The Bannock Indians from the Fort Hall reservation in eastern Idaho scouted for the Army in the 1877 Nez Perce War. But in 1878 a group of Bannocks attacked white herders on the Camas Prairie. Led by Chief Buffalo Horn, they attempted to join forces with the Paiutes in northern Nevada. Buffalo Horn was killed early in the war but the Bannocks and some Paiute allies marched north toward the Umatilla Agency in Oregon. They were scattered in a number of fights with soldiers, volunteers and Umatilla Indians. The hostiles fled east trying, like the Nez Perce a year earlier, to link up with Sioux Chief Sitting Bull in Canada. Following a final skimimish in Wyoming the survivors either returned to Fort Hall or blended into peaceful bands of Shoshones.

In 1879, another conflict arose involving the Shoshones and related bands of southern Idaho. The result was the Sheepeater War (named after a band of Shoshones whose diet included mountain sheep). The Sheepeater War ended in defeat for the Shoshones and they were moved to the Fort Hall Reservation in eastern Idaho, which, in a size diminished from its original measure, still exists.[17]

The small Lemhi Tribe was a separate band of Shoshones who lived near what is now the city of Salmon, along the Lemhi River. They numbered about 500 around the time of the Civil War, and stayed out of the other tribal-federal conflicts of that time. In 1875, President Ulysses Grant ordered into place a Lemhi reservation on the banks of that river. But in 1907, the remaining tribal members were removed to the Fort Hall Reservation, about 200 miles southeast. In the late 1990s, the Lemhi band of the Shoshones began to seek federal tribal recognition as a unique tribe apart from the other Shoshones living at Fort Hall.

ANTI-MORMONISM

Idaho leaders throughout the 19th century often seemed to target some group of people within the state boundaries, and as the Indian conflicts subsided, politicians turned their wrath on the growing number of Mormons. Few places in the country exhibited sharper divisions between two dominant groups—the individualistic miners and timbermen in northern Idaho and the moralistic Mormons of southern Idaho. Their basic behavioral and philosophical approaches were diametrically opposed.[18]

The gentile politicians railed against the practice of polygamy, or plural marriage, which the Mormon Church sanctioned (though it never was widespread in Idaho, since only about two to three percent of Mormon families were at any point polygamous).[19] Politicians objected to these "peculiar people" whom they feared were puppets of the church leaders in Salt Lake City. But these Idaho officials did not invent the issue; it held the national attention. President Rutherford B. Hayes was, on the basis of polygamy, fervently anti-Mormon, and when he appointed a new territorial governor in 1879, he made sure that man—John B. Neil—felt the same. Neil laid the groundwork for anti-Mormon sentiment and legislation, and cleverly won sympathy in the Democratic north by appealing to anti-Mormon sentiments there while quieting the longstanding Republican talk insisting the Panhandle remain part of Idaho. With that effort, Neil may have launched the movement toward dominance by Republicans in Idaho. In effect, annexation and anti-LDS rhetoric became effective wedge issues.

Neil's campaign swung enough votes in 1882 to give five Republicans their first territory-wide wins since the fraudulent elections of 1863, and set the pattern for Idaho politics for the next decade and beyond. Ex-Southerners, who had formed a large part of the Idaho mining population, increasingly were outnumbered by arrivals from the Republican Midwest, and both increasingly were willing to support the party of the anti-Mormons. These circumstances led in the 1880s to Republican domination and created the political conditions needed for statehood: Republican territory working with a national Republican administration and Congress. This set of circumstances eventually settled into the long-term Republican domination of the state that exists today.

Neil lost the governorship in 1883 when he was not reappointed. Soon however, the anti-Mormon torch was picked up by another Republican leader who, as United States marshal, had joined Neil in pushing for stringent anti-Mormon laws and who had enforced them as strenuously as he could—Fred T. Dubois of Blackfoot. Dubois was the son of Jesse Dubois, for years a powerful politician in Illinois and a neighbor of Abraham Lincoln. While anti-Mormon ferment was not great as the decade began, the fear-mongering of Dubois and others coupled with the growing population of non-Mormons in the eastern Idaho farm country, gradually increased Republican strength. Dubois built a strong Republican Party organization in many counties of the state for the first time. Running for the territorial seat in the U.S. House, he defeated incumbent Democrat Governor John Hailey in 1886, and won again in 1888.

The anti-Mormons' political strength grew as well, and by the end of the decade they were effectively able to bar Mormons from voting, holding office or serving on juries. In 1885, enough anti-Mormons were elected to the territorial legislature to pass the Test Oath law which required prospective voters to swear that not only were they not polygamists, but that they did not belong to any organization that supported the practice. (Mormons fought the law as a suppression of civil liberties to the U.S. Supreme Court, where in the 1890 decision in *Davis v. Beason*, they lost.) At the 1889 constitutional convention, anti-Mormon forces pushed through insertion of language essentially barring Mormons from the franchise. The courts overturned its validity within a few years, but it remained formally in the constitution (though not enforced) until 1982 when Idaho voters approved its repeal.

Dubois' other cause was Idaho statehood, and he was key to pushing it through Congress. He worked closely with Edward Stevenson, the Democratic territorial governor appointed by President Grover Cleveland. Stevenson was a long-time Payette Valley farmer, and the first Idahoan appointed as governor of the territory. When Cleveland lost the presidency to Benjamin Harrison in 1888, the political conditions for Idaho statehood finally ripened. The territory, the President, and the Congress all were finally of the same party— Republican. All were aligned on the matters of polygamy and Mormonism,   and leaders in Idaho as well as Washington favored statehood. That status was granted in 1890, and the Idaho Constitution adopted at a convention the year before went into effect.

TURBULENCE AT STATEHOOD

Ironically, the debate over Mormonism fell away almost as soon as Idaho became a state. For one thing, the president of the LDS Church, Wilford Woodruff, in September 1890 told Mormons to comply with all civil laws related to marriage, and the church, soon after, officially renounced polygamy. Second, an Idaho Supreme Court under direction of its first major leader, James F. Ailshie (a loyal Republican), struck down the validity of several of the most important anti-Mormon laws. Third, the Republican who served as the last territorial governor and first governor of the State of Idaho, George Shoup, was a no-nonsense military man from Salmon (which he had helped found) who had little interest in the battles over the LDS Church. Finally, Dubois wound up with another of the new U.S. Senate seats from Idaho, removing him from internal state politics for several years.

But another major conflict soon took the place of anti-mormonism.

The Idaho of statehood was in many ways substantially more "civilized" than that of 1863. The territory's population more than doubled in both the 1870s and 1880s, and in 1890 stood at 88,548; that number would nearly double again in the 1890s.[20] The largest county was Bingham, which at the time included most of eastern Idaho north of the small counties near the Utah border (and was then a hotbed of anti-Mormonism). Boise and Pocatello, the two largest cities, were becoming established frontier towns of nearly 30 years' duration, with approximate populations of 2,300 each. Around 1890, major irrigation projects abruptly created what is now the Magic Valley and much of the farm country in Canyon County as well. The days of small freelance mining were mostly gone, and large-scale mining, undertaken by large companies, had taken over, most notably in the Silver Valley. Then as mining became a smaller portion of the state economy, timber took up much of the slack. In the late 19th century, timber companies began buying huge tracts of land in northern Idaho, and numerous towns—Sandpoint, Orofino, St. Maries, Potlatch, Kamiah, Kooskia and many more—owe their early existence to the sudden growth of the timber economy.

The state had started out Republican, but as the party's linchpin of anti-Mormonism faded, Idaho voters swung wildly. Individualism and populism were perhaps never so much in evidence in Idaho as in that first decade of statehood, when party loyalty seemed to vanish. Far from settling down to calmly create a new state, these Idahoans expressed a determination to be neither defined nor constrained. National economic turbulence in the 1890s had its effect in Idaho as well. Political allegiances had more to do with such matters as railroad regulation, the rise of unions and the status and price of silver (and, briefly, the returning specter of anti-Mormonism), than with steady political alliances. Legislatures in that first decade were deeply split between Republicans, Democrats and Populists. Far from being the reliable Republican state anticipated in 1890, Idaho voted for Populist James Weaver for president in 1892, and for the next two elections (lower-case populist) William Jennings Bryan, a Democrat. Seven Republicans and four Democrats served as governor in the state's first three decades.

Shortly after statehood the Idaho Republican Party shattered over the question of free coinage of silver and inability to cope with the latest economic downturn, to the point that in 1896 Idaho had six political parties. The gubernatorial winner was Frank Steunenberg, a Populist-Democrat supported by the Silver Republicans. Populist-Democrat "fusion" groups dominated the Idaho Legislature after that election as well. Even though Steunenberg was a relative newcomer to Idaho, he was able to get support from four of the six parties. A faction of Republicans loyal to William McKinley (who got only about 20 percent of the Idaho vote that year) and the new Prohibition Party were the only holdouts. Steunenberg got 76.8 percent of the vote, the highest ever received by a candidate for governor of Idaho. (The next two highest figures, surprising in a Republican state, also were recorded by a Democrat: Cecil Andrus, in 1974 and 1990.)

But Steunenberg's coalition fell apart almost as swiftly as it was created. He was re-elected in 1898 by only a plurality and then became bogged down in the Silver Valley mining war. The mining companies and the workers engaged in bitter battles from the early 1890s through the next quarter-century over pay, working conditions and the right of the workers to organize, starting with a flare-up in 1892. Steunenberg himself had a background as a labor union member as well as a merchant (newspaper publisher), and he was at first sympathetic with the workers. But when almost a thousand of them marched on the Frisco Mill and blew it up, Steunenberg called in federal troops and suspended civil liberties in Shoshone County.[21] For a time, this action—martial law was maintained in force for almost two years—broke the unions. But immediately after, and for several decades to come, it radicalized the unions that sprang up to replace the early organizations.

On the last day of 1905, five years after leaving the governorship, Steunenberg was assassinated—killed by a bomb outside his house at Caldwell—in apparent retribution for his actions in the Silver Valley conflict. His murderer, Harry Orchard, was quickly captured and convicted. Orchard implicated several major labor leaders, including the nationally-known "Big Bill" Haywood, in the killing. The three key labor figures identified by Orchard were seized in Denver, hustled by train to Idaho, and put on trial for murder. That trial, in which such legal luminaries as William Borah, William Hawley and Clarence Darrow came to national attention, was the trial of the century in Idaho.[22] Haywood and the others were acquitted though their exact role in Steuneneberg's assassination remains a matter of dispute even today.

Labor relations in the Silver Valley remained bitter for more than another decade, during which time the radical Industrial Workers of the World found fertile ground there. Governor Moses Alexander eventually helped to defuse the situation in the patriotic fervor of World War I. Union influence stayed strong in the region, however, and the Silver Valley remained one of the few Democratic strongholds in Idaho at the end of the twentieth century.

While labor turned radical in the Coeur d'Alene district, it was deeply distrusted elsewhere in the new state. The newspapers warned against "combinations," whether of corporations or of labor unions. In his book about the Haywood trial, *Big Trouble*, writer J. Anthony Lukas referred to a turn-of-the-century sense in Caldwell, "the mounting uneasiness that Caldwell's citizens weren't fully in control of their own lives, that malign forces threatened their well-being."[23] In many Idaho citizens' views those "malign forces" were represented by organized labor.

Over the next decade the state slowly settled into a calmer pattern of electing an increasingly large number of Republicans in most elections, even though Republicans continued to be split into factions. The new factions were conservatives, based on the McKinley free-enterprise principles, and the progressives, who modeled themselves more after Theodore Roosevelt. The Progressives had the highest-profile and the most successful Idaho politician ever in William Borah. Fresh off his work in the Orchard trial and other high-profile cases, Borah was elected to the United States Senate in 1907 by the Idaho Legislaturee, once more dominated by Republicans. The Legislature would continue to elect United States senators until passage of the

Seventeenth Amendment to the United States Constitution, which provided for the popular election of senators rather than by the state legislature. Borah, a strong proponent of this change, once called the party system "the vice of democracy," and just before his death in 1940—when he still was a senator—he planned to support Burton Wheeler, a liberal Democrat from Montana, for president. Borah became internationally known for his role as a leader of the isolationists and for progressive legislation. Among voters in Idaho he was impregnable. When he ran against the only strong Democratic opponent he ever faced, Governor C. Ben Ross in 1936, in a strongly Democratic year, the voters overwhelmingly re-elected Borah.

Borah may have been a national figure, a credible candidate for president in 1936—but he was not a driving force in Idaho politics. Back home, progressives were not a major factor and, with Borah's departure across the continent, they were essentially leaderless.

The roots of the modern Idaho Republican Party instead go back to a bitter rival of Borah's, businessman Frank Gooding. A native of England, Gooding moved to Ketchum in 1881 and became involved in a wide range of businesses, eventually becoming a founder of the state's sheep industry and one of Idaho's wealthiest men. The current city and county of Gooding are named for him. Gooding was elected to the state Senate in 1898, state Republican chair in 1902—where he was instrumental in rebuilding the party organization—and governor of Idaho in 1904 and 1906. He did all of this before he became a United States citizen (an oversight finally corrected before he later won election to the United States Senate); but then Gooding was not a man to let little obstacles get in the way. After serving his two terms as governor, in which he pushed for state aid to irrigation, and for railroads and other business development, he was able to install as his successor an ally, James Brady. Brady and Gooding later reversed roles in the U.S. Senate, Gooding replacing Brady there when he died. Another close ally of theirs (and associate in the livestock industry), John Thomas, also served in the Senate. He replaced Gooding there when Gooding died in 1928.

All this suggests a strong political machine, beginning with Gooding's organization of the GOP just before his governorship, that became the dominant political force in Idaho until the Great Depression. It was a machine of much greater subtlety than those of, for example, Chicago or New York. It was nearly invisible. It operated relatively loosely. The political machinery was dominated not by an office holder such as Gooding or Thomas but by a Rexburg attorney and lobbyist named Lloyd Adams, one of the powerful, barely-seen, forces in Idaho politics. Adams was a power in Idaho from 1912, when he helped Gooding's forces win a razor-thin gubernatorial election, until he died in 1969. Though careful to maintain good relations with Democrats during the years when they did well, Adams' loyalties were never in question, and he was the organizer who kept Republicans increasingly dominant through the 1920s.[24] Such an informal organization probably was as much political organization as many Idahoans were willing to endure.

Democrats increasingly were dependent on a few strong leaders, and except for a couple of decades in mid-twentieth century, they have been ever since. While Democrats occasionally elected governors and members of Congress from 1902 to 1932, they controlled the Idaho Legislature only once in that time, in the election of 1916—and then mainly as a show of support for the liquor prohibition that Democratic Governor Moses Alexander had just signed into law.

Alexander, mayor of Boise and then elected governor of Idaho in 1914 and 1916, is probably best known for being the nation's first elected Jewish governor, and secondarily as Idaho's foremost prohibitionist. He should also be known more for two major achievements. He was the mediator who managed to finally broker peace in the long-running labor war in the Silver Valley, which set the stage for a return to Democratic dominance there that has lasted to this day. Secondly, he brokered another string of agreements in another kind of conflict among irrigation water providers in southern Idaho. Until Alexander's involvement, independent providers of water and canals had often run into conflict and were at cross purposes, stunting continued growth of irrigation in the Magic Valley and other areas. Alexander was the catalyst for developing negotiated settlements and agreements which, in many places, continue to govern the critical distribution of water in southern Idaho and have allowed for tremendous growth in its farm economy.

But leaders such as Alexander (who ran once more, unsuccessfully, in 1922) were not easy for the Democrats to find. Their party was deeply split in the 1920s between traditional Democrats and farm activists who formed a new Progressive Party, which at times drew more votes than did the Democrats.

Depression and the return of competition

The prime organizing element on the left in Idaho in the 1920s was the Nonpartisan League, an agricultural group founded in North Dakota, deeply dedicated to its version of economic justice—which in its view included public ownership of many large businesses and utilities. Thanks in part to a strong local leader, Ray McKaig, the organization grew to more than 12,000 members in Idaho by 1919. Its political arm was the Progressive Party, which elected eleven state legislators in 1922, nineteen in 1924 and twelve in 1926. That marked the last appearance to date of a third-party or independent elected official anywhere in the Idaho Legislature or statewide offices.[25]

The Democrats' solution—uniting themselves and the Progressives—eluded them until 1930, when they benefitted from two lucky (for them) occurrences. One was the Great Depression, which had beat upon rural Idaho through the late 1920s but was becoming increasingly severe by 1930. The other was the party's failed 1928 candidate for governor, C. Ben Ross, who decided to try again in 1930 —and this time lightning struck.

Ross was a farmer, from both Parma in Canyon County and from the Pocatello area (where he served as mayor), and was a founder of the state's Farm Bureau. Unlike most Democrats, he had strong rural ties.[26] He was also one of the premier campaigners in Idaho history, a true entertainer and something of a demagogue. A mystic who believed for many years that his destiny was to become president, Ross has been compared to Huey Long of Louisiana as a popular leader. The 1932 general election that swept Franklin Roosevelt into the presidency – with the help of Idaho's hitherto Republican votes— also swept out almost every Idaho Republican on the ballot, even many judges who then ran on partisan tickets. Ross won a second term that year—and emerged the dominant figure in the state. Farmers who long had voted Republican instead allied themselves with Franklin Roosevelt, who gave them some hope for better times ahead.

In decades to come Idahoans would strongly support some national leaders (such as Ronald Reagan), but never again would they seek top-down leadership in quite the same way as they did with the Roosevelt election of 1932. Despite Roosevelt's coattails, few Idaho Democrats elected in the 1930s were true liberals or New Dealers, and most who were did not last. Before the New Deal was very old, traditional Republican conservatism reasserted itself in Idaho.

The electoral cataclysm did give Ross the opportunity to create a powerful and long-lasting Democratic Party. In some states, new Democratic political leaders did just that, but Ross failed. A charismatic leader he may have been, but Ross was no organizer or uniter, and his New Deal-related initiatives came to naught. He made his mark with the reinstitution of the direct primary and the passage of the state's first income tax. He also pushed through the state's first sales tax but it was repealed within 18 months in the state's first referendum. Ross was personally popular enough to become the state's first three-term governor (terms then lasted two years), but smashed his political career in 1936 in a losing campaign for the Senate against the unbeatable Republican, William Borah.

Plenty of other Democrats were elected in the Democratic sweep of the early 1930s, including several members of a remarkable Idaho Falls family. Chase Clark, an attorney who had practiced in Mackay before moving to Idaho Falls, ran for U. S. Senator in 1928 but lost in that Republican year. He went on to run for governor in 1940, won, and was later appointed a federal district judge after narrowly losing the 1942 election. His brother Barzilla, who, like Chase, served as a mayor of Idaho Falls, was elected governor to succeed Ross in 1936. Their cousin, D. Worth Clark, was even more successful, winning two terms in the U.S. House and then a term in the U.S. Senate in 1938. (He made two more unsuccessful tries for the office in 1944 and 1950.)

Part of the reason for Democratic progress in mid-century was Tom Boise, a Lewiston businessman, a Republican until 1936, but thereafter for thirty years the most powerful Democrat in Idaho. Boise was a conservative, as was, in many respects, the farm and labor vote he drew upon to form the backbone of the Democrat organization.

The Idaho Democratic Party through those decades was usually quite conservative—not drastically different from the Republican. The individualism, the skepticism of government, the moral traditionalism that marked Republicans was different only in tone and degree among many Democrats. The "economy bloc" of conservatives, who often fought for smaller budgets, dominated the Democrat controlled Legislature of the 1930s and passed more tax cuts than did the Republican majorities of the time. Such legislative leaders as Charles Gossett (later a governor and U.S. senator) were among the most powerful in Idaho history, partly because of close bipartisan working relationships. Few Democrats won substantial office in those years without backing by the party's conservatives.

One who did was Glen Taylor. A vaudeville entertainer who operated a traveling song and dance show, Taylor was the most liberal major-office politician Idaho has ever produced. The conservative Democratic organization was usually able to block his efforts, such as when he ran for the U.S. House in 1938 or Senate in 1940 and 1942. But by 1944, Taylor had become such a polished candidate, with such a large, loyal personal following, that he won the Democratic primary and, in that strong Democratic year, narrowly beat Clarence Bottolfsen, a two-term Republican governor. Taylor's political mistake came in accepting the 1948 vice-presidential nomination, with Henry Wallace topping the ticket of the left-leaning Progressive Party. Taylor was promptly branded a communist sympathizer, and he lost his 1950 Democratic primary election, and again in 1954, and a primary in 1956.[27]

The Red Scare, coupled with the national turn toward conservatism in 1950, took Idaho politics into another hard turn—to the right. Harry Truman in 1948 was the last Democrat to win Idaho's electoral votes with a strong margin and that year Democrats won up and down the ticket. Since then, only Lyndon Johnson has repeated the feat, but although he won nationally by a landslide he took Idaho only by a slim margin.

Through the Roosevelt and Truman years, Idaho Republicans remained active and powerful. By 1938, Republicans were recovering sufficiently from their shock of the previous few years to begin winning again, and the decade that followed was a closely-matched seesaw between the parties; major offices such as governor, senator and U.S. representative often switched from one party to the other.

In 1950, almost all the major-office Democrats up for election were swept out, and their party had to start virtually from scratch. With that election, Idaho entered a new pattern of partisan politics that, with but one short break, has lasted ever since.

NATIONAL POLITICS

The federal government has always been a strong presence in Idaho. In 1890, the initial year of Idaho statehood, Congress passed the Federal Forest Reserve Act, which set aside large chunks of the state as national forests. The forests covered, then as now, most of central and northern Idaho, and substantial swatches of the south. Much of the remainder of Idaho was reserved as federal land which was never obtained by private landowners through homestead or otherwise, and not given to the state. This land is today operated by the Bureau of Land Management. This federal presence in Idaho goes back to the first part of the century, and has been a central part of life in the state ever since.

But ever since World War II, the federal government has steadily become an even more obvious participant in Idaho.

World War II brought several major military developments to Idaho. One was Gowen Field, a military air base south of Boise which survives today as the headquarters of the Idaho National Guard. The Farragut Naval Training Station at Lake Pend Oreille became, in 1942, the second largest naval training station in the nation, though it was drastically scaled down after the war. A small Navy facility remains at Lake Pend Oreille: it functions as a submarine testing facility. In Pocatello, an army air base and a large military manufacturing station (for gun relining) was built, forming the initial base of that city's non-railroad manufacturing industry. And Mountain Home Air Force Base, created by Congress in 1942, barely survived several shutdown proposals to become Idaho's largest military base. It expanded in the 1990s.

The largest single federal development grew out of the National Reactor Testing Station, founded in the eastern Idaho desert near Arco in 1949. This grew into the Idaho National Engineering & Environmental Laboratory (Now called the Idaho National Laboratory) which established its base at Idaho Falls, and became eastern Idaho's largest employer.

The 1940s and 1950s in Idaho saw a shift from the statewide emphasis on smaller organizations like local, home-grown businesses and local governments, toward larger, more concentrated units, that operated on a more regional and national scale. Chain and branch banking, bitterly fought by a variety of interests for many years, led the way, coming to Idaho in the thirties. The little Idaho First National Bank, the first bank in Idaho, established in 1867, eventually became the largest, with branches in most of the large and mid-sized communities in the state. But bigness cropped up in other industries as well. In Boise, the Morrison-Knudsen Corporation, which started early in the century as a typical small construction company, obtained several large international contracts and became a massive international construction giant, all the while remaining based in Boise. Back in 1939, Joe Albertson founded his first grocery store in Boise; by the time he died in 1993, he had hundreds of stores in most states of the country, and the fastest-growing major supermarket chain in the nation.

During World War II, J. R. Simplot made money selling Idaho potatoes to the military, and later supplying french fries to restaurant chains such as McDonald's. His increasingly diversified company eventually became Idaho's largest single employer, with branches operating internationally. In the 1980s, Simplot helped found Micron Technology in Boise, which became one of the largest computer chip manufacturers in the nation, and Idaho's largest private employer.[28] Numerous small timber companies were gradually swept up by a few industry giants, so that by the 1960s such large companies as Potlatch and Boise Cascade (now called Boise Cascade LLC), dominated the field.

Concern about the impact of the outside world has remained potent as well. While Idaho has moved to expand international trade, many in the state expressed concern about the North American Free Trade Agreement (NAFTA). Timber producers in northern Idaho complained that Canadian producers were undercutting them because of unfair advantages. And southern Idahoans noted in 2002 that when the J. R. Simplot Company closed facilities in Caldwell and Heyburn, it announced expansion of locations in Canada and overseas. The streak of isolationism that has recurred through Idaho history has never vanished entirely.

REDEFINING THE PARTIES

The first major Republican figure of the post-World War II era was a moderate. St. Maries physician C. A. Robins, who was elected Idaho's first four-year-term governor in 1946, was actually the choice of a number of relatively liberal Republicans and Democrats. In his term, state government expanded rapidly and was reformed in many respects. The most controversial of reforms saw the number of school districts reduced from about 1,200 to about 120. Many Idahoans decried this consolidation as part of a communist plot.

In 1950, conservative Republicans took over for a time, led by new Governor Len Jordan, a Grangeville sheep rancher, car dealer, and former one-term legislator. Misapprehending the state's financial situation, Jordan ordered massive state budget cuts including the closure of two teacher colleges at Lewiston and Albion. The new senator elected that year was Herman Welker, a close ally of Wisconsin Senator Joseph McCarthy.

Jordan's Republican successor not only was one of the most activist governors in Idaho history but served longer than any governor before him. Robert Smylie, a little-known attorney elected as attorney general in 1950, admired the centralization and professionalization of state government begun by Robins (who had appointed Smylie as attorney general), and during his twelve years as governor, Smylie aggressively followed the same path. Smylie encouraged government action in areas such as roadways, parks and social services that succeeded in moving Idaho from near the bottom of state rankings, to somewhere near the middle. Smylie also found ways to increase taxes, arousing antagonism from conservatives in both parties.[29]

In the middle 1950s, a Democratic revival began and proceeded on two fronts. One was the organizational building of Tom Boise of Lewiston, who was able to set many labor union members and conservative farmers against the conservative Republican policies. The other track was that of 32-year-old Frank Church, who in 1956, after defeating Glen Taylor in a comeback attempt and then Republican incumbent Herman Welker, won a U.S. Senate seat in Idaho, and kept it for twenty-four years. Church was reliant on the Boise organization's support in his first win, but rapidly set about creating his own organization so as not to be overly dependent. He became the leader of the liberal Democrats, those willing to expand government activities and spending, especially on education. At the same time he took care not to veer too far from standard Idaho views on such sacred subjects as gun control. During the time of this revival the Democrats were highly competitive, and for four years in the 1960s held three of the state's four seats in Congress.

For a decade, both parties maintained internal equilibrium, balancing themselves between their two wings. These unstable politics imploded dramatically for both sides in 1966, resulting in the end of party organization, (or "machine") politics in Idaho.

The crucial race was for governor that year. Robert Smylie sought re-election to a fourth term, but faced strong opposition from the many Goldwater Republicans who had nearly carried the state for their candidate in the Johnson sweep of 1964. Smylie, who had supported New York Governor Nelson Rockefeller rather than Arizona Senator Barry Goldwater in the 1964 Republican presidential primaries, underestimated his opposition. He lost the 1966 primary to conservative state Senator Don Samuelson, one of a string of moderate losses to conservatives that year and for the next several elections. The key issue at that point was the sales tax, which Smylie had proposed and had pushed through the 1965 Idaho Legislature; Samuelson declared neutrality on the tax, but as a state senator had voted against it. Samuelson's win drew an independent candidacy for governor from liberal Republican State Senator Perry Swisher, who had been one of the prime legislative architects of the sales tax; Swisher's entry further diminished the Republicans' moderate base.[30] Among Democrats, a different picture emerged. The main primary contenders were Charles Herndon of Salmon, (who was backed by the Tom Boise organization), conservative Senate Minority Leader Bill Dee of Grangeville, and relatively liberal State Senator Cecil Andrus of Orofino. Herndon won the August primary, but was killed in a September plane crash. The Democratic central committee meeting that followed, held to fill the ballot vacancy, was hotly contested. Andrus, as the second-place finisher, campaigned for the nomination but was opposed by the Tom Boise forces, which backed another conservative Democrat, Max Hanson. The Church forces chose this moment to break with Boise and throw in with Andrus. Andrus won the nomination by two votes.

The effects of that vote were far-reaching. It was a death blow to the Boise organization, whose leader was gravely ill in late 1966, and to any Democratic Party statewide organization as such. Instead, it solidified Church and Andrus as the leading Democrats, and one or the other, or both, dominated Idaho Democratic politics from 1966 to

1994. Andrus lost the 1966 general election to Samuelson, but became the Democratic nominee again in 1970. He won that election and went on to win re-election three times, in 1974, 1986 and 1990.

The effect of all this was to pull many conservative Idaho Democrats out of the party, and into the Republican fold. Increasingly, the parties in Idaho took on more definite philosophical casts; the Republicans as conservatives, the Democrats as moderates or liberals.

Idaho since has elected a number of conservatives to long stretches in Congress. State Senator James McClure (who like Andrus got his big political break because a plane crash killed his party's front runner) was elected to the U.S. House in 1966, ousting a Democrat, Compton I. White, Jr., who also opposed Tom Boise in the fight over the Andrus nomination. McClure served three terms in the House then three terms in the U.S. Senate before retiring in 1990.

McClure's replacement was Larry Craig, who also had been a state senator representing McClure's home territory in Payette. Craig served a decade in the U.S. House, then was elected in 1990 to the Senate, and re-elected in 1996 and 2002.

In 1980, the Republican tide, initiated by Ronald Reagan's presidential campaign, swept Democrat Frank Church from the Senate. He was beaten by Steve Symms, who had served four terms in the U.S. House from the First Congressional District, and who stayed in the Senate two terms. Symms, in turn, was replaced by another Republican, Boise Mayor Dirk Kempthorne, and Kempthorne in 1998 by another Republican, Mike Crapo of Idaho Falls.

Apart from the popular Andrus and Church, who developed strong personal popularity around Idaho, most Democrats who won did so under unusual circumstances. A good example grew out of the unusual history of a prominent Republican, one of the best Idaho campaigners ever, George Hansen.

The former municipal official from the Pocatello area (former mayor of Alameda) was elected to the U.S. House in 1964, turning out two-term Democrat Ralph Harding. Hansen then opposed Senator Frank Church in 1968. Church had by then become a nationally prominent senator, particularly because he was one of the early "doves" on American military action in Vietnam and had been the keynote speaker at the 1960 Democratic National Convention. Hansen, by contrast, was a "hawk," and the lines formed clearly. Church, however, had already been given, by his opposition, a chance to put in-state damage from that issue behind him. In 1967, as Church became more outspoken on the war, a group in northern Idaho led by ex-Californian Ron Rankin tried to recall him. The effort backfired, as Church skillfully won over many Idahoans, if not on his view of the war then at least on his sincerity. The recall movement collapsed when it turned out to have been financed by a wealthy southern Californian from Orange County.[31] Church won that 1968 election in a landslide, his biggest ever, and went on to lead Senate investigations of the Central Intelligence Agency, chair the Senate Foreign Relations Committee, and to run for president in 1976.[32]

But Hansen's story in Idaho politics, one of the longest and strangest in the state's history, was just beginning. After another failed bid for the U.S. Senate in 1972, he recaptured his old House seat in 1974 by defeating incumbent moderate Orval Hansen (no relation) in the Republican primary. His campaign debts mounted, however, and problems associated with campaign finances would ultimately wreck his political career, cost him re-election in 1984 (losing to Democrat Richard Stallings, a professor at Ricks College) and send him to federal prison. Through most of that, Hansen remained popular in much of Idaho. A wonderfully skillful campaigner, he blamed many of his problems on Washington, D.C. Democrats and the Eastern, liberal news media, and entered on several crusades, notably against the Internal Revenue Service. Even when he lost in 1984— after conviction on four felonies related to finance reporting—the election results were so close they were recounted. Hansen went to prison not long after leaving Congress.[33] Years later, some of Hansen's convictions were overturned by an appeals court.

Hansen's successor Stallings served four terms in the House from the second district, one of the most Republican districts in the country, but he lost his 1992 Senate bid to Republican Boise Mayor Dirk Kempthorne. Stallings failed in a try to regain his former House seat in the 1998 election.

Since the 1940s, Democrats have had only a couple of high water marks. One was in 1958 when they took over the Idaho Legislature and every statewide office except governor. They campaigned on the strength of the recession and a Right to Work referendum which generated strong labor turnout. The other Democratic success was in 1990. Incumbent Democratic Governor Andrus led the ticket and Democrats won every major race except the U.S. Senate seat. They also held half of the seats in the Idaho Senate. Republican Lieutenant Governor Butch Otter cast the tie-breaking vote to give the Republicans control of the Senate. In both cases, the Democratic high water receded with the next election.

The year 1994 would become the best election year in decades for Republicans. They won every statewide and major race except the race for state auditor, won by Democrat J. D. Williams. Their landslide victory reduced the Democrats in the Legislature to a handful. Perhaps most significantly, the Republicans had recaptured the governorship. Republican Canyon County farmer and former party leader Phil Batt captured the office Democrats Cecil Andrus and John Evans had held between them for twenty-four years. Idaho's 1995 Legislature was, in fact, the most Republican in the nation with an 80 percent legislative majority. Each election year since has left overwhelming Republican margins in place. When Batt opted not to seek a second term, his successor, Republican Senator Dirk Kempthorne, won the job in a landslide and was easily reelected in 2002.

Idaho is a rapidly growing state, with large numbers of people coming and going, and its voting habits and patterns—and the laws governing them—have changed substantially over time. Even with the recent history of one-party dominance, Idaho's political future can never be considered permanently locked in place. There is little reason to believe that Idaho politics will not change again even though the Republicans since 1994 have maintained strong dominance. Once known as a fairly competitive two-party state with very exciting elections, Idaho, in the first decade of the 21st century, is the most Republican state in the union featuring rather dull elections with many offices uncontested.

Chapter 3 notes

1 Carlos Schwantes, *In Mountain Shadows* (Lincoln, NE: University of Nebraska, 1991), pp. 39-43.
2 Figures from Bureau of the Census, reported in various editions of the *Idaho Blue Book* published by the Idaho Secretary of State.
3 In general, see Sven Liljeblad, *Indian Peoples of Idaho*; Beal & Wells, *The History of Idaho* (Lewis Historical Publishing, 1959); Deward Walker, *Indians of Idaho* (University of Idaho Press, 1978).
4 Brigham Madsen, *The Bannock of Idaho* (Caxton, 1958).
5 See especially David Lavender, *Let Me Be Free: The Nez Perce Tragedy* (New York: Harper Collins, 1992); and Alvin Josephy, *The Nez Perce Indians and the Opening of the Northwest,* (New Haven, 1965).
6 See the Journals of the Lewis and Clark Expedition, various publishers and dates.
7 Cort Conley, *Idaho for the Curious* (Cambridge, ID: Backeddy Book, 1982), pp. 250-251.
8 Examples of such people (and their stories) can be found in many books, notably Rick Ripley, *The Ridgerunner*, (Cambridge, ID: Backeddy Books, 1987); Cort Conley, *Idaho Loners* (Cambridge, ID: Backeddy Books, 1994); and *Harold Peterson, The Last of the Mountain Men*, (Cambridge, ID: Backeddy Books, 1969), an account of Sylvan "Buckskin Bill" Hart, a long-time trapper on the Salmon River.
9 Conley, *Idaho for the Curious*, pp. 451-453.
10 Schwantes, *In Mountain Shadows*, p. 63; Idaho Blue Book 1993-1994, pp. 21-33; Ronald Limbaugh, *Rocky Mountain Carpetbaggers* (Moscow, ID: University of Idaho Press, 1982), pp. 18-19.
11 Schwantes, *In Mountain Shadows*, p. 46.
12 Schwantes, *In Mountain Shadows*, pp. 49-53; Conley, in *Idaho for the Curious*, for references to Pierce, pp. 62-70, and Florence, pp. 593-595.
13 Schwantes, p. 129.
14 Schwantes, pp. 88-89.
15 Carl Bianchi, ed., *Justice for the Times* (Boise, ID: Idaho Law Foundation, 1990).
16 Limbaugh, *Rocky Mountain Carpetbaggers*, pp. 28-65.
17 Josephy, *Nez Perce Indians*, pp. 32-88.
18 Peirce and Hagstrom, *Book of America*
19 Schwantes, p. 124.
20 Idaho *Blue Book* (State of Idaho, 1935), pp. 85-87.
21 A brilliant study of the trial and the circumstances, both local and national, surrounding it, is the exhaustive *Big Trouble*, by J. Anthony Lukas (New York: Simon & Schuster, 1997).
22 Lukas, *Big Trouble*,
23 Lukas, p. 50
24 Randy Stapilus, *Paradox Politics: People and Power in Idaho* (Boise, ID: Ridenbaugh Press, 1988), pp. 96-99; interviews with John Porter, John Corlett, Robert Smylie; article "W Lloyd Adams," by William Davis, Idaho Yesterdays, Summer 1968.
25 Hugh Lovin, "The Nonpartisan League and the Progressive Renascence in Idaho, 1919-24," *Idaho Yesterdays*, Fall 1988.
26 See Michael Malone, *C. Ben Ross and the New Deal in Idaho* (Seattle: University of Washington Press, 1970); it is the one full-scale biography of Ross.
27 Ross Peterson, *Prophet Without Honor* (University Press of Kentucky, 1974); Glen Taylor (autobiography), *The Way it Was With Me* (Secaucus, NJ: Lyle Stuart, 1979); Stapilus, *Paradox Politics*, pp. 81-84.
28 George Gilder, *The Spirit of Enterprise* (New York: Simon & Schuster, 1984).
29 See especially Robert Smylie, *Governor Smylie Remembers* (Moscow, ID: University of Idaho Press, 1998).
30 Accounts of this year's governor's election can be found in autobiographies by all four

major participants: Smylie, *Governor Smylie Remembers*, pp. 212-214; Andrus, *Politics Western Style*, pp. 16-18; Perry Swisher, *The Day Before Idaho* (Moscow, ID: News Review, 1995), pp. 52-63. An overview account appears in Stapilus, *Paradox Politics*, pp. 126-137. See also LeRoy Ashby and Rod Gramer, *Fighting the Odds: The Life of Sen. Frank Church*, pp. 234-235.

31 Ashby and Gramer, pp. 235-243.

32 For the Hansen story see generally, Stapilus, *Paradox Politics*, pp. 171-186.

33. Stapilus, *Paradox Politics*.

CHAPTER 4
VOTER PARTICIPATION AND PARTIES

M uch as the Deep South was rock-solid Democratic for many decades after Reconstruction, so Idaho since the early 1990s has headed toward one-party status. So solid is the Republican hold on Idaho that the Gem State may be the most Republican state in the country.

In the elections from 1992 to 2004, Republicans won U.S. Senate seats five times out of five; U.S. House seats 13 times out of 14 (and every time after 1992); the governorship three times; the down-ticket constitutional offices nine races out of twelve. Especially remarkable was the Republican record in state legislative races. From 1992 to 2002, Idaho's 105 legislative seats were up for election five times; of those 525 outcomes, Republicans prevailed 428 times. The fact that Democrats did not even contest more than a third of those seats does not diminish the Republicans' feat. Even county offices—each county elects nine officeholders—saw a sharp decline in the number of Democrats.

This situation has drastically changed politics in Idaho. Traditionally, Idaho politics has been dominated by a Republican majority but has been competitive, with no more than brief periods when Democrats were shut out from major office or a strong legislative presence.

Democratic representation has fallen before in the state's history (with the elections of 1894, 1904, 1912, 1920 and 1924 but at those times third parties split what might have been Democratic votes; first the Populists, later the Progressives. Only in 1920 was Republican dominance so complete as in recent elections.

Idaho has had all-Republican congressional delegations before, but only once since the 1920s has the monopoly endured for more than one election in a row (and then just for two elections, from 1980 to 1984). Republicans also held almost all statewide elective offices during the twenties. But attach a big asterisk: the Republican dominance in the twenties and in occasional elections early in the century resulted in large part from strong third-party activity. The Republican dominance in the 1990s and early in the new millennium is unprecedented in the state's history. All the statewide and major office positions except judicial are partisan—chosen in races where the parties nominate candidates. On the local level, county offices are partisan, but city, school board and other local district offices are not.

Even this does not convey the whole story. In 1994, 1998 and 2000 state Supreme Court contests—officially nonpartisan—took on a decisively partisan cast when large numbers of Republican Party workers and elected officials lined up to support one contender against another. One of those elections featured a former Republican attorney general and state senator, Wayne Kidwell, running against a former state Democratic Party chair, Mike Wetherell; Kidwell won. Partisan undercurrents have appeared in nonpartisan city elections, most notably a mayoral election in Boise in 1993 pitting the incumbent Brent Coles, who had strong Republican support, against Tracy Andrus, the daughter of Democratic Governor Cecil Andrus. The nonpartisan sector of Idaho government increasingly has taken on partisan coloration—with the Republican, whether official or unofficial in designation, winning virtually every time. But in 2003, Democratic state representative David Bieter was elected Boise mayor in a three-way race with Republican County Sheriff Vaughn Killeen and former Republican gubernatorial candidate Chuck Winder.

This partisan dominance has brought sweeping changes to the Gem State. It has narrowed the range of political debate; ideas, concepts, patterns of thinking about public matters which are part of civic life in nearby states are absent in Idaho. One-party dominance has reduced the influence of independents as a force "up for grabs." And it has diminished regionalism in Idaho, since all major regions of the state are now dominated by one party in contrast to the days when, for example, the north might be Democratic while other regions went in different directions.

What led to this overwhelming Republican dominance?

COMPETITIVE PARTY SYSTEM?

Idaho long has been a Republican state by most standards.[1] But historically, Idahoans have been notorious ticket splitters. They elected Democratic governors from 1970 to 1994 while electing Republican legislatures throughout that time. They sent Democrat Frank Church to the United States Senate for four consecutive terms along with some of the nation's most conservative lawmakers, including Congressmen George Hansen and Steve Symms.

Like most states, Idaho politics and government have primarily been in the hands of two major political parties—the Democratic and Republican—for most of its history. And most of that time, Republicans have held a rough majority or at least a strong plurality.

In many ways, the supporters for these parties in Idaho are similar to parties in other states. Business people, including the leaders of resource industries and many professionals support the Republican Party. So do an overwhelming number of farmers; strong Democratic inroads in the farm community in the thirties and forties all but vanished a generation later.

If that were all, one might suspect that the Republican Party should be weakening, since Idaho is becoming less reliant on resource industries, and the percentage of people involved with them has been in decline. But Republicans have picked up support from other groups.

The percentage of Mormons in Idaho has grown, (roughly doubling in the last half-century), and LDS church members are overwhelmingly Republican. The church's doctrines on social and economic issues neatly mesh with those of the Idaho Republican Party. Although the church itself goes to great lengths to declare itself nonpartisan. A number of Democratic officeholders also have been Mormon including the only two Mormons to serve as governor of Idaho, Arnold Williams and John Evans, and the last two Democratic second district congressmen, Ralph Harding and Richard Stallings.

Social conservatives generally have—increasingly in the last generation—gravitated to the Republican Party, and that includes many people who have migrated to Idaho from other less socially conservative locations. Many retirees who have moved to Idaho appear to be Republicans.[2]

The Republicans have developed a solid organization; voter education and superior get-out-the-vote efforts have elected Republicans even when Democrats have fielded strong candidates in competitive districts. The GOP also does a better job of encouraging absentee voting which boosts voter turnout. Absentee ballots and information are sent to prospective voters well in advance of election and absentee voting deadlines. All of that takes money, which the Republicans also have had in greater abundance.

"Election day" registration, starting in 1994, allows voters to register at the polls on Election Day. In the 1994 election, 31,704 people registered and voted the same day, five percent of the total number of registered voters. The impact of election day registration was especially high in Ada County, the state's most populous. In 1996, approximately 13 percent of the total number of registered voters registered at the polls—68,064 out of the total 508,030 votes cast. From 1998 through 2002, the numbers of same-day voters were again significant. No survey of these voters has been conducted to determine how they voted, but examination of polling information strongly suggests that many of these new voters were Republicans attracted to the polls by very strong Republican Party get-out-the-vote efforts.

These new voters have been crucial in elections in the 1990s and up to 2002. The vote for many Democrats remained about the same in 1994 as in several previous elections, adjusted for overall population gains. For example, Democrat Larry LaRocco, elected to Congress in 1990, actually won more votes in 1994 (even adjusted for district population gains) though he decisively lost that year to Republican Helen Chenoweth. The overall number of voters rose substantially in 1994 and 1996 over the previous elections; those new voters mostly favored Republicans.

Another factor suggests the Republicans advantage from election day registration. In some counties, such as Shoshone in the northern Idaho Panhandle, the numbers of election day registrants in 1994 and 1996 were almost negligible. In these counties, Republican and Democratic candidates won percentages more in line with their parties' historical records.

Precincts populated largely by new subdivisions and other new development, where many out-of-staters have settled, have generally favored Republicans. Many of these newcomers arrive from places on the Pacific coast, especially from California and the Seattle area and may have been voting with their feet. Their transit appears to have helped make Idaho more conservative, and their former homes more liberal, at the same time.

Meanwhile, traditional sources of Democratic support have been in decline. Organized labor, which once provided the core of Democratic strength, has fallen in membership and financial capacity since the seventies, a decline hastened by the (Republican-supported) Right to Work law passed in 1985. Democrats have become deprived of a once-strong army of campaign workers, and no other comparably large group has arisen to replace it. What is left of organized labor has been relatively divided between the parties. Many environmentally-oriented Democrats have clashed with timber and other resource industry labor union members over environmental and other issues, and those labor union members have given increasing numbers of their votes to Republican candidates who are closer to them on environmental (if not always some economic or social) issues.

What is left for Democrats is a collection of interest groups, which, individually, are relatively small. The once-central role of the Idaho AFL-CIO as a key organizer and fundraiser for Democrats has been largely taken over by the Idaho Education Association, a school teachers union (and in some years, the largest single donor to Democratic legislative campaigns). Environmental groups such as the Idaho Conservation League and Idaho Rivers United are much more disposed to Democrats than Republicans, and so are a number of social welfare groups. Even combined, however, their resources are small compared to those available to the Republicans.

Environmentally-oriented ("wine and cheese") Democratic candidates have cost Democrats votes in farm and labor-oriented communities.

Idaho Democrats also have had to contend with unpopular national figures. Such national Democrats as Jimmy Carter, Edward Kennedy, Bill Clinton and Al Gore have been deeply unpopular in Idaho, and have served as weights around the necks of Idaho Democratic candidates. Unpopular national liberal figures have continued to hurt Democrats—even when some of them live in Idaho. In 1980, Democratic Senator Frank Church held a fundraiser featuring the singer Carole King who lived in central Idaho. She urged Church to close INEEL—a position Church did not share, but which may have hurt him anyway.

Democrats also have suffered from diminishing expectations as losses have led to expectations of loss—and a resulting diminished ability to field quality candidates, raise money and find volunteer help. News media reports, not only opinion columns but also news articles in Idaho, often describe Democratic candidates, even many months ahead of the election, as longshots or underdogs. That further undercuts Democrats' ability to compete.

Still, nothing stays the same forever in politics.

Speaking to the most Republican legislature in the country, Governor Phil Batt said in his first "State of the State" address in 1995 that "(w)e Republicans should not read (the message of the 1994 election) wrong. Let us not overemphasize the approval of our party. The voters have a very tenuous relationship with any political party. We Republicans can be removed from power in a single election, if we put politics above the desires of the electorate."[3]

Governor Batt understood that Republicans are more dominant in the ranks of state elected officials than in the electorate. As he implicitly suggested, partisan attachments remain subject to change.

PARTICIPATION

Involvement in party politics is just one of many avenues of participation available to Idahoans.

One could simply argue that Idahoans accept the logic of the old saying, "you can't complain about government if you don't at least vote"—and they do like to complain. Or, one could say that Idaho's voter turnout rates help validate Elazar's classification of much of the state as being moralistic. There lies in the Idaho political culture an attitude that voting is a civic obligation, a duty that must be performed. Voter turnout rates are typically above the national average, and in some elections Idaho turnout rates have been among the highest in the country.

Idaho remains a relatively "easy entry" state for participating in politics. Both political parties often are on the lookout for party and campaign workers, and are often looking for candidates as well. The competition for entry is tougher on the Republican side, but that often means an ambitious candidate simply needs to put in a few more years working in the party structure or helping with campaigns. Many elected officials in Idaho work their way up the system in that fashion.

David Leroy, a Boise Republican, has remarked on this: "One thing that is eminently obvious in Idaho politics, Ada County politics included, is that a young person with a better mousetrap who's willing to work hard can actually get elected."[4] Leroy, an attorney and Lewiston native, started his legal career in New York City but moved to Boise and entered politics. Before he turned 40, Leroy was elected as an Ada County prosecutor, Idaho attorney general and Idaho lieutenant governor (and very nearly governor as well).

POLITICAL PARTIES

For most of its history the United States has had a two-party system, but never a national system. The American system is characterized by a decentralized system of state parties that exercise considerable autonomy. Unlike the British or Canadian models, state and local parties are more concerned about winning elections than they are about having their policy positions adopted. According to political scientists Hrebenar and Benedict, "party positions and platforms drive policymaking in only a few, and often not the most significant areas of public concern."[5] Whatever the differences between the Democrats and Republicans, for either party to be successful, it must compete where a majority of the voters are positioned—close to the center of the political spectrum where policy distinctions are often blurred.

Despite their lack of ideological orientation, political parties at all levels play an important role in American democracy. In fact some say they "are essential to the effective operation of modern democratic societies."[6] They are viewed as "the best medium of representation between the mass public and government."[7] They perform this representative function by mobilizing a variety of groups—economic, ideological, trade, professional—to participate in the political process, amassing voters to compete for elective office. They encourage participation and help legitimize the process and, in a real sense, simplify the process by providing cues to the voters as to which party or candidate to support.

Voters historically have believed that Democrats and Republicans stood for different policy positions whether they actually have or not. For substantial periods of Idaho history the differences may have been subtle, but at other times—such as during the Great Depression—the differences have diverged sharply. Since the mid-1960s, conservatives have migrated away from the Democratic Party, and moderates and liberals away from the Republican, with the effect that in the 1970s and 1980s the Democrats had moved generally further to the left and Republicans further to the right. The overwhelming Republican control in Idaho in the recent election cycles has made such analysis more difficult but the voters clearly perceive party differences. A "Republican" nomination of a candidate is only a slight step from election in many parts of the state, a strong indicator of the power of that party label and what stands behind it.

Parties also help organize the government. The parties, for example, provide leadership in the legislative branch. Members of the Legislature voting through their party caucuses determine the composition of legislative leadership.

State law largely determines state party structure. Every aspect of the organization is set forth in the Idaho Code from the very foundation of the party, the precinct organization, to the state party chair.

Idaho is divided into about 900 voting precincts, the exact number and boundaries determined by county clerks and commissions. Each party is entitled to elect (at the primary elections) precinct committee members for each precinct. The precinct committee members collectively form the county central committee, which does have some official and unofficial roles. Both major parties usually try to fill as many of these positions as possible, but often few county organizations manage to fill them all.

Party leaders generally are more interested in filling precinct positions than in encouraging contests for them. Still, contests do occasionally happen—ordinarily when an ideological faction decides to take control of a party organization from another faction. This has happened more often among Republicans than among Democrats, usually when moderate and conservative groups field competing sets of precinct candidates. Challenges by conservatives against moderates fell short in the 1970s in Bannock County and in the 1990s in Kootenai County. However, a 1990s challenge by conservatives in Ada County did succeed. It resulted in the election of a conservative Republican chair in Idaho's most populous county.

Precinct workers often contribute the hours necessary to circulate the party's message throughout their neighborhoods. They are the party foot soldiers; they reflect little glamour and do a lot of work.

Historically, county organizations have exerted much clout in party politics in Idaho. County chairs and central committee members, composed of chosen precinct committee persons have played key roles in the election of federal, state and local officials. At one time, the county organization, particularly the chair, had patronage power—considerable say over who received state jobs; in 1967 new state merit system legislation undercut this power.[8]

The U.S. Supreme Court in the 1964 *Baker v. Carr* decision and subsequent decisions also weakened the power of the county organization. These decisions required both houses of the Legislature to redistrict on the basis of population and throw out old systems that included equal representation for each county in the Idaho Senate regardless of population. The House was apportioned on a population basis. Implementation of "one-man (person), one-vote" undermined county representation and control and, in Idaho, led to the creation of a whole new structure of party organization—almost a parallel organization— the legislative district committee. Legislative districts are the basis for legislation representation but are not coterminous with county boundaries. They include a portion of a county or a combination of counties. The new reapportionment rules virtually required in some instances the combining of counties to get the kind of balance in population required to satisfy the new criteria set by the U.S. Supreme Court in the 1960s and 1970s. Now county organizations share power with another set of local party officials who may be from another county.[9]

Both county and legislative district organizations are represented in the state party central committee, along with members who serve in an ex-officio capacity. Even though the state and local party organization may appear to be a hierarchy from the top (state) to bottom (local), no command and control authority exists. Just as the national party apparatus does not dictate to the states, the state does not dictate to the locals, except when it has dollars to contribute to campaigns.

There is, depending on the strength of the party system, considerable coordination of efforts. The Idaho Republican Party has been particularly effective in making this coordination work. Some of that can be attributed to the strength of the talent in the organization as well as the dominance of the Republican Party in Idaho politics.

Central committees, led by a chair who is a spokesperson, and by an executive director who handles staff efforts, govern both major political parties statewide. Both parties maintain full-time offices in Boise. Chair and executive director positions have, through most of the last half-century, rotated regularly, as few people have served more than two or three years—and no one in many years serving as long as a decade.

PRIMARY ELECTIONS

Primary elections, which tend to attract far fewer voters than general elections, have been the subject of much debate and speculation.

In Idaho, as in many other western states, primaries grew out of a turn of the century reform spirit. The purpose of the direct primary is to give the voters and not the party elites the power to select party nominees. The direct primary was established in 1909 in Idaho, over the objections of a number of political party leaders, especially a number of Republicans. When they swept into power in 1919 after a brief period of Democratic dominance, they abolished the primary. But popular pressure for it kept building, and in 1931 Democratic Governor C. Ben Ross and a Republican legislature brought it back. Idaho has had the direct primary ever since.[10]

Idaho has an open primary system. A voter can cast a ballot for candidates in any party without having to declare a party preference. (A voter can vote for candidates only within a single party at a time, however, and cannot jump back and forth between parties.) Absent party registration in Idaho, no conclusive statistics about the number of Republicans or Democrats exist. Strategists in both political parties long have presumed that, while there are more self-regarded Republicans than Democrats in Idaho, the number of either still falls short of a majority, and a large slice of Idaho voters consider themselves independent. *Public Policy* surveys validate their presumption. For example, in the 2004 survey, statewide survey respondents indicated that 29 percent considered themselves to be independents, 18 percent Democrats, and 47 percent Republican.[11]

That has sometimes led to discussion of the impact of "crossover" voting, as voters with a loyalty to one party vote in the other's primary, either to push for a weak opponent or to vote against an especially odious (to them) candidate. No major study of crossover voting in Idaho has ever been attempted, however, and its real impact remains a topic of much debate and considerable mystery.

The political process in Idaho is very open. Parties have little control over the entrance of candidates into their nominating procedures. Such openness has hurt both parties at times. In the 1950s and 1960s, the Democrats chose pro-gambling candidates, two of whom won the party's nomination for governor by plurality votes in the Democratic primaries, Al Derr in 1958 and Vernon K. Smith in 1962. Republicans sometimes have had difficulty nominating their strongest candidate from a crowded field of hopefuls. In 1978, seven Republicans ran for the gubernatorial nomination; the winner was a candidate with strong support in eastern Idaho but not elsewhere, and Democratic Governor John Evans won the general election. In 1994, Republican Phil Batt entered his party's primary campaign partly to ensure that, unlike 1978, a strong candidate would be nominated. Democrats have had similar problems, such as when a supporter of national splinter figure Lyndon LaRouche won a nomination for the Ada County Commission; Democratic voters apparently had not realized which candidate in the race was the mainstream Democratic candidate.

Idaho's primaries have had no measurable impact on presidential nominations. Since the early 1980s, the national Democratic Party has refused to accept returns from the Idaho primary as a basis for selecting delegates to its national convention, since the open primary system allows Republicans to participate if they choose. In response, Idaho Democrats have held county caucuses to determine presidential preferences and select delegates. The caucus procedures are relatively complex and require handbooks for even experienced party leaders. In general, any self-declared Democrat can attend and vote in a caucus, which can last several hours. Delegates are selected to the state party convention; at the state convention, delegates are picked to attend the national convention.

The Idaho Republicans do make a little more use of the primary— their national organization does not bar its use in delegate selection— but it has had almost no impact on national events because it is held in late May (close to Memorial Day), long after the presidential nominating decisions have been made.

The May primary has been attacked as useless in the presidential sweepstakes and for providing an early start for statewide general election campaigns. For a time in the 1970s, the primary was held in August; that was criticized because it was held during what is for many people vacation time, and candidates campaigning then found relatively little interest among voters.

Regardless of the primary date, turnout has been light, typically ranging from 30 percent to 35 percent. Participation in the May 2004 primary was even worse: 25 percent. Ada County, home to Idaho's capital city, had only a 16 percent turnout. It is believed that those who turnout in such primaries are mainly party activists and often people on the philosophical extremes. They tend not to be representative of their party membership, often being either more liberal (Democrats) or more conservative (Republicans).

LOCAL ELECTIONS: FROM COUNTIES TO SEWER DISTRICTS

Turnout for local elections usually is even lower than for primaries. Though turnout rates vary significantly among the more than 1,000 local units, the typical pattern is low turnout, 10 percent to 20 percent. Consolidation of most local government elections was approved by the Idaho Legislature in the 1990s with the intent—or hope—of increasing voter turnout. Prior to passage of this legislation, local elections could be held on almost any day of the calendar year. Such scheduling discretion appeared to free officials to manipulate voter turnout, placing elections on dates that almost guaranteed low turnouts and holding elections quickly before the opposition could mount an effective campaign against a bond issue or a levy override.

THIRD PARTIES

In 1992, independent Ross Perot—running under the banner of the Reform Party—made a mighty if temporary wave in Idaho politics. Idaho provided one of Perot's best showings that year, taking 27.1 percent of the vote and almost edging Democrat Bill Clinton for second place. (As it has every time since 1968, Idaho voted Republican for president.) Idahoans appeared to enjoy Perot's bluntness and his criticism of normal party politics in Washington—always a potent theme in Idaho. The year 1992 marked unusually high voter turnout, and some indications were that Perot drew as many as 60,000 new voters to the polls. Voter analysis also suggests that most of these voters were Republicans—meaning that in Idaho, Perot may have contributed to the Republican tide that dominated for a decade to come. As did George Wallace's 1968 independent presidential candidacy in the south, Perot's independent candidacy may have provided the crossroad for a number of conservative Democrats (especially in northern Idaho) to make the switch to voting Republican thereafter.

The Perot constituency, as such, did not survive 1992. His Reform Party fielded statewide and local office candidates in the elections that followed, but none of them came close to winning. When Perot ran again in 1996, his portion of the Idaho vote dropped to 13 percent. By that point, his Reform Party had become just another in the shifting groups of small-scale parties which pop up in Idaho election years.

The two main parties have not been seriously contested by a third party for many years, not since early in the state's history. In Idaho's first two decades, silver issues badly split the Republicans and created a strong Populist Party (which sent one senator and two representatives to Congress, as well as a number of state legislators to the Statehouse). In the twenties, the Progressive Party elected a number of legislators. However, since 1900 only Republicans and Democrats have served in Congress from Idaho, and since 1928 only major party candidates have been elected to the Idaho Legislature.

Since the Progressives, only one third party has persistently fielded candidates in Idaho: the Libertarian Party. It has run candidates for offices from U.S. Senate through the Idaho Legislature, but has never come remotely close to filling a ballot for positions statewide. It ordinarily runs about a dozen candidates for various offices in a given election—and it has never come very close to winning an office. The Libertarians generally have operated on a shoestring, with small budgets and little or no campaign organization. In 2002, they received some funding from national term limits organizations, and used the money to field candidates for several dozen state and federal offices.

The Natural Law Party has presented candidates for congressional offices and has gained some statewide visibility by participating in public television debates. None of the candidates have done very well but they have been in a position to be a "spoiler" in at least one close race. In 1996, the Natural Law Party candidate may have altered the outcome of the First District Congressional race when she received 2 percent of the vote while the winner Helen Chenoweth got 50 percent and her challenger Democrat Dan Williams got 48 percent.

Like most state political parties in the West, Idaho's parties are not very strong in either policy influence or candidate selection. Both draft and adopt platform documents every other year; these are swiftly forgotten and rarely referred to, other than as occasional grist for attack by the opposition. Neither party has a large amount of discretionary income, though candidates in both parties do rely to some extent on party organization contributions for their campaigns. Both parties hold election-year summer conventions (often at the same time at opposite ends of the state) but—especially since the primary election day was moved from August to May after 1978—little serious business is conducted, and these affairs are little more than pep rallies.

These are among the reasons Republican Governor Batt warned his colleagues about the risk of losing support. He correctly understood that even as the state became more one-party-Republican, the citizens will have only a loose attachment to political parties.

Chapter 4 notes

1 See James B. Weatherby, "Idaho: Growth and Change in A Conservative State" (paper prepared for delivery at the American Political Science Association Annual Meeting, Washington, D.C., August 1997) and Randy Stapilus, *Paradox Politics: People and Power in Idaho* (Boise, ID: Ridenbaugh Press, 1988).
2 Michael Barone, "Divide and Rule," *National Journal*, no. 28 (July 12, 1997): 1411.
3 Phil Batt, 'State of the State Address," (Boise, ID, January, 1993).
4 Stapilus, *Paradox Politics*, p. 243.
5 Ronald J. Hrebenar and Clive S. Thomas, eds., *Interest Groups in the American West* (Salt Lake City: University of Utah Press, 1987).
6 Clive Thomas, *Politics and Public Policy in the Contemporary American West* (Albuquerque: University of New Mexico Press, 1991).
7 Ibid.
8 Stephanie L. Witt, "Idaho," in State Party Profiles: A 50-State Guide to Development, Organization, and Resources, eds. Andrew Appleton and Daniel S. Ward (Washington, D.C.: Congressional Quarterly, Inc., 1998).
9 Witt, "Idaho."
10 Boyd Martin, *The Direct Primary in Idaho* (Stanford: Stanford University Press, 1947).
11 *16th Annual Public Policy Survey* (Boise, ID: Social Science Research Center, Boise State University), 2005.

THE PROMINENT ROLE
OF INTEREST GROUPS

Individuals have a stronger voice acting in concert than acting separately. An Idaho schoolteacher may have little influence on federal education policies or state funding decisions. But as a member of one of the largest statewide organizations in Idaho—the Idaho Education Association—that teacher's voice can be magnified many times. What is true in education is equally true in many other arenas.

Even at the grass roots, interest group activity is accelerating. Neighborhood organizations, a relatively new concept in Idaho, are forming in many of Idaho's largest cities. Boise has more than 30 officially recognized neighborhood organizations many of which were formed around issues involving a proposed new development in their neighborhood; cities such as Nampa and Pocatello also are developing such groups. These activists are sensitive to neighborhood protection issues and let the planning and zoning commissions and local governing bodies know their positions when they feel their neighborhoods are being threatened.

In Boise, activists in the city's North End have periodically become major players in city and Ada County Highway District (ACHD) politics. Some of these activists favor slower growth and more reliance on mass transit operations, and have become more directly involved in land use planning decisions. That growth position developed into a local political controversy as other parts of the city sought faster growth. The Idaho Legislature finally intervened, reorganizing the ACHD into representation by districts, eliminating the North End's dominance on the ACHD commission.

Interest groups represent a source of influence in the political system that can compete with political parties. Their impact can be especially strong in states such as Idaho, where loyalty to political parties —and the lack of party "machines" of the type that exist in some states—opens other conduits for those seeking to influence public policy. Ordinarily, however, interest groups and political parties do not compete as such. Rather, interest groups usually align themselves with parties, candidates and office holders—a set of affiliations that can change dramatically over time.

Political rhetoric is full of references to "special interests" which are often cast as evil forces bent on subverting the will of the people. Less noted is that most of the critics of "special interests" are themselves members of interest groups. In fact, most Idahoans are members of interest groups whether they know it or not. As an example, the Idaho Farm Bureau sells many insurance policies in the state; its policyholders directly or indirectly contribute to the organization's lobbying efforts. Various religious organizations have weighed in on one or more public policy issues.

Keeping large groups united across a range of issues, however, can be difficult in a state as spread-out as Idaho. As much as the state is dominated politically by a single party, dominance in policy-making is much more amorphous, with periodic development of unexpected coalitions. These people who have come to their "last place" in Idaho, will go to great lengths to defend their interests, to the point of joining forces with those conventionally considered the "enemy."

GROUP TACTICS

Access is a primary goal of any group seeking to influence policy-making. Before a group can effectively deliver a message, it needs to get the attention of the key decision makers; that means having access at critical stages in the decision making process to influence the final outcome. Gaining this access and sharpening one's message requires many activities.

Interest groups take direct action by providing financial contributions to endorsed candidates and mobilizing their membership to vote for their endorsed candidates. There are also many indirect actions that can be taken including providing a forum for candidates to speak at organizational meetings and publicizing favored candidacies in organizational publications. One of the most potent tools the interest groups have is money, "the mother's milk of politics," the ability to make significant contributions to highly valued incumbents or to promote the candidacies of sympathetic new candidates.

These groups do not remain static, however. Their contribution amounts have changed from year to year, and many of the largest are ad hoc, formed around specific issues or interests. For example, there was a major presence of the group "Idahoans Against One Percent" in 1992 but they were invisible in 2002 when there was no tax limitation measure was on the ballot. Taxpayer groups gave way to ideologically and economically oriented Political Action Committees (PACs) in 2002, groups such as Citizens for Term Limits and Yes on One: The Idaho Coalition for Indian Self-Reliance.

Listed here are the five biggest-contributing political action committees—financial organs that interest groups create to manage and distribute political funds—in the 1992 election year cycle in Idaho.[1]

1.	$554,090	Idaho Education Association PAC
2.	$338,451	Idahoans Against One Percent
3.	$185,455	Morrison-Knudsen PAC
4.	$103,246	YES! We Want No Casinos
5.	$61,134	Idaho Business PAC

Now, here are the five largest from the 2002 election cycle, ten years later:

1.	$3,860,752	Yes on One: The Idaho Coalition for Indian Self-Reliance
2.	$349,515	Idaho Education Association PAC
3.	$279,509	Committee to Repeal the Repeal
4.	$230,475	Citizens for Term Limits
5.	$192,349	Realtors PAC

The largest single PAC in recent years has been one operated by the statewide teachers' organization, the Idaho Education Association (IEA), but its impact has been less than one might expect. The IEA has supported mostly Democrats at a time when Democrats have been losing and have consequently trimmed overall spending. That means they have little clout with the people who lead state government (who are almost all Republicans), and they have less ability to affect a change. By the end of the 1990s, the organization was contributing to more Republican candidates, but that change did not succeed in winning the IEA new friends in that party. Republican candidates often referred to it as the teachers' "union," rather than as the professional organization teachers consider it to be.

The IEA also has been involved in many ballot issues, including property tax limitation initiatives in 1992 and 1996. These activities drew down the resources it could otherwise direct to sympathetic candidates. Its involvement with candidates has been sporadic—sometimes highly active, at other times withdrawn, even in major races.

Many of the other large PACs are issues-oriented, centered around such topics as term limits, abortion and gambling. Almost $4 million expended by the tribal gambling interests in 2002. But big-ticket issue PACs are only part of the story: dozens of individually smaller business PACs do contribute to candidates, and their totals are far larger than the IEA or most of the issues PACs. In all, political action committees contributed about $6.7 million to candidates or ballot measures in Idaho in the 2002 election cycle. That is big money in the context of Idaho political campaigns.[2]

In their drive to influence decision makers, interest groups try to shape public opinion, gaining general approval for their organization and some of its policy positions. They seek to define their policy positions as being consistent with state priorities, the "public interest." In the 1980s when Idaho's economy was stagnant and economic development was virtually every official's public policy goal, most major legislation was presented as "economic development legislation" whether the label really fit or not. City sponsorship of Tax Increment Financing (TIF) in the late 1980s benefited from this economic development emphasis. A similar measure had failed in the late 1970s when TIF was more associated with urban renewal and an unpopular program to redevelop downtown Boise during a period of rapid growth. But in the 1980s the mood and priorities had changed, the financing device became known in the late 1980s as "revenue allocation" and the successful bill was officially called "The Economic Development Act of 1988." City lobbying efforts nicely coincided with the mood of the public.[3]

To the extent that they can link their goals with current state priorities, groups can be effective. According to political scientists Clive Thomas and Ron Hrebenar, ". . .despite the rhetoric of many groups that their goals are 'in the public interest' these goals are often narrow and sometimes very self-serving; gaining a tax break, getting an exemption from a regulation, securing a budget appropriation,. . ."[4] Perception is often reality in politics.

Groups operate not only in the policy formulation and adoption arenas but also in the implementation arena. Thomas and Hrebenar, note that ". . .as state government expands and becomes more complex, more and more lobbying is directed toward the bureaucracy"[5] and to an increasing extent, to the courts. Groups seek to make sure that their legislation is carried out according to the original intent. The sheer volume of new regulations compels them to shepherd their legislation through the rulemaking process or work to undermine the impact of a bill they have opposed. Policy making does not end with the passage of a bill.

The judicial arena is also an access point for further policymaking in that a suit or a threatened suit can raise issues that reluctant legislators are often obliged to address. A group of Idaho school districts, for example, sued the state over what they contended is a failure by the Idaho Legislature to comply with the state constitutional mandate to provide a "thorough" education. These suits and what they could do to the state budgeting process have attracted a lot of legislative interest. For years, the "thoroughness" issue was at or near the top of the legislative agenda. On one occasion, the Legislature even passed a bill seeking to, in effect, dismiss the suit against it—by turning the complaining districts into defendants, on the charge that *they* had failed to provide a thorough education. At this writing, the whole issue still is in court.

Much lobbying still remains focused on the legislative process. The key policymakers in the state are the legislators and in a pluralistic democracy legislators beget lobbyists. They need each other. Lobbyists need votes and sponsorship; citizen legislators need informed expertise on complex legislation and, while we like it or not, campaign contributions.

Idaho has averaged approximately 300 lobbyists during the past several years compared to Utah's 800-900, Montana's 750, and Oregon's 700. In some states, governmental employees are required to register as lobbyists even though much of their work entails testifying on technical impacts to their agencies—raising, for example, Arizona's roster of registered lobbyists in 1996 to 5,500—but that is not a requirement in Idaho. Government officials often do play a major role in the lobbying arena, however, not only advising legislators of the impact of some legislation but also pursuing their own agency priorities. There are also many volunteers and volunteer organizations who lobby but need not file because they are not paid for the work. They make their presence known in the capitol when a bill affects them.[6]

Some of these amateurs can be the most effective of all.

In the 1980s, the Association of Idaho Cities (for which one of the authors was then a lobbyist) proposed a bill to authorize cities to impose fees on all tax-exempt properties, including churches, for the payment of police and fire services. The bill was reported out of the House Revenue and Taxation Committee on a Friday and sent to the House floor, but the following Monday the committee chair rose on the House floor and asked that the bill be returned to committee, in effect a killing maneuver (with which the House agreed). The chairman did not do this out of personal opposition. He had read the reaction of legislators returning from their weekend stay at home, where they had been exposed to a wave of sermons preached that Sunday about the bill to "tax churches."

One of the most valuable resources lobbyists have is information; during much of Idaho's history, before the creation of the Legislative

Council (the first legislative staff) in 1963, lobbyists were virtually the sole source of legislators' information. The Council filled some of this void, especially as it grew into a substantial number of research specialists. But lobbyists are still major information providers to legislators. As legislation has become more complex, the need for increasing amounts of information has led legislators to remain heavily reliant upon lobbyists, particularly those lobbyists who have credibility and expertise.[7] If legislators want to know about the impact on doctors of a particular piece of legislation they will contact the Idaho Medical Association. Consideration of environmental legislation may lead them to call on either the Idaho Association of Commerce and Industry or the Idaho Conservation League.

Lobbyists generally are highly regarded in the Idaho Legislature. They are members of the so-called "Third House," recognized as legitimate players in the legislative process. The relationship between legislators and lobbyists in Idaho usually is amiable and symbiotic.

Marilyn Shuler, while a graduate student at Boise State University, conducted extensive interviews with 100 of the 105 members of the 1975 Idaho Legislature and reported: "Many legislators indicated that lobbyists deserved to have a better reputation among the general public. Legislators viewed them as offering accurate and helpful information, and it was often reported that the Legislature could not function efficiently without their help."[8] Another 1975 study of the Idaho Legislature also indicated that lobby groups were well respected by Idaho legislators. A third study provides evidence of the positive role of lobbyists in the Legislature.[9]

Lobbying regulation, particularly registration, is used to identify who the lobbyists are, whom they are representing and what issues are getting their attention. This allows greater opportunity for public scrutiny of who is really concerned about a particular issue and what resources are being used to influence policymakers. Such regulations are also important given the negative public attitude toward lobbying groups. Idaho was one of the last states to pass regulatory legislation. A 1970 publication on Idaho lobbying noted that: "the only provision in current law relating to the regulation of lobbying is a 1907 law which prohibits any person from attempting to influence the vote of any member of the Legislature except by appearing before a committee, by newspaper publication, by public addresses or by written statements, arguments or briefs. Violations of this section are misdemeanors and are punishable by fine and/or jail sentence. (18-4707). . . In addition, House rules forbid lobbying within the chambers and the Senate prohibits lobbying while the Senate is in session unless the individual senator authorizes the lobbyist to speak to him."[10]

In 1967, the Citizens Committee on the State Legislature recommended "the legislature adopt legislation which would require lobbyists to register and disclose their expenses in their efforts to influence legislation. Such legislation is common in most states."[11] Legislation was introduced to implement the committee's recommendations but was never passed. Given this legislative inaction, an initiative petition was circulated that ultimately led in 1974 to the passage of the "Sunshine Act" that imposed many of the committee's earlier recommendations. The timing was perfect. The initiative passed in the wake of the Watergate scandals and the disclosure about huge amounts of money mishandled in the 1972 presidential campaign. Lobbyists are now required to report any expenditure over a minimal level and to indicate the specific bills they are lobbying.[12]

TYPES OF LOBBYING GROUPS

There are many types of lobbying organizations in Idaho. Some of the most influential are the economic interest groups like the Idaho Association of Commerce and Industry (IACI) and the many corporations who have their own lobbyists but also work under the umbrella of IACI. They lobby to protect primarily the economic interests of their membership but they also have been active on more general issues, such as their leadership of the campaign against the property tax limitation initiatives and, and support for education and tort reform.

There are also professional groups including the Idaho Medical Association, Idaho Dental Association, Idaho Hospital Association, and Idaho Trial Lawyers Association. Ideological groups such as the Idaho Chooses Life, the American Civil Liberties Union, or the Idahoans for Tax Reform also are often active. Their motivation is to promote a particular cause or principle.

"Good government" groups, such as the League of Women Voters, primarily stress the provision of information without ostensibly trying to promote a policy agenda. They provide information and monitor committee activity but rarely testify or take positions unless they have reached consensus through a thorough study and review of a selected issue.

Last but certainly not least are the governmental lobbies. Intergovernmental lobbying is on the increase. The variety of government lobbyists in Idaho is significant, even including university presidents. They encompass whole categories of state and local government entities and individual governments as well. The Association of Idaho Cities and the Idaho Association of Counties are two of the most respected and visible lobbying organizations. Other local government organization such as the school, highway and fire districts along with employee organizations, especially the firefighters and public educators, also are significant players.

Clout by these groups in Idaho, as elsewhere, is derived from a number of factors, such as those noted in the Hrebenar-Thomas study. How important is the group to the state? Does it arrive at the Statehouse with hat in hand, or does it have important bargaining chips—does it arrive with a strong negotiating stance?

For decades, Idaho Power Company was in just such a position. Though a regulated utility, it was in a strong financial position and had support among many Idahoans because of its low electrical rates and its many community service offices. It also was a major taxpayer, partly because it owned a string of expensive hydropower dams (which in turn were partly responsible for the low rates). That public support, combined with a skillful lobbyist corps, made Idaho Power a force for many years. It is still important in Idaho, but less than in decades past. In the early 1980s the company was forced (by stockholders) to defend its water rights at one of the Snake River dams and to file suit against thousands of farmers in southern Idaho. Abruptly, legislative candidates arose specifically to march against Idaho Power Company. The firm's standing at the Legislature diminished from that point on. Lawmakers could, if they chose, vote against Idaho Power on some issues with apparent impunity.

Other economic groups that have large constituencies, including the Idaho Farm Bureau and the Intermountain Forest Association, and large businesses that employ Idahoans in many regions of the state, including the J. R. Simplot Company, Albertson's, Potlatch, Micron Technology and others, similarly have been able to use their economic position as a major bargaining chip. They can and some have threatened to leave Idaho. They can point out how the welfare of their Idaho employees will be affected by what they view as a harmful public policy decision.

Interest groups more often on the side of the status quo than on the side of change generally have an edge. Legislation usually is harder to pass than it is to kill. For years, for example, a collection of anti-tax groups laid in wait at the Senate Local Government and Taxation Committee, which acts on tax measures which already have been approved in the House. The committee's makeup historically has made it a killing ground for tax legislation. Pushing a bill all the way through the process can be far more draining on resources than a targeted one-shot approach to kill a bill at any single point. Even most major groups will carry only a small number of bills in any given legislative session. To kill, there is no need to convince 105 legislators; it may need only one or a handful of people—legislative leadership or the committee chair who can sit on the bill, or the governor who could veto it.

Some groups have many adversaries; others have few, and these latter are fortunate. The mere appearance of some groups' legislation can amount to an automatic red flag for others. (Activity by some conservation groups, for example, will lead to a quick response on the part of some farm or industry groups.) Certain groups, such as the senior lobby or the League of Women voters, have few natural enemies, but may pick up a few depending on the issue at stake. Smart lobbyists extend this principle and look for allies among other interest groups. Many major bills can only be passed through the work of coalitions, and effective lobbyists often work with other lobbyists to gain support and disarm the opposition. The Idaho Liability Reform Coalition was the largest legislative coalition in the history of Idaho politics. It successfully lobbied passage of comprehensive tort reform legislation in the late 1980s. Such diverse groups as the Boy Scouts, the cities, the Idaho Association of Commerce and Industry, and the Idaho Farm Bureau joined in common cause to cap damage awards and provide protection from certain civil suits. There is an old legislative axiom: Legislators like to ratify solutions presented to them rather than struggle with problems dumped on their desks by sharply competing interests. Broad-based coalitions satisfy this legislative preference very well. Such coalitions also have worked well in elections as well. An extraordinarily broad coalition—with members ranging from the business lobby to teachers organizations—in 1992 and in 1996 beat back proposed property tax limitation initiatives.

The size and statewide reach of a group reveals its potential power base, the ability to mobilize voters to enthusiastically support elected officials who are "friendly" to a group's interests. The clout which the Idaho Education Association brought to bear—considerable in the 1980s, diminished in the 1990s—is based on its ability to mobilize thousands of schoolteachers. On the other hand, the thousands of state employees nominally represented by public employees' associations have achieved relatively little legislatively since the 1970s. Recent freezes on state employee pay drew little resistance.

Organizational unity is a critical factor. The Association of Idaho Cities hotly debated among its membership during the 1970s and 1980s a proposal to seek repeal of mandatory collective bargaining laws for Idaho firefighters. Even though many city officials supported the effort, the law was never repealed largely because the organization could not muster a consensus among its membership. This statewide organization with union strongholds in northern and southeastern Idaho could not agree on this issue even though the repeal proposal had significant budgetary implications for all of the largest cities.

Influence of interest groups is not static; it can change over time, sometimes as the organizations change and sometimes as do their top issues.

Consider, for example, this analysis:

> The character of the political and economic system within which the group operates will affect its power and effectiveness . . . A group whose goals are in contrast with widely accepted values, for example, will have less success in securing favorable public policy than one which can give its demands legitimacy by clothing them in accepted ideology. Thus proponents of gambling in Idaho have frequently faced strong opposition from churches and church sponsored organizations.[13]

That statement was correct in 1970, when it was made, but attitudes toward gambling changed. In 1988, a constitutional amendment was approved to allow lottery and other gambling games. Even though some legislators oppose gambling they would not dare propose repeal of the lottery; it has become too popular. On the Utah border, the lottery has become a key element of the local Idaho economy. The top seller of Idaho lottery tickets is a convenience store called La Tienda in the small farm town of Franklin on the Utah border. The second and third top lottery sellers also are in similar rural towns on the border of lottery-less Utah. One public opinion survey indicated that an overwhelming majority supported the continuance of the lottery (70 percent plus) and a majority also supported expansion of tribal gaming.[14]

Another type of lobbying has emerged in recent years—contract lobbying. These lobbyists are well-connected people, often former legislators and in several cases attorneys, who handle lobbying activities for various clients. Some of them, such as former state senator Bill Roden, former state representative Skip Smyser and attorney Ken McClure are considered to be among the most influential political people in the state. Of the approximately 300 registered lobbyists in Idaho, about a tenth are contract lobbyists.

RELATIVE STRENGTH OF INTEREST GROUPS IN IDAHO

A survey conducted by James Weatherby and Glenn Nichols at University of Idaho in the early 1970s asked legislators and lobbyists whom they thought were the most influential. Both legislators and lobbyists agreed that the two most influential groups were the Idaho

Education Association and the Associated Taxpayers of Idaho. The other six groups that were rated in the top ten by both groups were the Associated Industries of Idaho (now the Idaho Association of Commerce and Industry), Idaho Power Company, Idaho Cattlemen's Association; Idaho Chamber of Commerce; and the Idaho League of Women Voters.[15]

But in the early 1980s, political scientist Sally Morehouse identified the most powerful groups as Idaho Power Company, Idaho Farm Bureau, mining and forest industries, railroads, county officials, the Mormon church, Idaho Education Association, AFL-CIO.[16]

Boise State University Professor Gary Moncrief, in looking at the results of both of these studies, in a 1987 publication noted an

> *abundance of economic interest groups—particularly 'producer' groups like the Idaho Power Company and mining, timber, and ranching groups. We also find economically oriented trade associations, like IACI and the Idaho Chamber of Commerce. Weatherby and Nichols add that some individual companies (Boise Cascade, J. R. Simplot, Morrison-Knudsen) may be underrepresented in the rankings because they are often well served by the broad-based industry or trade associations. . . Labor unions and associations are also represented on both lists in the form of the AFL-CIO and the Idaho Education Association, although both are less influential today than in the late 1960s. The Mormon Church is generally considered powerful, particularly in the southeast. The church's influence is, however, more subtle than that of some economic interest groups, since the church rarely takes a stance on political issues in the state...Both the League of Women Voters and the Associated Taxpayers of Idaho also enjoy respect stemming from their reputation as well-organized groups capable of extensive research. They are usually perceived as very legitimate sources of information.[17]*

There are no current surveys indicating interest group strength but it is safe to say that dominance by a few groups is more difficult today in a more complex, growth-oriented state.

The Idaho Association of Commerce and Industry remains, however, one of the state's most powerful groups. Founded in 1974, it has been a major player for years but cannot make campaign contributions because of its nonprofit tax status. Its individual members have their own PACs. For this reason it is sometimes difficult to distinguish the IACI clout from some of its own powerful individual members—Union Pacific Railroad, Idaho Power Company, Albertson's, J.

R. Simplot Company, Washington Group International and the Intermountain Forest Association. Their member firms typically contribute more dollars in the major statewide elections than any other group of interests. IACI has many interests: school reform, regulatory reform, human resources, and environmental concerns. Under the leadership of its current president, Steve Ahrens, it has taken several "public interest" stands such as leading the opposition to the One Percent property tax limitation initiative that appeared, at least on the surface, to be more of a concern of public sector rather than private sector groups.

It would be a mistake, however, when discussing the business lobby to generalize about its importance or assume it is monolithic. For example, in the 1998 legislative session, the trucking and railroad interests clashed over legislation to increase the weight of trucks on certain routes in Idaho. The truckers won with the strong support of the governor but only barely and after a bitter fight. General business groups and professional groups have wrangled over managed care legislation and electrical deregulation, among other topics.

The Associated Taxpayers of Idaho, founded much earlier (in 1947) than IACI, has a constituency similar to that group and is a highly credible source to the Legislature on tax and finance issues. Even though the president, Randy Nelson, is a registered lobbyist, the organization typically does not take explicit stands on legislative issues, except to point out the impact of certain legislation on the balance of the current tax structure. It monitors budgets and works with the State Tax Commission in the implementation of tax laws. It holds an annual conference in late fall that is a popular gathering place for Idaho policymakers prior to the beginning of a legislative session.

The Idaho Farm Bureau has been dominant almost from the beginning when southern Idaho's arid soil was turned into agricultural lands. At the Statehouse there's an oft-repeated joke that any bill can be passed as long as it carries an "agricultural exemption." No legislative sponsor would dare ignore the agricultural lobby. As growth has changed the demographics of the state, making it more service oriented, the assumption has been that the Farm Bureau and other agricultural groups would lose clout. The passage of workers compensation for farm workers is indication of the loss of some of that clout, but only by small degrees. No one in Idaho discounts an organization with over 57,000 member families and representing an industry that is still of critical importance to the state.

The American Federation of Labor and Congress of Industrial Organization (AFL-CIO) in Idaho also has less clout than it once did. In the mid-1950s its membership included about 35 percent of the workforce; at century's end, it had between 10 to 14 percent.[18] When timber and mining were among the most significant elements in the economy, the AFL-CIO drew large numbers of their workers into its membership. But when mining declined in the 1980s so did labor's power, to the point that the Legislature was able to override the governor's veto on a "right-to-work" bill in the 1985 session. The voters upheld the new law in a referendum in 1986. There were few repercussions from this anti-labor activity. Democrat Cecil Andrus' return to the governor's office by a narrow margin, after serving as Interior Secretary for President Jimmy Carter (who was very unpopular in Idaho), was helped by a big turnout in the labor strongholds of Lewiston and Pocatello.

This list of interest groups is subject to change—and will change, as this dynamic state does. The number and variety of interests groups in Idaho has grown as the state has grown and diversified. Their relationships, involving ever more coalitions, have become increasingly complex as well. Interest groups at the Idaho Legislature and in the background of political campaigns reflect many of the interests of the state at large, which have changed greatly and will continue to change.

Chapter 5 notes

1 Campaign Financial Disclosure Reports, Office of the Secretary of State, 2002.
2 Randy Stapilus, *The Idaho Yearbook/Directory 1998* (Boise, Id.: Ridenbaugh Press, 1998).
3 A district court decision cast some doubt about the constitutionality of many types of tax increment financing projects. District Judge Robert Newhouse ruled in August, 1998 that most projects should be subject to a popular vote. See Urban Renewal Agency of Boise City, Case No. CVOC 9800978D, 4th District Court Judgement.
4 Ronald J. Hrebenar and Clive S. Thomas, eds., *Interest Groups in the American West* (Salt Lake City: University of Utah Press, 1987), p. 129.
5 Ibid.
6 Lobbyist Expenditure Reports, Office of the Secretary of State.
7 Randy Stapilus, "Lobbyists," *Boise Magazine* (December, 1990/Janaury, 1991).
8 Marilyn Shuler, "An Analysis of Legislative Role Behavior As An Alignment of Role, Reference Sources and Issue Definition in the Idaho Legislature: A Case Study of the 1975 Public School Kindergarten Law" (Master of Public Administration Thesis, Boise State University, 1977).
9 Gary Moncrief, "Interests of Sectionalism," in *Interest Group Politics in the American West*, eds. Ronald Hrebenar and Clive Thomas (Salt Lake City: University of Utah Press, 1987), p. 70.
10 James B. Weatherby and Glenn W. Nichols, "Interest Groups in Idaho Politics," in State and Local Government in Idaho: A Reader, eds. Glenn W. Nichols, Ray C. Jolly and Boyd A. Martin (Moscow, ID: Bureau of Public Affairs Research, University of Idaho), p. 65.
11 Weatherby and Nichols, "Interest Groups," p. 66.
12 John Peavey, "Government - Let The Sunshine," Idaho Cities (Boise, ID: Association of Idaho Cities, October 1974): 13.
13 Hrebenar and Thomas, *Interest Groups*.
14 David R. Scudder, John Crank, and James B. Weatherby, Idaho Public Policy Survey #9 (Boise, ID: Social Science Research Center, Boise State University).
15 Weatherby and Nichols, "Interest Groups," p. 62.
16 Sarah M. Morehouse, *State Politics, Party and Policy* (New York: Host, Rinehart and Winston, 1981).
17 Moncrief, "Interests of Sectionalism," pp. 69-70.
18 Lorraine Nelson, "Why did the public side with Teamsters?; Economics professors disagree on whether unions are coming back," *Lewiston Morning Tribune,* August 25, 1997.

CHAPTER 6
THE IDAHO CONSTITUTION

State and federal constitutions are drafted for fundamentally different reasons. The federal Constitution grants powers to the national government; under provisions of its Tenth Amendment, powers not granted or delegated to the national government are "reserved" to the states and/or to the people. In contrast, state constitutions provide that powers are primarily limited, not granted. If limitations are not imposed in certain areas, then the state government is free to act. As Daniel Elazar noted generally about state governments: "Because states are plenary governments, they automatically possess all powers not specifically denied them by the U.S. Constitution or their citizens. Consequently, a state constitution must be specific about limiting and defining the scope of governmental powers, especially on behalf of individual liberty." Similar statements can be found in Idaho Supreme Court decisions. In the 1957 *Eberle v. Nielson* case, the Court said: "We look to the State Constitution, not to determine what the legislature may do, but to determine what it may not do."[2]

For these reasons and others state constitutions are, like Idaho's, far more comprehensive than the federal. Prohibitions and restrictions on state actions or programs are detailed. This somewhat exhaustive approach was designed by framers suspicious of government officials and seeking to control overly ambitious politicians. The federal Constitution is rarely amended, and its meaning changes most often by judicial interpretation. State constitutions are typically amended at each general election; Idaho has followed this pattern. However, in both the 2002 and 2004 general elections there were no constitutional amendments on the ballot; the first such elections since 1958.

Idaho, more than many other states, today operates very much the way its state founders had in mind. It still has essentially the same constitution, with a number of specific but largely marginal changes. On one hand, that reflects a constitution that many Idahoans have long felt is a fundamentally sound governing document for the state. On the other hand, it is also a demonstration of Idaho's innate conservatism and unwillingness to change a great deal. One serious and well-supported attempt to revamp the Constitution by a constitution revision commission was rejected in 1970.[3] But living with the old and very detailed document sometimes has created problems, whether embarrassing skeletons in the closet such as the anti-Mormon provisions (repealed in 1982) or limitations on handling certain state education funds (amended in 1998).

The fact that there have been fewer attempts to amend the Constitution in Idaho than in some of its neighboring states tells us something more about Idaho. Even though Idaho is part of the populist West and its citizens often use direct democracy mechanisms of initiative and recall, Idaho citizens cannot use the initiative process to change the Idaho Constitution. That is an important difference between Idaho and her neighboring states where constitutional amendments are regularly placed on statewide ballots through the initiative process. Property tax limitation or term limits measures that pass elsewhere in the West are enshrined in most state constitutions. But not in Idaho. Initiative petitions contain proposed new laws subject to amendment or repeal by the Legislature as are other laws. Idahoans are more cautious and less willing to upset the status quo, and in some ways that has served them well.

The state's founders were not only people of their time but also, in most cases, people of other territories and states as well. Members of the constitutional convention had been actively involved in politics, and many had been elected to office, in places such as South Carolina, Washington, Oregon, Nevada and the territory of Montana (which achieved statehood shortly after the Idaho Constitutional Convention but before Idaho's statehood). Many of them had been to California, and the California Constitution was emulated in a number of respects.[4] They also closely examined and referenced the California, Colorado, and Montana constitutions.[5] A few had actually helped write other state constitutions; in some ways they were an uncommonly experienced group.[6]

HISTORICAL BACKGROUND

Idaho's constitutional convention met months before the state came into existence. This early meeting indicated considerable momentum for statehood, born of a deep resentment of the territorial government whose officials were considered "carpetbaggers." These

"Idaho" officials had come in from other parts of the country to implement what was essentially national control over Idaho territory. Also there was strong interest in gaining control of federal lands that would be ceded to the new state. Beneficiaries of these new lands would be the public schools, University of Idaho as the land grant institution, the state penitentiary and some state social services.[7]

Territorial Governor Edward A. Stevenson, who had been working for statehood with Delegate Fred T. Dubois, received word from Washington that statehood was possible for Idaho, under the right conditions. In other words, he was told, members of Congress—having already established that Idaho would vote Republican, the party then in congressional majority—wanted to know what principles would govern the new state before they gave their assent.[8]

So in 1889 Stevenson took the unusual step of calling for a convention to draft a constitution for a then-non-existent state. Weeks later Stevenson was replaced as governor by George Shoup, an appointee of the new Republican Benjamin Harrison administration; but Shoup reiterated the call for a convention. It met in Boise in July, 1889. Neither governor apparently had any specific authority to call such a convention, but took the action on their own initiative as did other states, including Alabama, Louisiana, Mississippi, Missouri, Ohio, Indiana and Illinois. They all held similar conventions without congressional approval.

The delegates were trained to think in conventional legal structures because about 40 percent of them were attorneys. (In fact, 12 percent of all the attorneys in Idaho Territory at that time were delegates.)[9] The attorneys were even more dominant at the convention, however, than their numbers suggest. Alexander Mayhew, the leader of the Democrats at the convention,Weldon Heyyburn (later a U.S. senator from Idaho), John T. Morgan (later a Supreme Court justice) and Willis Sweet (later a congressman). all were active participants.

The key figure at the convention was William Clagett, the president of the convention, the leading Republican and the driving force behind many elements of the document. Clagett, a native of Maryland, became a lawyer in Iowa in 1858 and moved around Nevada, Montana, Colorado, the Dakota Territory and Oregon. In Nevada, he met writer Samuel Clemens and was Mark Twain's travel companion in the memoir "Roughing It." Clagett came to Idaho— his last place—in the wake of one of the gold rushes with a record of activism in politics and law almost everywhere he lived. "William Clagett was the architect of Idaho's Constitution," Colson wrote.[10] He described him as Idaho's James Madison, the driving intellect behind the document—and as well, the leading orator at the convention and the constitution's leading advocate outside it.

As the verbatim record of the convention proceedings attests, these delegates were a contentious bunch, with widely varying views of what this new state should be like. Legal scholar Dennis Colson observes: "There were miners vs. irrigators, laymen vs. lawyers, Democrats vs. Republicans, small counties vs. large, the north vs. the southeast vs. the southwest, consumers vs. railroads, the common man vs. monopolies, traditionalists vs. progressives, the people vs. the politicians, skinflints vs. spendthrifts, promoters vs. pioneers, Rebels vs. Yankees, fervent Christians vs. skeptics and virtually everybody vs. the Mormons."[11] No one and no one philosophy would be the author of this constitution; it would be hammered out by negotiation and compromise.

Still, some basic themes did emerge. The basic elements of the Constitution reflect Idaho's territorial political culture, and its conservatism. One of the prevailing frontier values was individualism, and local control and freedom from governmental constraints were also cherished values.[12] Idahoans were strongly anti-government, particularly resentful of the territorial government and the national government's slow handling of its statehood efforts. The "carpetbagger" governors had substantial powers in dealing with the Legislature and in the appointment of state and local government officials but showed little interest in the welfare of the state. With all this in mind, the framers included a long list of individual rights that were to be protected from abuse of governmental power.

The Idaho Constitution followed, in broadest outline, a pattern common in American states and based on the federal structure. It outlined three branches of government—executive, legislative, judicial— and made provision for local governments, primarily consisting of counties as the basic local units, and secondarily of others including cities and school districts. Two legislative branches, the senate and house of representatives, were set up. The populist tradition that was manifest in an active Populist party at the time called for the creation of eight independently elected constitutional officials in addition to the governor: lieutenant governor, secretary of state, state auditor, state treasurer, attorney general, superintendent of public instruction, and inspector of mines.

The eight constitutional officals was reduced after 1970 to seven with elimination of the position of inspector of mines. And one of the remaining seven was renamed in 1994 when the state auditor became the state controller. The legislative and executive branches of government have changed only slightly since statehood.

A supreme court and lesser courts (later reorganized during court reform of the 1960s, 1970s and early 1980s) were formed. Although unlike the federal model, all judges in Idaho were to be elected, as they still are, again reflecting the state's populist heritage. These structures and official positions are similar in general outline to those found in most other states. Some of the political considerations in the setting up the first judiciary reflected the very bitter regional rivalries that were represented in the convention. The court system was divided into districts so that judges' chambers could be spread throughout the state and there was and is a requirement that the state supreme court meet periodically in northern Idaho each year.[13] Idaho sectional interests heavily influenced these decisions.

At the time of statehood, Boise City and several territorial counties had run up heavy debts. The framers' distrust of government officials and their fear of government debt led to taut restrictions on Idaho state and local government. Restrictions were especially tight in the area of collecting taxes and other revenues, and in spending—some of the most stringent restrictions anywhere in the country, before or since.[14] Not until 1998 was the Constitution amended to remove the $2 million limit on state government indebtedness. The sections on taxation involved considerable debate and discussion between the agricultural and mining interests, the pre-eminent economic groups at that time, both of whom wanted their property exempt from taxation but wanted the other economic interests to pay property taxes. Eventually, they decided to make both groups' property subject to taxation.[15]

Voting rights was another contentious issue. Chinese workers who were brought to labor in the mines, and "other Mongolians" (presumed to include Japanese) were specifically disenfranchised, though at one time in the 1870s they constituted about 25 percent of the population. Indians and women also were denied the right to vote.

The hottest issue in Idaho in the 1880s was the "Mormon question," a matter of intense national interest as well. Anti-Mormon sentiment at the constitutional convention, which ran strong, conflicted with and finally overran the delegates support for a bill of rights and individual liberties. Mormons were denied the right to vote; not only polygamy (at that time still allowed by the church) but also a number of purely religious beliefs were indicated as reasons.[16]

The anti-Mormons feared that expansion of the electorate would increase the pressure to extend the franchise to Mormons. Representation in the Legislature was then based on the number of voters, not the number of people. In 1889, the church had not yet renounced polygamy and some non-members described it as a dangerous cult. Although Mormons had founded many of the farm communities in eastern Idaho, they formed a clear majority of the population only in Bear Lake County. In 1885, the right to vote and to sit on juries was denied to Mormons through use of a "test oath" law that allowed any voter to challenge the qualifications of any other voter and would require voters to swear they did not believe in plural or "celestial" marriages. The mood in Idaho generally was anti-Mormon; that was one of the reasons Idaho became a Republican-leaning territory during those years, since Republicans were considered to be more anti-Mormon than Democrats.

Weldon Heyburn, a Republican from Shoshone County, wanted to effectively incorporate the "test oath" into the Constitution. The delegates adopted language that would deny voting and jury rights to believers in celestial marriage and certain other tenets of the LDS faith.[17]

Anti-Mormon activism at the convention was bipartisan. Even the Democrats who were supposedly closer to the Mormon cause, had little good to say about them. Boise County Democrat George Ainslie had been elected as a territorial delegate to the U.S. House in 1880 partly on the strength of Mormon votes (and lost the next election partly because of controversy over his Mormon backers). At the convention, when the *Salt Lake Tribune* reported that Mormon leaders had been in touch with the Democratic caucus, Ainslie took to the floor to bitterly denounce the *Tribune* ("the most infernally filthy sheet that was ever published on the face of God's green earth") and led off a series of attacks on Mormons by Democrats.[18] Only delegate P. J. Pefly from Boise opposed the anti-Mormon provisions and later was to be the only delegate to vote against the entire Constitution.

The anti-Mormon section remained in the Constitution, partly because of sentiment in the territory and partly because key officials in Washington had made clear that they would not admit Idaho to the union if it appeared to waffle on its Mormon attitudes. Ironically, the whole debate toned down after statehood, even as some politicians continued to stir the pot.[19] The church banned polygamy soon after Idaho statehood. A series of state Supreme Court decisions around the turn of the century effectively short-circuited the anti-Mormon provisions, and Mormons became active in Idaho political life. But not until 1982 did the Idaho Legislature place on the ballot a constitutional amendment deleting the discriminatory language, though it had been rendered ineffective decades earlier by court decisions. There was no substantial public debate about removing the provision, and it passed overwhelmingly. Even so, more than 100,000 Idahoans voted to retain it.[20] (apparently the fear of generating an even larger vote in that direction had kept it off the ballot for years.) Suffrage rights were given to the Chinese and Indians by the Idaho Constitution in 1962, though changes in federal law had accomplished the purpose in 1943.

Other religious and moralistic matters came to the fore at the convention. In the late 1880s mining was entering a comparative slump in Idaho, and the sometimes-wild mining towns were looked on with disfavor by the faster-growing population of farmers and professionals. Southern Idaho was fertile ground for the Women's Christian Temperance Union, which was then picking up steam nationally in its crusade for prohibition of alcohol.[21] Idaho did nor join Wyoming in enacting women's suffrage in 1990. Part of the reason for the failure of women's suffrage then was the close relationship between women's right to vote and prohibition, which many of the convention delegates, opposed, especially the miners and timber men.

This subject apparently brought some bemusement to the delegates, most of whom (to judge from comments made during debate) were steady or even heavy drinkers. A formal request from the Temperance Union to insert a prohibition plank in the Constitution failed. But the delegates were uneasy at leaving matters there, and agreed to a provision saying that "the first concern of all good government is the virtue and sobriety of the people and the purity of the home . . ."[22]

Just over a quarter-century later, however, Idahoans did vote to amend their Constitution to enact prohibition, ahead of national prohibition, one of the first states to do so. That provision remained in force until 1934, when voters legalized beer, and later other liquors as well. When that happened, Idaho established a state liquor control agency in 1935, and the State Liquor Dispensary remains a part of Idaho government. State liquor stores are scattered through most mid-sized and larger communities in the state, including a number of low-consumption Eastern Idaho (Mormon) communities.

PROTECTING FARMING AND INDUSTRY

Governmental regulation of the economy was not high on the personal agendas of the convention delegates—another reflection of their conservatism. They were more interested in promoting a favorable business climate than in imposing regulations that might hamper the development of businesses. But the fact that the delegates were anti-regulation did not necessarily mean that they were totally "pro-business." In fact there was throughout the convention a very significant strain of populism that manifested itself in the anti-corporate sections in the Constitution. One of the noteworthy populist victories was in the sections dealing with the regulation of the railroads. The delegates were concerned about protecting people from the abuses of the "large and stupendous corporations."[23]

The rise of farming in Idaho during the 1880s, spurred by the rapid increase in irrigation farming in southern Idaho (which was about to be expanded dramatically in the Magic Valley), and the regional differences they highlighted, was reflected in a number of constitutional provisions.

Irrigation had begun in Idaho with the first Mormon settlers (who had refined the practice to a high art in Utah). By 1889, most of the land close to large streams had been claimed, and additional irrigation needed more complex organizations and infrastructure. Ditch companies were formed, and the question of relative water rights in Idaho, as in many other western states, was coming to the fore. While the Snake River gave Idaho a more substantial water base than most western states had, it was limited. Water use was very much on the minds of the convention delegates, especially those from southern Idaho, whose members dominated the irrigation committee.[24] The northern parts of the state had much less farming, and more of it was dryland, not irrigated farming.

The convention approved language saying that domestic water use should have priority over all other kinds; irrigation would then have priority over manufacturing, But the delegates also adopted the prior appropriation doctrine, including in the Constitution the "first in time, first in right" principle of water rights that still governs Idaho water usage. The principle says that the first person to put a given source of water to a beneficial use (which can include agricultural, domestic, manufacturing or other uses) has priority over later users if water supplies run low. That approach, which almost all western states have adopted, is sharply different than the "riparian" principle in use in most eastern states. "Prior appropriation" is seen as more useful in places where water is scarce, because it provides a clear principle for who can and cannot use water when supplies run low. The riparian principle, which generally allows for use of water running near or through property, does not address the question of scarcity so squarely—usually not a problem in most of the wetter eastern states.

That central tenet of Idaho water law, a standard provision in water "appropriation" states throughout the West, was never forgotten but often breached. For many years, the usual approach to settling water disputes involved neighbors sitting down together, often with attorneys, and hammering out an agreement, which ordinarily would be rubber-stamped by a judge. The first really thorough adjudication of water rights would not come until the 1987 filing of the

Snake River Basin Adjudication. At that point, "first in time, first in right" became inconvenient for many long-time farmers, and legislation began to be passed in the Idaho Legislature to redefine or circumvent it. That process is still ongoing at this writing.[25]

There was a serious proposal at the convention to make Idaho a "riparian" state, using the major theory of water rights extant in the country, and an approach used by nearly all eastern and a few western states. Under riparian doctrine, the owner of property through which water flows can use it. Delegate Lycurgus Vineyard argued that "if you propose to protect agriculture in this territory, I think this is the first step toward their protection." His proposal was denounced by a clear voice vote.[26]

In general, the water and resource issues were dominated by farming interests. The business, manufacturing and irrigation committee was made up entirely of southern Idaho farmers, except for future Governor William McConnell of Moscow, who earlier in his career had been one of the first irrigators in southwest Idaho. One exception to irrigation's priority for water was granted, however. Because of the efforts of conservative mining lawyer Weldon Heyburn, water rights in mining districts went first to mining interests.[27]

DEBT AND SPENDING

One of the key arguments for creating a state was the potential for putting the territory on a sounder financial basis, and expanding government to carry out some needed projects. Most of the delegates at the convention seemed to agree with those general principles; but they differed widely on how far the state should go in debt, and what it must pay for.

In his book *The Idaho Constitution: The Tie that Binds*, Dennis Colson wrote, "the debt limit was the source of considerable confusion during the debate."[28] A committee report said that debt would be allowed up to 1 percent of the value of property in the state, so long as it was scheduled to be repaid within twenty years. That proposal was finally scrapped, along with many others proposed and rejected. The basic requirement that the state government keep its operating budget in balance has remained in force.

Idahoans have, however, changed the indebtedness and financial management provisions of the Constitution many times. Changes since have been made, for example, to allow debt accumulation by state-created "public corporations" such as the Idaho Housing Finance Administration.

The convention did not impose a vast range of costly duties on the new state government, but it did build into the Constitution a provision requiring public schools. It said: "The stability of a republican form of government depending mainly upon the intelligence of the people, it shall be the duty of the Legislature of Idaho, to establish and maintain a general, uniform and thorough system of public, free common schools."[29]

That provision—with its implicit question of what constitutes "uniform and thorough"—has generated discussion over the years. As previously noted, in the 1990s it exploded into a major statewide lawsuit brought by a group of school districts, whose attorney was a former Idaho Supreme Court justice, Robert Huntley. The issues it raised have not yet been resolved.

RATIFICATION

In his book *Rocky Mountain Carpetbaggers*, historian Ronald Limbaugh noted that "the sixty-six page document was uninspiring and complex, more like a legal code than a framework of government, but such political instruments were fashionable in their day and the framers were proud of their handiwork."[30]

Prospective threats to the Constitution—which was drafted without yet having the benefit of a state to attach it to—quickly arose. The most notable area of opposition came from the northern part of the territory, which was still interested in separation from southern Idaho and joining with Washington state. But northern Idaho was given some choice spoils in return for support, especially an assurance that the University of Idaho would remain at Moscow. (Some of the strongest votes in favor of the Constitution came from the Panhandle.)

The Mormons in eastern Idaho were unhappy with a constitution that barred them from voting or holding office, but they were not allowed to vote on the document. Most Idahoans of the day, apart from some concerned that their cost of government would greatly increase upon statehood, strongly favored full state status for Idaho. There were others even in southern Idaho who were greatly concerned that the state simply did not have the resources to operate a viable state government.[31] Even so,, in November of 1889 the Constitution passed overwhelmingly, 12,333 to 1,776.

CHANGES

The Idaho Constitution can be changed in two ways, through amendment of specific sections, or through revision of the entire document in a constitutional convention. No constitutional convention has been convened since 1889 and there has been no serious call for the creation of one.

Constitutional amendments require a two-thirds vote of each chamber of the Legislature and a simple majority approval on a general election ballot. As of 2004, the Idaho Constitution has been amended 123 times, including six changes in 1998, two in 2000 and none in 2002 and 2004. One additional 1998 proposed amendment was approved by the Legislature, and by the voters at the general election, but rejected by the Idaho Supreme Court in a 1999 ruling. The court's decision held that two questions were improperly combined into one ballot issue, contrary to constitutional requirements.

Unlike constitutional amendments in many other states, constitutional amendments in Idaho are directly incorporated into the text upon adoption and not published in a separate appendix.

The most dramatic and most numerous set of amendments proposed at one time was in the 1912 general election, the high water mark for progressivism in the country. In the 1912 election, Idaho voters approved the initiative and the referendum process, provided that each county in the state would have its own senator in the Idaho Legislature, allowed the state to assume more debt, made all elected state officials subject to recall, and more. Idaho progressive and populist movement leaders who not only pressed for more direct democratic devices but also for overhauling the state Constitution influenced these amendments. They succeeded in getting a proposal on the ballot to make those changes but it failed by a decisive margin in 1918.

Despite the frequency of the amendments, few major changes have been made to the document. Most are of the "housekeeping" variety, involving essentially technical, incremental changes. The most amended Article is VIII which addresses county government organization. A minority of articles have never been amended: Articles II (separation of powers), XIV (militia), XVI (livestock), XVII (state boundaries), and XXI (schedule and ordinance).

The first amendment required that counties have an independent elected county superintendent of public instruction, rather than give that title ex-officio to the local probate judge. Later, both positions were eliminated from the Constitution.

TRYING FOR A REDRAFT
Only once has an attempt been made to completely redraft the Idaho Constitution.

It started with a proposal by Governor Robert Smylie in 1965 that state officials and voters take a fresh look at a document encumbered with "cobwebs of bigotry and suspicion and restraint that are not useful to the people in the conduct of this, their government."[32] He offered only two specific proposals himself—or increasing the terms of county sheriffs from two to four years, and creation of a state water resources agency, both proposals which have since been approved—but said that many other areas should be considered. A review commission was established; it was intended to develop a proposal to be delivered to the Legislature, which would eventually call a state constitutional convention, which in turn would adopt the revised document.

The commission included a number of officials prominent in Idaho then and later, such as future U.S. Senator James McClure and 1966 gubernatorial candidate Perry Swisher. Through five years of meetings and 32 hearings the members displayed some difficulty coming to grips with the most needed reforms.[33]

In its final report, the group did say that "the constitution we live under today is not one of our own making nor of our forefathers but one resulting from the political considerations needed for statehood in 1889. It was written hurriedly to seize a sudden opportunity for Idaho to enter the Union and was worded to answer every conceivable question, objection, prejudice and demand of factions in the state as well as of a congressional committee. It was not a document growing out of and meeting the local needs of Idaho people."[34] The commission proposed keeping about two-thirds of the original Constitution but also proposed extensive revisions. The new document would have guaranteed Idahoans a "right of privacy" and "to have the quality of their environment preserved and enhanced," and would have inserted an equal-protection clause into the state Constitution. It proposed to limit the size of the Idaho House to twice the size of the Senate (earlier provisions allowed for a number three times as great), and four-year terms for senators.

These proposed changes seemed to have broad support; backers included many members of both political parties. But opponents aroused strong concerns across Idaho. Seventh District Judge Henry Martin was concerned about provisions that eliminated the popular election of judges, and even more about federal acceptance of Idaho water rights. He noted that the language concerning water rights in the original Constitution had, in effect, been approved by Congress on statehood. Would the federal government, he asked, continue to accept state policy on water rights under the new Constitution?

Such concerns were enough to stop the revision effort in its tracks. On election day, 66 percent of the voters opposed the revised constitution; only two counties (Latah and Bannock) voted in favor. No follow-up revision effort has been made since.

Chapter 6 notes

1   Daniel Elazar, "Series Introduction," in *Arizona Politics and Government: The Quest for Autonomy, Democracy, and Development* by David R. Berman (Lincoln, NE: University of Nebraska Press, 1998), p. xix.
2   *Eberle v. Nielsen*, 78 Idaho 572, 306 P2d. 1083 (1957).
3   Idaho Constitutional Revision, explanatory document published by the Idaho Secretary of State's office, 1970.
4   See Dennis Colson, Idaho's Constitution: The Tie That Binds (Moscow, ID: University of Idaho, 1991), pp. 6-14; and compare with California state constitution.
5   Donald Crowley and Florence Heffron, *The Idaho State Constitution: A Reference Guide* (Westport, CT: Greenwood Press, 1994), p. 5.
6   Colson, *Idaho's Constitution*, pp. 6-15.
7   Crowley and Heffron, *The Idaho State Constitution.*
8   Ronald Limbaugh, *Rocky Mountain Carpetbaggers: Idaho's Territorial Governors* (Moscow, ID: The University Press of Idaho, 1982), pp. 175-181.
9   Colson, *Idaho's Constitution*, p. 6.
10 Ibid., p. 8.
11 Ibid., p. 6.
12 Robert H. Blank, *Regional Diversity of Political Values: Idaho Political Cultures* (Washington, D.C.: University Press of America, 1978).
13 Crowley and Heffron, *The Idaho State Constitution.*
14 See especially Colson on the indebtedness matter, pp 105-110; Idaho Constitution, art. VII sec. 11 and art. VIII sec. 1-5; the Idaho Constitution has frequently been amended in this area, usually to provide for greater allowance of public indebtedness
15 Crowley and Heffron, *The Idaho State Constitution.*
16 Colson, *Idaho's Constitution*, pp. 30-39. For background on anti-Mormonism in Idaho, see Limbaugh, pp. 140-183.
17 I. W. Hart, Proceedings and Debates of the Constitutional Convention of Idaho (Caldwell, ID: State of Idaho, Caxton Printers, 1913), numerous sections but especially pp. 128-145, pp. 185-211, and pp. 931-956.
18 Hart, pp. 184-185.
19 Notably, Fred T. Dubois after 1900. See Robert Sims, *Governors of Idaho* (Boise, ID: Boise State University, 1998), p 43.
20 Election records, Idaho Secretary of State.
21 Colson, pp. 25-30.
22 Idaho Constitution, art. VII, sec. 8.
23 Crowley and Heffron, *The Idaho State Constitution*, p. 16.
24 See Colson, pp. 161-177; Hart, pp. 1119-1136, and the Idaho Constitution, art. XV: Water Rights.
25 See the Snake River Basin Adjudication Digest (Boise, ID: Ridenbaugh Press, March 1993-present).
26 Hart, Proceeding and Debates of the Consitutional Convention of Idaho
27 Colson, pp. 169-172.
28 Ibid., pp. 106-109.
29 Idaho Constitution, art. IX, sec. 1.
30 Limbaugh, *Rocky Mountain Carpetbaggers*, p. 183.
31. Crowley and Heffron, *The Idaho State Constitution*, p. 16.
32 Robert E. Smylie, "State of the State," Boise, Idaho, 1965.
33. Report of the Secretary of State on revision of the Idaho Constitution, document produced by the Idaho Secretary of State, 1970. And guest opinion drafted by Merle Wells, November 1970.
34 Ibid.

C. W. Cornell

Idaho Statehouse reflected in adjacent Hall of Mirrors.

CHAPTER 7
LEGISLATIVE PROCESS AND POLITICS

The Idaho Legislature matches the Idaho attitude toward government: less is better, full-time politicians are distrusted, and closeness to the constituency is valued. As a result, Idaho's legislators have remained part-time citizen lawmakers representing relatively small districts. Idaho has, for example, about a third the population of Oregon and half the population of Utah, but more state legislators than either.

The Legislature is bicameral, with a senate composed of thirty-five members and a house of representatives composed of seventy members. All 105 serve two-year terms. Among other western states, only Arizona uses the same two-year term pattern for the senate as Idaho does. Other legislatures utilize staggered terms, intended to provide some continuity in the body.

Qualifications for service in the Legislature are minimal. Legislators must be United States citizens, qualified electors, and residents in the legislative district at least one year prior to the election. They must also maintain their district residence during their term of office.

In Idaho, members are sworn into office in early December following their November election. They meet in an organizational session to elect leadership and appoint committee members. They do not consider legislation until January, when the regular session convenes.

The Idaho Legislature has met in annual session since 1969, before then they met in biennial sessions. Typically the sessions last about three months from the second Monday in January into the last weeks of March. Compared to other states, Idaho's sessions are relatively short.

There have been occasions, especially during the struggles over reapportionment when the Legislature has been called into special session after the adjournment of the regular session. The Legislature cannot call itself into special session. The calling of a special session is a gubernatorial prerogative and the governor sets the agenda; but legislators are not obliged to support the intent of the call. In the early 1980s a special session was called by Democratic Governor John Evans. In response the "veto-proof" Republican Legislature met briefly, killed all of the governor's bills, and adjourned.

Women serve in several leadership positions in both the House and Senate and there are a considerable number in the entire membership. Currently 29 out of the 105 Idaho legislators are women. The 28 percent this represents exceeds the national average of 23 percent. Idaho ranks 16th nationally in 2005 in the percentage of women serving in the Legislature.[1]

Unlike many other legislative bodies, there are few lawyers in the Idaho Legislature; historically, Idaho has had fewer lawyers than in most other state legislatures. The relatively low pay and the need to keep at work year-round in smaller communities may be contributing factors. Since December 2000, legislators have received $15,646 annually, plus expenses. Per diem, covering food, lodging and related expenses, is $99 a day for legislators who live outside the Boise area, and $38 a day for local legislators. In addition, members are paid an annual $1,700 constituent service allowance for attending meetings and other expenses, and $50 a day plus expenses for participating in interim committee meetings.

Legislative compensation is determined through a two-step process. Salaries are recommended by the Citizens Committee on Legislative Compensation created by a constitutional amendment in 1976. Their recommendation becomes official if the Legislature does not officially reject the new pay schedule. Legislative pay is a tricky issue for a "citizen legislature". Low pay typically guarantees that the majority of legislators will be retired, farmers, or independently wealthy individuals. The apparent intent of legislators is to make salaries "low enough to prevent people from making legislative service a full-time job. But it must also be high enough to make it possible for a broad range of Idahoans to take the necessary time away from their other jobs to serve."[2]

The Legislature is a member of the National Conference of State Legislatures (NCSL) and legislators are paid to defray expenses for participation. The American Legislative Exchange Conference is preferred by some legislators over what they consider to be the more liberal NCSL. Some of these organizations may help influence the flow of legislation with their reports and model legislation.

LEGISLATIVE FUNCTIONS

Like other state legislatures, the Idaho Legislature performs a variety of functions including policymaking, constituent services, and oversight of state agencies.

Policymaking

Legislators are policymakers or problem solvers to whom the Idaho Constitution has given substantial lawmaking powers. They largely determine what government will or will not do. Much of their work is rather uneventful—deliberating about proposed minor corrections to current law. But legislators also have to make many tough decisions that have serious consequences determining who the winners and losers are. Limited resources force more "zero-sum" than "win-win" outcomes. Whether it is a major budgetary decision, giving more money to one agency project and less to another, or choosing between insurance companies over trial lawyers, legislators decide who will be advantaged by a resource or regulatory decision and who will be disadvantaged. Will more money be allocated to the faster growing urban areas and denied the rural areas? Will insurance companies receive liability protection or will trial lawyers be free to ask for uncapped damages for their clients?

The range of issues confronted by legislators includes environmental protection, economic development, corrections, abortion, health care, welfare reform and many others. Legislators propose their own solutions to these problems, as do groups and individuals outside the legislative arena. The extent to which solutions advocated by these groups are enacted by the Legislature is a testament to the strength of these groups. It also may say something about the varying degrees of access different groups have in influencing the legislative agenda. After all, pressure is an integral part of the legislative process; the Legislature is not just a debating society.

Legislators operate within an intergovernmental context. They interact with officials from all levels of government and other branches of state government. Governors can have a major impact on the legislative agenda. Through their annual state of the state and budget addresses presented early in the legislative sessions (ordinarily on the first and third days of the session), governors are well positioned with significant media and public attention to shape legislative agendas, to focus public attention on the problems they have identified and the solutions they propose.[3] This often puts legislators in a reactive posture, spending most of their time reacting to the governor's initiatives.

Both state and federal judiciaries influence legislative policymaking. Court orders that require state and local governments to upgrade

their correctional facilities or address the inequity in funding for public education have had major budget and policy implications.

Federal mandates impact the legislative process. Passage of the
1996 federal welfare reform legislation is an example of a federal initiative that required state responses and implementation. Legislation
on welfare reform played a major role in the proceedings of the 1996
Idaho legislative session. The anticipated reauthorization of welfare
reform in 2005 may again have an impact on legislative activity.

As essentially creatures of the state government, local governments (cities, counties, school districts, etc.) must look to the
Legislature for new authority—for funding and new programs. State
legislative laws limit local government's ability to raise local property
tax revenue. Local governments are very active in asking for relief
from state mandates or seeking new legislative authorizations.

A major issue for policymaking bodies in a democracy is how well
they represent the people they are elected to serve. There are various
models of representation in American state politics: delegate, trustee
and politico. According to several studies of legislative perceptions, it
appears that on most issues legislators see themselves as being delegates. In other words, as delegates, they vote as they think their constituents would vote or would instruct them to vote. They are proud
of their legislative records that they believe effectively represent their
constituents' points of view. Public opinion surveys on major public
policy issues appear to support this delegate orientation among Idaho
legislators. Seventy-seven percent of the respondents to the *15th
Annual Public Policy Survey* want their legislators to act as delegates
rather than trustees.[4]

The 1990 legislative session featured the debate and passage of the
most restrictive abortion bill in the United States. There were clear
examples of legislators acting as delegates, especially some
Democrats who expressed opposition to this stringent anti-abortion
legislation but still voted for it knowing that their southeastern Idaho
constituents, many Mormons, strongly supported the legislation.

As legislative issues have become increasingly complex even the
most "delegate"-oriented legislator assumes a trustee role. "Trustees"
make their own independent judgments regardless of constituent
input. For example, the late 1990s debate over telephone deregulation
was an exercise that not only shows how dependent legislators are on
lobbyists for technical information, but how difficult it is for legislators to get a good reading of their constituents' attitudes about a complex issue whose ramifications may be hard for the average citizen to
understand. Sometimes they just have to make their own decisions.
Some observers have suggested that legislators have two effective

"constituencies"—the people in the home districts who elect them and the "statehouse crowd" they see during the three months they are in session.

Still other legislators are considered "politicos," changing their approach from delegate to trustee depending upon the issues. For example, on proposals calling for a tax increase most legislators know where their constituents stand—"no new taxes." The tax-service dilemma—calls to improve services but not increase taxes—appears to be universal. Typically, Idaho legislators vote "no" until a major budgetary crisis, such as the state experienced in the 1980s and in 2003. The crisis leaves them with no practical alternative but to raise taxes and risk the wrath of the voters.

Constituent service

Responding to constituent requests is a growing area of responsibility for state legislators, especially as state government becomes more intrusive and technical. To be effective, Idaho's legislators must be involved in helping constituents deal with state agencies and policies. Legislators typically also attend many public meetings and hearings throughout the year to explain their voting record or to hear citizen complaints or requests. In a sense, this is a year-around job that must be attended to whether or not the Legislature is in session.

Administrative oversight

Oversight is another major legislative function and becoming increasingly important given the growing range of legislative issues and the need for greater staff expertise in the application of complex laws. Oversight involves moving into the administrative realm by interacting more directly with state agencies in reviewing administrative rules and regulations.

Historically, the extent of legislative oversight in Idaho was limited to budget hearings where legislators questioned agency heads about their operations and use of tax dollars. Little real attention was given to most rules and regulations promulgated by state regulatory and administrative bodies except for attention from the directly affected parties. These groups or individuals monitored and sometimes attempted to influence the administrative process, or change the intent of the legislation through the rule-making process.

The passage of the Administrative Procedures Act (APA) in 1993 has had a significant impact on the administrative process. During the early part of the legislative session, legislators undertake a systematic review of rules adopted by state agencies under the APA. As part of their review, committees take public testimony from agency representatives and from individuals and groups who are impacted by the proposed regulations. Under the Idaho law, the Legislature has the authority to reject agency rules that do not reflect legislative intent. The 2004 legislative committees reviewed 425 separate collections of rules, or a total of 4,200 pages. One analyst noted that: "Stacked end-to-end, the volume of rules reviewed by legislators in just a few weeks would measure over two-feet high."[5]

Another aspect of the oversight function is to evaluate agency performance. The Office of Performance Evaluation is charged with the responsibility of assessing administrative effectiveness and measuring how successful agencies are in achieving their goals. To do this, the OPE has been given a degree of independence and a bi-partisan supervisory committee. The OPE oversight committee is equally divided between Democrats and Republicans. "Under the direction of the Joint Legislative Oversight Committee, a staff of performance evaluators examines the effectiveness of state agency administration, makes recommendations to the Legislature about ways in which state agency operations might be improved, and helps legislators ensure that agencies operate as intended."[6]

LEGISLATIVE PROCESS

"During the 2004 legislative session, 933 proposed pieces of legislation were prepared for legislative committees and individual legislators," a state legislative summary noted. "From that initial group of draft proposals, 619 bills were actually introduced, along with another 80 resolutions, memorials and proclamations. By the end of the session, 395 bills had passed both houses. Six bills were vetoed by the Governor. Following his review, 63 percent of introduced bills entered the law book. In all, 389 bills became law."[7]

To understand the Idaho legislative process is to understand the crucial role committees play in the process. Deference is given to the committee system. Rarely are bills killed on the floor of either the house or the senate. Typically, killing actions occur in committee. This specialization in functions and responsibilities works because of the "lay" complexion of the Legislature and the strong tradition in support of the committee process engendered by the many years of Republican majority rule.[8]

Individual legislators may introduce legislation either by pre-filing or during the early days of the session but few of these bills are seriously considered.

Legislative leadership

Legislative leadership is key to guiding the flow of legislation. It is the responsibility and privilege of leadership to appoint committee chairs and make committee assignments. These assignments are often made, especially chair selections, within the general framework of the seniority system, more so in the Senate than in the House. But recent turnover rates in the Legislature have opened up opportunities for relatively new legislators.

Leadership also plays a role in keeping members in tune with the majority party or governor's agenda. This is particularly difficult in a predominantly one-party legislature. There is always the risk that an overwhelming majority will turn into a *de facto* multi-party legislature. Often on major issues, there is more than one group speaking out on an issue; often Republicans are fighting among themselves.

House leadership is embodied in the speaker who sets the tone of the House deliberations if not of the Legislature. The speaker is fourth in line of succession to the governor and potentially the most powerful member of the Legislature. Other leadership positions include the majority leader, assistant leader, caucus chair and committee chairs.

Leadership of the Senate is split between the lieutenant governor and the president pro tempore. The lieutenant governor is elected statewide by the voters, but has few official functions in the Senate other than presiding over the chamber. The real leader is the president pro tem, who is elected by the senators of the majority party. The pro tem is the counterpart to the speaker of the House, except that he ordinarily does not preside over the chamber.

Committee chairs

In this committee-oriented system, committee chairs are very influential. They control the committee agenda—determining what legislation will or will not be considered with the exception of some high profile bills that leadership has targeted for expedited action. Committee chairs can single-handedly kill bills they do not like and rarely are they successfully challenged. One celebrated case occurred when a committee chair from eastern Idaho actually took the original copy of a bill that he did not like (the bill would have imposed the state sales tax on purchases by the then Idaho National Engineering Laboratory), locked it in the trunk of his car, and drove home with it to eastern Idaho so that it could not be reported to the floor or assigned to another committee while he was absent from the Legislature. Obviously, chairs' decisions to hold bills in committee are not totally immune from attack. There are procedures that allow for the calling of a bill from committee after it has resided in the committee for a certain period of time. But motions to pull bills from committee rarely succeed given the respect for the committee system and the power of the majority influence.

Most bills, and almost every piece of legislation that gets anywhere, is introduced or printed by committee. There are time limits for committee introduction, except for "privileged" committees that do not have such restrictions. Given the penchant of most Idaho legislators to postpone major decisions, especially fiscal decisions, it should be understandable that committees like the House Revenue and Taxation and the Joint Finance and Appropriations Committee are given a "privileged" status. They must be able to introduce new bills, particularly when major spending and tax decisions are at issue, in the closing days of a legislative session.

Introduction and first reading

Introduction involves the preparation of a "routing slip" (or, variously, routing service, or most simply "RS") by the bill drafting staff of the Legislative Service Office (LSO); the RS is a preliminary bill draft. Interestingly, a tax-supported public body (the LSO) produces it, literally, but it is viewed as essentially the personal property of the sponsor. With the exception of committee members and staff, no others are allowed to see it unless the sponsor approves or until after it has been introduced.

Historically, introduction of bills has been fairly *pro forma* with no extensive hearing or committee debate. Proposals were printed as a courtesy to the sponsors and in recognition that a relevant problem was being addressed. This trend is changing as the legislative process has become more contentious. Some RSs currently have a full hearing and have a real struggle to even be printed. Once an RS is printed, it is distributed to libraries and other agencies and is also available on the state of Idaho home page or on-line service.

Committee introduction of a bill does not guarantee that it will come back to that same committee. Given the critical role committees play in the legislative process, assignment of bills to committee can be a decisive act—the difference between life and death resting upon the assignment to a "friendly" or "unfriendly" committee. Typically the presiding officer (speaker of the house or president pro tem) assigns most bills to the originating committee. But not always. The sponsor may not be a member of the appropriate committee but still seeks introduction in a committee in which he is a member. Or there may be a technical question as to where the bill should be assigned. Given the subject matter designation of committees, the presiding officer has this discretion in order to more properly channel or "deep six" what he considers to be either a good or bad bill. For example, local government or education committees may introduce tax-related bills because they affect cities or school districts, but the legislation may be more properly the province of the Revenue and Taxation Committee if it is viewed as a revenue raising measure rather than as a general local government or public education matter. Or an insurance or liability reform bill may be assigned to either the Business (Commerce) or the Judiciary Committee (with more lawyers) depending upon the presiding officer's reaction to the legislation.

There is yet another assignment route. Leadership may also use the Ways and Means Committee in the House—which is actually a tool of the House leadership, and consists of members of the leadership—or the State Affairs Committee in the senate to carefully manage some controversial bills. In some respects they are used as "holding" committees. The membership of the holding committees is primarily composed of leadership.

Committee consideration

A high percentage of bills are never reported out of committee. Some are never fully heard or considered once introduced. A few are introduced as a courtesy to a constituent but with no real intent to push them through to passage. Most committee chairs take the view that if no one asks for a bill or shows any substantial interest, it usually stays in committee and therefore dies.

While awaiting full committee consideration, a bill may also be assigned to a subcommittee for hearing and recommendations back to the full committee. This specialization of labor has advantages but also pitfalls. Some decisions are effectively made in a small subcommittee with little visibility. Full committee consideration may be pro forma.

Just prior to final action by the committee, considerable testimony may be given by both sides, by lobbyists and by grass roots supporters. The committee may carefully, and sometimes sharply, question witnesses on both sides and engage in internal debate. Technical and non-controversial bills, which many are, may receive little testimony or debate. But the procedures and practices apply to virtually every committee except the Joint Finance and Appropriations Committee, where virtually no public testimony is taken. There are no RSs and bills may originate as Senate or House bills even though a minority of Senate or House members supported introduction of the legislation.

Several types of motions may be considered when the committee is moving to final action. The bill may be held in committee, reported with a "do-pass" recommendation, "do not pass" recommendation or no recommendation at all. Typically a bill is "on life support" if it is reported out with less than a "do-pass" recommendation. Any recommendation other than "do-pass" sends a strong negative message; the other members typically defer to committee direction.

In addition, a bill could be sent to another committee or to the amending order. Committees do not amend bills in Idaho as they do in many other states. They are amended on the floor in the amending order (general orders in the House and fourteenth order in the Senate). However, committees often indicate in their formal motions, when reporting the bill to the amending order that amendments are attached. Committees may indicate their recommended amendments. Those may be the amendments that are adopted in the committee of the whole. But in the amending order, any member may propose any amendment he or she wishes to attach to the legislation.

Yet another way of handling a major bill that needs amendment is to prepare a new RS incorporating committee changes rather than subjecting it to the vagaries of the amending order. Amendments to major controversial legislation often draw unfriendly amendments from opponents who would like nothing better than to change the intent of the legislation. If such a disaster occurs to a bill, all that is left to the sponsors in order to rescue their bill from ignominy is a unanimous consent request or motion to return it to committee where it is sent to a graceful death.

Second reading

Unlike many other state legislatures, the level of activity on Idaho's second reading calendar is essentially a non-event, merely a point along the way toward final consideration on third reading. Third reading is where the action is, which is just the reverse of most other states, when a vote is taken. Realistically, the only substantive actions taken on second reading would be mischievous unanimous consent requests or motions to divert the bill to the amending order or to return it to committee. Otherwise, there is no debate or action, the bill just moves to the third reading.

Third reading

Many different motions can be made in third reading. A bill could be sent to the amending order, which is more likely on a controversial bill where opponents want to delay the measure or as a defensive measure by the sponsors who recognize they do not have enough votes to pass the legislation without amendment.

But in most cases, the third reading is the point in the calendar where there is a final reading of the bill (actually the rules are suspended requiring a full reading), it is debated by both sides and then a vote is taken. Simple majority approval is required on all measures except constitutional amendments. Final votes in the House are recorded by an electronic voting machine (which displays the votes of each member above the chamber), and in the Senate by a voice vote. Members are allowed to change their votes until the final vote is announced, and they sometimes do.

Upon final vote, the measure—if passed—is sent to the other body to go through essentially the same process.

Amending order

The General Orders in the House, called 14th Order in the Senate, is the amending order where the "committee of the whole" can choose to amend legislation. The House and Senate convene into the committee of the whole infrequently, only after a number of bills accumulate. Most of the legislative process is fairly orderly but that has not always occurred in the amending order. Orderliness is often dependent upon the total number of amendments that may be considered and the mix of technical, minor or substantive amendments.

Once a bill is amended, it again goes through the reading process on the floor; rarely is it re-routed to a committee on its way toward final reading. Other bills may not be amended and can be reported back to the reading calendar or to the committee that reported the legislation to the floor. Each bill is required to contain an "enacting clause," as mandated by the state constitution: "Be it enacted by the Legislature of the State of Idaho." Occasionally during the amendment process a legislator will try to slip in an amendment striking the enacting clause, in effect killing the bill. The omnibus local option tax bill, House Bill 80, suffered this fate in the 1975 session in a move the *Idaho Statesman* called a "cowardly act."[9] The then Senate Majority Leader Phil Batt admitted that if the bill had been voted on in the third reading it would have passed. Rather than taking a public vote, the senators resorted to a parliamentary maneuver that did not require them to cast a recorded vote.

Within certain time limits, a member who has voted on the prevailing side (voted with the majority) may ask for reconsideration of the vote. If it is accepted under a unanimous consent request or passed by a motion (if there is objection to the request) another vote on the bill's passage is taken. That vote typically reflects changes due to last minute lobbying and/or the discovery of new information, meaning that the reconsidered vote will often result in a changed outcome.

Under rules suspension, a measure can be introduced and passed within a matter of a few hours. Rules suspension is typically used during the closing days of a session to expedite important legislation, particularly appropriation measures that the leadership is anxious to move through the process just prior to adjournment.

Adjournment

Typically the Legislature adjourns close to the end of March. Some lobbyists have suggested an informal adjournment "law"—never before St. Patrick's day and never after Easter.[10] At adjournment, many bills may be "left hanging on the calendar." They are either non-consequential bills or controversial bills that cannot be salvaged as either being out of favor or not being a priority. Time always runs out on some legislation, but not on all. In the final days of a session, a governor and legislative leadership may agree on a list of bills, measures which must be addressed before the lawmakers can end the session. These bills receive expedited attention.

Sponsors of legislation that has not been earmarked for expedited consideration as adjournment arrives will have to start all over in the next session. The Idaho Legislature is not a continuous body, and none of the legislation carries over from one session to another in Idaho as it does in other states. If, for example, a house originated bill is amended in the Senate, but the House refuses to concur with the Senate amendments, the bill goes to a conference committee composed of members from both houses selected by leadership of each party. If the conference committee cannot agree on a report or both houses do not accept the report, the bill dies. Conference committees rarely are used in Idaho, and when they are legislators seem to be confused about the rules governing them.

Governor's approval or disapproval

The governor is also a key player in the legislative process not only in helping set the legislative agenda (through the state of the state address) but also through presenting legislative proposals (his own and agency requests approved by the governor) and for final approval (signature) or disapproval (veto). The governor may also allow a bill to become law without his signature indicating that he really does not like it but defers to the legislative majority.

A governor's signature means that the bill becomes law upon reaching the effective date of the legislation. Most bills do not have a specified effective date; in that case the default date is July 1 of the same year. Others may have emergency clauses that provide for more immediate dates, even upon the actual date the bill is signed. Still others may have staggered dates—different sections of a complex new piece of legislation become law on different dates.

DIRECT DEMOCRACY - VOTERS AS LEGISLATORS

The Idaho legislative process involves two different dimensions. The more widely used is the traditional route for enacting legislation. This is called *representative democracy*. Voters choose their representatives to make policy decisions rather than the voters making such decisions themselves. In effect, the voters are one step removed from the actual legislative process.

The other approach is called *direct democracy* where legislative powers are shared with the voters. Voters pass their own laws through the initiative process or approve or reject a measure passed by the Legislature through the referendum process. The other direct democratic device is the recall. The recall is not directly related to the legislative process but can be, and is, used to remove legislators and some other office holders from office. The recall has only rarely been used against legislators (once in the 1970s against three eastern Idaho legislators who voted for a legislative pay increase many voters disliked), but is used most often against elected city officials.

Idahoans can participate in other ways too. They do not have to rely entirely on legislative bodies to write the laws: With the initiative process, Idahoans can—and do—attempt to write laws themselves. They can propose a new law or an amendment to existing law and gather signatures of at least 6 percent of the registered voters statewide. The initiative is placed on the next general election ballot. If a simple majority of the voters approve, it becomes law. But the new law has no greater legal status than other laws and can be amended or repealed by the Legislature. Unlike the neighboring states of Oregon, Nevada, and Montana, Idaho voters cannot amend the constitution through the initiative process.

The use of the initiative in influencing state policymaking is becoming more prevalent in a number of western states, particularly in California, Oregon, Washington, and Colorado. It has been used less in Idaho, in part perhaps because in this smaller state legislators are closer to their constituents. Proponents may also be aware that ballot issues have had only limited success in Idaho. In the 70-year history of the initiative process in Idaho, only 26 proposed initiatives have gained general election ballot status and only 14 have passed. Some of the more notable initiatives that have become law include the 1978 One Percent Initiative (property tax limitation measure), "the Sunshine Act" (campaign finance disclosure) of 1974, the 1982 home-owners exemption (property tax relief), and the 1994 term limits measure. In addition to these initiatives, since 1978, there have been repeated attempts to pass additional property tax relief measures. In both 1992 and 1996, in expensive statewide campaigns, property tax limitation measures similar to the 1978 One Percent Initiative were defeated by the same two to one margin. There have been other tax policy initiative attempts as well. In 1984, an initiative to exempt groceries from the state's sales tax was defeated. Opponents successfully argued that the initiative did not provide for replacement revenues if grocery sales were exempted from the sales tax.

Despite the rather checkered history of initiative proposals, there is a growing concern in Idaho about following the lead of California and Oregon, where voters have typically dealt with extensive laundry lists of measures. Some of those measures have affected Idaho, such as the passage, in June 1978, of California's Proposition 13 which surfaced in virtually identical form as Idaho's One Percent Initiative.

In the 1996 Idaho election four initiatives won a place on the general election ballot, but there was a real possibility that 12 measures could have gained ballot status. The four initiatives were successful in large part because their supporters contracted with out-of-state firms who provided paid signature gatherers to collect enough signatures to secure ballot status. The emergence of professional signature gathering firms may change the dynamics of the initiative process in Idaho from a grass roots model to a special interest based model. Some measures seem to have as much to do with national interest groups as with statewide policy concerns. Idaho's 1996 bear baiting initiative was sponsored in large measure by a national association that had sponsored similar measures in other states. The 1994 and 1996 congressional term limits measures were significantly aided by the national term limits movement.

During the 1997 legislative session the initiative process was revised to make placement of initiatives on the ballot more difficult. Supporters were required to obtain signatures equal at least to 6 percent of the registered voters in 22 counties. Advocates of the change feared that the required number of petition signatures could be obtained from a few of the urban centers of the state, particularly in southwestern Idaho, or at major gatherings such as regional fairs. With the revisions, fewer initiatives made the ballot in succeeding elections. In 2001 the law was challenged in federal court and Judge Lynn Winmill struck down the 22 county provision in the *Idaho Coalition United for Bears v. Cenarrusa* case.[11] Winmill's decision was affirmed by the U.S. Court of Appeals for the ninth Circuit in September 2003.

LEGISLATIVE STAFF

Legislative staff is limited though it has expanded considerably in the past decade. Staff is provided by the Legislative Services Office, which was created in 1993 to combine the functions of the legislative auditor, legislative budget office and legislative council. It marked a substantial expansion over three decades from the original Legislative Council staff, which was created in 1963 with one full-time staffer.

The LSO is primarily involved in drafting legislation and staffing interim legislative committees. All proposed bills must go through the LSO drafting process, whether they are presented to the council in complete draft form or as an idea that requires extensive research and staff drafting. All proposals whether actually originated by a legislator or not must be officially sponsored by a legislator to be processed through the LSO procedures.

The Legislature's only standing joint Senate-House committee, the Joint Finance-Appropriations Committee (JFAC), which has equal membership from each chamber, develops budgets and introduces appropriations bills. It is the only standing committee in the Legislature established by statute, and the only one with its own staff. The legislative budget office staff provides analysis of agency budget recommendations and provides general assistance to the committee. The legislative auditor's office, also overseen by JFAC, conducts financial audits of state agencies and may recommend management or accounting improvements.

That staffing, and the general growth in the LSO office, indicates more professionalization of the Idaho Legislature. But these are limited steps. Apart from the budget committee, no other committee has its own staff other than secretarial help, and part-time citizen lawmakers still have only limited resources to help them in reaching independent decisions.

Office space in the capitol has steadily expanded so that all of the members of leadership and committee chairs, and many other legislators, have an office. Most of the other members use their desks on the floor of the house or senate as their office. The state's purchase in 1999 of the Ada County Courthouse, located across Sixth Street from the Idaho Statehouse, was intended to increase office space capacity. But tight budgets have precluded any remodeling of the courthouse and at the time of this writing, debate was still continuing over whether the old courthouse should be torn down or remodeled.

Media coverage varies among the different type of media. The Associated Press wire service is permanently located in the basement of the capitol building. During the sessions, desks are also available nearby for several Idaho daily newspapers, for public radio news and for Idaho Public Television. Newspapers from Spokane, Idaho Falls, Twin Falls, Pocatello and Lewiston usually send reporters to cover the session; the *Idaho Statesman* in Boise usually assigns two reporters to the session.

As for Idaho Public Television, budgeting cuts have had an impact. Public television for years provided a nightly one-half hour statewide broadcast during legislative sessions; these have been curtailed to weekly broadcasts.

Each year the Legislature funds interim study committees made up of legislators from both houses and staffed by the Legislative Services Office. The subject matter of each committee is determined by concurrent resolution. Typically the committees meet from early summer through late fall, but few have had a major impact on state policies. Their ineffectiveness can be attributed to dealing with issues over which a consensus is almost impossible; usually the result of a disconnect between the membership on the interim committee and the germane standing committees. A "quiet burial" is often the fate for such issues as legislators decide not to take a final vote.

REDISTRICTING AND REAPPORTIONMENT

Both state and federal constitutions require reapportionment. It must be accomplished after each United States Census.

Over the years the size and composition of the Legislature has changed rather dramatically. Much of this change has been forced by federal court decisions.

From statehood to the 1960s, the Idaho Legislature was dominated by rural interests—particularly agricultural, timber and mining interests. The "cowboys" prevailed on most major votes. The evidence for this dominance was the "agricultural exemption" that was almost a mandatory part of any major piece of legislation. Idaho was an agriculturally dominated state and agriculture interests were essentially kings in the Idaho Legislature.

During this period the basis for representation was county based. Each county, regardless of population, was represented by a legislative delegation—a senator and two representatives based on population with the important proviso that each county had to have at least one senator. Clark County with fewer than 1,000 people had as much representation as Ada County, with many thousands.

This rural dominated representation scheme came to an end in the mid-1960s. The U.S. Supreme Court ruled in the *Baker v. Carr* decision that the Fourteenth Anendment guarantee of equal protection applied to legislative representation. The court held that merely representing territory and economic interests would not suffice under the "equal protection clause" of the United States Constitution. In *Reynolds v. Sims* (1964) the United States Supreme Court held that both houses of the Legislatures had to be apportioned according to the "one-man, one-vote" standard, rejecting the practice many states employed in which state senate districts were counties rather than equivalent numbers of people.[12]

Reapportionment became a long and bitter issue in Idaho. The first reapportionment plan, finally implemented in 1966, came after three special sessions of the Legislature and several federal court decisions.

The pattern of federal court decisions overturning special legislative session decisions continued throughout the 1970s and 1980s. In 1983 a Idaho district court judge, with behind-the-scenes input from the governor's office, came up with a creative reapportionment scheme. The judge imposed a system of seven "floterial districts" that were imposed on top of the existing 35 districts. This resulted in a two tiered system in which floterial district legislators represented five times as many people as other legislators. The system was not as bad as some feared but it was quite a challenge for legislators trying to "represent" what were essentially mini congressional districts.

In 1994 the Idaho voters approved a constitutional amendment to provide for a redistricting commission. Only 11 other states have such a commission. Idaho's first commission met through the second half of 2001, after the 2000 census results were released to the state. It held 24 meetings around Idaho. Its six members, evenly split between Republicans and Democrats, frequently deadlocked in considering numerous plans, and critics questioned the usefulness of the whole idea. Though its life span under the statute was 90 days, the commission wound up meeting over a 10-month period. Two plans from the group were rejected by the Idaho Supreme Court; but a third was approved and implemented.

Through all of this, reapportionment has had only limited impact in Idaho. Democrats thought the reapportionment of 1983 would help their party; the next election, in 1984, turned out disastrously for them (though reapportionment was not a significant contributor). The reapportionment of 2001 may have helped Democrats in at least two legislative districts in the 2002 election—the point is debatable, and has been debated—but probably had little practical effect on outcomes anywhere else.

TERM LIMITS.

Within an eight-year period, from 1994 to 2002, Idaho adopted term limits through the initiative process, reconsidered and upheld them through an advisory vote, and then later upheld the Legislature's repeal of term limits. Even though term limits is no longer effective in Idaho, the policy's impact on the state in the last few years should be reviewed to better understand the state's unique political culture.

The state term limits movement began in 1990 as initiatives were proposed in California, Colorado and Oklahoma. Most Western states have some form of legislative term limits and all but Utah's were enacted through the initiative process. In 1994, Idaho voters approved an initiative to impose term limits on state and local officials. Federal officials were included but their limits were struck down by the U.S. Supreme Court (*US Term Limits, Inc. v. Thornton*, 514 U.S. 779, 1995) which ruled that congressional qualifications for office could not be established by state law.

Public opinion surveys supported term limits but evidence did not support the need for such a measure. Empirical analysis showed significant turnover in elected office without the limits.[13] Despite the evidence, the measure passed with the strong support of the United States Term Limits movement. The focus appeared to be on wresting control of Congress from the Democratic majority. State and local limits were apparently secondary, though the proponents denied it. But with the U.S. Supreme Court decision in the Thornton case, federal term limits were scrapped while the state limits remained in place, thanks to the severability clause included in the initiative.[14]

In the 1997 and 1999 sessions fairly serious efforts were made to reverse the Idaho term limits for state and local officials. These efforts failed. The major effort in the 1998 session was to place the term limits issue on an advisory ballot in the November general election. The state's voters were given the opportunity to again visit the term limit issue for state and local officials now that the federal issue had apparently been resolved. By a narrow margin, the voters reaffirmed support for term limits.

In 2002, the Idaho Legislature became the first in the nation to overturn a voter-passed (by initiative) term limits law. Term limits backers then placed a referendum to reinstate that law on the November general election ballot. By a razor thin majority, the voters upheld the legislative repeal.

LEGISLATIVE ELECTIONS

The political party influence on the legislative process varies from state to state but, even in heavily Republican Idaho, many candidates decide on their own to seek legislative office. Parties still play a role in recruitment but not as much as in the past. The Republican Party has dominated the Idaho Legislature over the past forty years. **(See Table 1.)** However, interest groups also play major roles in the recruitment and fund raising for candidates. In the policy arena, interest groups are typically more influential than the party leaders and organization.

Very few legislative districts are competitive; much of the state has "safe" Republican seats. Historically those safe Republican seats have been in southern Idaho, particularly in the upper Snake River Valley and in the Magic Valley. The safe Democratic seats have been in northern Idaho and in Bannock County in southeastern Idaho. For much of the state's history, the northern Idaho legislative delegation was staunchly Democratic. But several elections after 1990 left the Idaho Democratic Party with only one "safe" district and that one, ironically, now is in the heart of the city of Boise, once a Republican stronghold.

Given the one-party nature of Idaho politics, most of the spirited legislative campaigns have come in party primaries featuring fierce competition between the moderate Republicans and the ultra-conservative wing of the party.

The Democrats have not avoided division either. A split between the "lunch bucket" (blue collar) Democrats and the "wine and cheese" (environmentalist) Democrats has persisted. Although these fissures have existed for many years, they became very evident in the 1996 election, particularly on the nuclear waste issue.

The "wine and cheese" faction lost in northern Idaho legislative races and also gambled heavily on a nuclear waste initiative that lost in the 1996 election. The "lunch bucket" faction stayed away from the issue fearing it would alienate working class voters, which it did.

In the years of divided government, there were many opportunities for partisan clashes, especially over public education funding. In the days when the Democrats had fairly respectable numbers in the Legislature, (the 1970s and 1980s) Democrats were able to develop coalitions with moderate Republicans (sometimes called "steelheads" after the fish that swims upstream) to move major pieces of legislation. With the overwhelming number of Republicans in some sessions, it was possible for the majority to work out their differences and strategies in caucus, especially when they had "veto-proof" majorities.

Unlike other governmental entities, the Legislature is not subject to the provisions of the open meeting laws. Therefore, the real decisions on major policy issues could occur in caucus without the public being privy to counter arguments and the deals that were struck. Or at least that is a potential scenario. But clearly not all of the work of the Legislature is determined on a partisan basis. There is much room for disagreement, especially within the Republican Party on a number of social and economic issues, particularly given their recent huge majorities.

The Idaho Legislature has typically reflected Idaho's traditional conservatism. The Legislature has been slow to adopt new programs that are relatively common in other states and to repeal such programs once established. It has been, for example, very reluctant to enact legislation authorizing alternative forms of revenue for local governments. It has moved very slowly in the area of economic regulation, even in the licensing or registration of contractors. Taxing and spending levels have reflected the state's underlying conservatism. Idaho is close to the bottom in a number of spending categories. Funding for education has been a priority in the state but some spending levels are considerably below most neighboring states. The state is virtually alone in not providing state assistance for local school construction and allowing schools to adopt development impact fees. Idaho also ranks toward the bottom in combined state-local per capita debt.

Considerable progress has been made over the years in increasing legislative capacity and professionalism. Annual sessions were instituted in 1969. Legislative staff agencies have expanded and many of the legislators now have their own offices and secretarial support. Salaries have increased slightly but still trail most other states.

Unlike its neighboring states, the Idaho Legislature enacts most policy decisions. In reality, little legislative power is directly shared with the people through the intiaitive process and rarely has a legislative act been the subject of a referendum. Representative democracy rather than direct democracy predominates in Idaho.

Chapter 7 notes

1   Dan Popkey, "Women pack a powerful punch in Idaho Legislature," *Idaho Statesman*, Jan. 26, 2005.

2   Jim Fisher, "Idaho Legislative Pay," *Lewiston Morning Tribune*, September 30, 1998.

3   David C. Saffell and Harry Basehart, *Governing States and Cities* (New York: The McGraw-Hill Companies, 1997), p. 135.

4   15th Annual Public Policy Survey.

5   See "Legislative Session Summary 2004" Boise, ID: Legislative Services Office, State of Idaho).

6   James B. Weatherby, *Idaho Legislative Manual 2002*. (Boise ID: Center for Public Policy and Administration, Boise State University, 1998) (see Office of Performance Evaluation profile).

7   "State Legislative Summary 2004."

8   James B. Weatherby, *Idaho Legislative Manual 2002* (Boise, ID: Center for Public Policy and Administration, Boise State University, 1998).

9   John Corlett, "Cowardly Act in the Senate," *The Idaho Statesman*, March, 1975.

10   Some lobbyists have developed their own "law on adjournment." University of Idaho lobbyist Martin Peterson says that it is "never before St. Patrick's day and never after Easter."

11   Idaho Coalition United for Bears v. Cennarrusa, 234 F. Supp. 2d 1159, 1160 (D. Idaho 2001).

12   Baker v. Carr, 369 US 186, 82 S. Ct. 691 (1962); Reynolds v. Sims, 84 S. Ct. 1362 (1964).

12   Gary Moncrief and James B. Weatherby, "Idaho should reconsider term limits' effect on state, local offices," *The Idaho Statesman*, June 23, 1995. B-1.

13   See U.S. Term Limits v. Thornton, 112 S. Ct. 1842 (1995).

CHAPTER 8
THE COURTS

The biggest lawsuit in Idaho history, ongoing as this is written, was ordered by the Idaho Legislature. That lawsuit has generated the most sweeping commentaries by the courts in Idaho history about the relationship of the branches of Idaho government. The story is worth telling in some detail.[1]

One big advantage Idaho has over most other western states is its relatively plentiful supply of water. While much of the state is natural desert, a big water resource runs through much of it. The Snake River, which starts just east of Idaho in Wyoming and dumps into the Columbia River in Washington state, runs like an arc through southern Idaho. Some 87 percent of the state's land area, and the bulk of its population, lies within the Snake River basin. The Snake has made possible Idaho's spectacular irrigation development and its hydroelectric power, which has kept electric rates in Idaho lower than in most of the country. Water indeed is "the lifeblood of Idaho." It was true when former Governor Len Jordan said it in the 1950s and it is still true today.[2]

The Snake's flow, and that of its tributaries, has been large enough to satisfy almost everyone's desires for most of the state's history. At the Milner Dam near Twin Falls, the Snake River is almost entirely dewatered—nearly all the water at this point is diverted for irrigation —and yet appears again as a full-flowing river a few miles farther on, with springs and tributaries bringing it up to strong flows.[3]

Whoever controls Snake River water controls much of the state of Idaho. That is why the *Swan Falls* case was so critically important.

Swan Falls Dam, located in the Snake River about 50 miles south of Boise, was built in 1901 (by the Tradedollar Mining Company, a company headed by Andrew Mellon) and came to be owned by Idaho Power in 1915 after a series of electric power consolidations. Idaho Power Company had water rights at Swan Falls, as elsewhere, but conditions were attached which appeared to require it to subordinate its rights to those of many irrigators upstream. Eventually, in the drought year of 1977, some of Idaho Power's shareholders sued the corporation, saying it had not been aggressive enough in protecting its water rights. Most Idahoans assumed that the Idaho Supreme Court would toss out the complaint, but in a stunning 1982 decision—called forevermore the *Swan Falls* decision—the court said that the shareholders' case had merit.

Political turmoil followed for several years, as worried irrigators faced a massive lawsuit from Idaho Power against their water right claims, and politicians struggled for a solution. Finally, in 1985, the state, the irrigators, and the corporation—which saw continued use of its electric power by irrigators as important to its business—the state and the irrigators agreed on a formula for assessing the water rights. Central to that was a complete, total Snake River Basin Adjudication (SRBA)—a legal determination of who owned what water rights.

THE SRBA

More than 160,000 water rights (about a third of them federal) ultimately were found to be involved. A separate SRBA Court (formed within the state's fifth judicial district) and a separate SRBA Courthouse in Twin Falls were established when the case was filed in 1987. Judge Daniel Hurlbutt, a district judge from the fifth district, was named to preside.[4]

Such an adjudication was inherently controversial, and for some water users risky. Many water rights had evolved over the years through informal agreements, often with little consideration to state constitutional requirements of "first in time, first in right." As procedural efforts on the case progressed, irrigators pressured the Idaho Legislature to change the law in order to help protect some of their traditional water right uses. A large batch of bills to that effect was passed by the 1994 Legislature.

This legislation was immediately challenged in SRBA Court as unconstitutional, an infringement on a judicial action that was already underway: changing the rules in the middle of the game. In a December 1994 ruling, Hurlbutt declared unconstitutional most of those new laws as an overstepping of legislative authority. He also said that in legal cases, the state must speak with "one voice"—that the Idaho Department of Agriculture and the state attorney general, for example, could not act as separate parties.

The decision outraged many legislators and was loudly criticized by many in the executive branch—including Governor Cecil Andrus. In angry response, legislators cut judicial budgets (eliminating, for example, Hurlbutt's court counsel position) as a direct expression of their feeling.[5]

The Idaho Supreme Court considered the case for several months before rendering its decision. It concluded in June 1995 that the Idaho Legislature had authority to make most of the changes—though not all of those it actually made—in the SRBA. It overturned most, though not all, of the Hurlbutt ruling. The decision generally turned on the Idaho Legislature's authority to "regulate by law, when necessary, the methods of proceeding in the exercise of their powers in all courts below the Supreme Court."[6]

The decision did not take headon the question of to what extent the Legislature can alter the direction of an ongoing legal action. It instead took a broader view—turning mainly on whether a particular element of legislation was "necessary" to the conduct of the SRBA.

In the decision, written by Chief Justice Charles McDevitt, the court said that it "has consistently recognized that Article V, Section 13 of the Idaho Constitution empowers the Legislature of this state to enact procedural rules when such rules are necessary because of changing times or circumstances or the absence of a rule from this Court. Whether legislative action in this context is necessary within the meaning of Article V, Section 13 is a constitutional determination to be passed upon by this Court."[7]

Which it did, ruling on one specific element of the legislation after another. The Supreme Court upheld portions of the 1994 legislation which directed that the Idaho Department of Water Resources (IDWR) director's reports constitute *prima facie* evidence, that awards of attorney fees and costs against the state be banned (though it did allow for a major exception) and that the director of the IDWR be removed as a party in the adjudication.

In the case of director's reports forming *prima facie* evidence, for example, the court noted that court rules allow for legislative presumptions concerning evidence. In this case, the court ruled, "Unless that evidentiary presumption is overcome by the evidence or the application of that presumption is clearly erroneous on its face, the facts set forth in the director's report are established."[8] The effect appears to give a stronger weight to the director's report than had existed previously.

But the Supreme Court also said that other elements of the legislation were not "necessary" and therefore could not stand: designation of the director as an "expert"; requirement that unobjected to portions of the director's reports be decreed as reported. The latter, the court said, was an unacceptable interference of the Legislature in a properly judicial function.

The decision set the SRBA off on a new course, after a year spent in considering how it should be practically applied to the case. But appeals and consequent re-evaluations of the SRBA continue, over a decade later.

Contentious courts

Idaho's courts since the reform of the early 1970s have been rated in national surveys as among the best structured and most efficient in the country. This is a result of aggressive court reform in the late sixties; up to that time, Idaho's courts were no bragging point.

The court reform is one of the most striking anomalies in Idaho government, a stunning exception to Idahoans' general opposition to dramatic change. This reform upended a century-long system; but in this case at least, few have quarreled with the end result.

Among the earliest institutions established in Idaho, courts functioned poorly through the territorial years. The first supreme court, appointed in 1863, did not even meet as a body until 1866, after all three original members had resigned.[9] Judicial turnover was high,[10] and at least one judge was chased out of the territory by a mob. One of the reasons for this was political: Idaho Territory was strongly Democratic, and all the judges were appointed by Republican administrations in Washington.

There were other causes for complaint too. The statement developed by the Idaho Constitutional Convention in 1889 for statehood suggested that "the most intolerable evil, however, under which we have lived for the past 25 years, has been the changing and shifting character of our judicial decisions, by which we have been deprived of the inestimable benefit of judicial precedents as a safeguard to our rights of person and property. Scarcely has one judge, sent to us from abroad, obtained even a slight insight into the laws and customs of the territory, before another coming into his room has undone the work of his predecessor . . ."[11]

At the constitutional convention, where lawyers made up much of the delegate population, the judiciary committee was one of the two largest, and the judiciary article of the state constitution was the longest, with 27 sections. The judiciary committee was closely split on whether Idaho Supreme Court justices should be elected or appointed to the post, only narrowly opting for election, though the convention overall supported that decision strongly.[12] The Supreme Court was first set at three members, to be elected on partisan ballots.

The convention also approved a variety of other courts below the Supreme Court: district courts, justices of the peace, probate courts, municipal courts and more. (The original version of the Idaho

Constitution also contemplated district attorneys, a system soon discarded, though occasionally suggested as a useful reform.) The constitution also included specific provisions for how the state should be apportioned into judicial districts, and specified (as a sop to the northern Idaho delegates) that the Supreme Court had to travel to Lewiston at least once a year to hear cases. That latter provision has been fully adopted in spirit. Today, the Idaho Supreme Court and Court of Appeals holds sessions in all of the larger communities in Idaho from Sandpoint to Pocatello (the Panhandle to southeastern Idaho), and sometimes to smaller communities as well.[13]

FORMATION AND ENDLESS CHANGE

Idaho had its own John Marshall in Justice James F. Ailshie, who served two separate terms totaling 24 years, starting in 1903 and ending in 1947.[14] He was the key to many of the early Supreme Court decisions that shaped much of Idaho law, perhaps most notably in his ruling in *Toncray v. Budge*,[15] a Supreme Court's decision that made illegal, and ended, anti-Mormon discrimination in Idaho.

The courts from statehood established a clear set of precedents for others to follow, but the structure of the courts underwent frequent changes. At the Supreme Court level, the three-member partisan court was made non-partisan from 1914 through 1918, then partisan again, then finally non-partisan from 1934 to the present. Voters in 1914 rejected overwhelmingly a proposed constitutional amendment that would have increased the number of justices to five; but six years later, apparently convinced the work load on three justices was too heavy, they approved an almost identical proposal. The number has stayed at five since.

The major structural change at the appellate level in Idaho courts in the last half-century has been the addition of a whole new level of court—the Court of Appeals. Through the 1970s, justices on the Idaho Supreme Court complained that they were overworked and their case backlog was growing. The number of court cases in Idaho did in fact, as in the rest of the country, explode during that time. After several years of debate, the Idaho Legislature created a new Court of Appeals that began operation in 1982. The court handles some appellate cases. Under this plan, all cases appealed from district courts, and all those which constitutionally must be decided by the Idaho Supreme Court, would initially go to the Idaho Supreme Court. But many of the more routine cases on appeal would go to the three-judge Court of Appeals. The system worked; the Supreme Court's backlog diminished Less cases were appealed from the Court of Appeals to the Supreme Court.[16]

The Supreme Court ordinarily is an appellate court, hearing cases sent up from trial courts or from some state agencies (such as the state Reapportionment Commission, the Public Utilities Commission and the Industrial Commission which according to the Constitution must be appealed directly to the Supreme Court.[17] In 2001, it received 847 appeals; ordinarily it issues about 250 written opinions each year.

Despite the fact that the Idaho Supreme Court has issued occasional controversial decisions, it has remained generally nonpartisan despite many political links. Although in 1990 all of the members of the Court had been appointed by Democratic governors, the Court had no difficulty reaching a speedy decision declaring that the Republican lieutenant governor could break organizational ties in the Idaho Senate, which was then split 21-21; the decision continued the 30 years of Republican control of the chamber.[18]

Although the Supreme Court justices are elected and serve regular six-year terms, most have reached the high court through appointment rather than election, because many of them resign in mid-term and replacements are appointed. Until 1998, the last justice elected to an open seat to the Court, in 1968, was Allan Shepard, who had been a state attorney general. In 1998 Wayne Kidwell was elected to a seat on the Supreme Court. For a time, all five justices were Governor Andrus appointees. But Andrus often liked to say that the justices tended to be independent of political considerations once they slipped on their black robes, and he, like others, often found that true.[19]

Through much of the state's history, Supreme Court seats were strongly contested, especially in the years when those seats were partisan. A contested election in 1970, however, was the last for a Supreme Court position until 1994. In 1994, Justice Cathy Silak was challenged by Wayne Kidwell, a former state attorney general. Justice Silak won. Another noteworthy judicial election was in 1998: Justice Byron Johnson, who had served since 1982, decided to retire that year at the end of his term, leaving the seat open for election. It was the first open Supreme Court seat in 35, and three candidates, including Kidwell, filed for the seat. Kidwell was forced into a run-off but won in the general election.

Another contest occurred in 2000, when Silak was challenged by Fourth District Judge Daniel Eismann. This time, numerous Republican leaders around Idaho lined up behind Eismann, and he defeated Silak, marking the first ouster of a Supreme Court justice in Idaho in more than half a century. The central issue was water: Silak had voted to uphold a controversial decision from the SRBA Court. In 2004, Justice Wayne Kidwell announced that he would retire at the end of the term, but that did not spark a political contest, as former Attorney General Jim Jones ran unopposed to fill the seat.

Idaho's Courts have tended to be centrist and, especially at the district level, generally conservative. Nationally, the end of the twentieth century saw the rise of the "new judicial federalism," in which litigants sought civil rights and other favorable rulings from state courts which they did not obtain on the federal level in the post-Warren Court era. Idaho has not, in general been involved in this trend, in contrast to some courts in neighboring states such as those in Oregon and Washington. But like other state courts, Idaho courts follow precedent from United States Supreme Court decisions.

THE LOWER COURTS

Much greater reform was needed below, where budgets were low and the quality of judges highly variable.

Most of the local-level judicial action was undertaken by justices of the peace, local residents who often were not attorneys and who were paid according to fees imposed upon conviction. In the book *Justice for the Times*, Alfred Perry, who served 37 years as an Idaho judge, recalled the experience of a friend who in 1940 was charged with a fishing violation. "Judge Perry's friend was required to appear in the back end of a dimly lit pool room before an elderly gentleman in red long johns with no shirt who was identified as a judge. No plea was taken, no trial held. The game warden stated the charge, and the judge stated the result: 'He arrests 'em, I fine 'em, that'll be $10.' Judge Perry vowed that when he became a justice of the peace in Gem County in 1952 he would not allow such goings on, but he noted the difficulties of doing justice. He inherited an outdated set of the Idaho Code, some complaint forms and warrants. He had no public courtroom, no staff, no legal training. He maintained his office in his dry cleaning plant."[20]

Because many of these low-level judges were paid out of fines and court fees, the courts were often derided as administering "cash register justice."

Beginning in 1949, Idaho legislators began to propose dropping several of the local courts, such as probate courts and justice courts, from the roster of those outlined by the Idaho Constitution, but those efforts failed. The Idaho Legislature in 1965 and 1967 passed judicial reform measures; which were vetoed by Governor Don Samuelson, who expressed concern that the public did not adequately support them. But in 1969, after some revisions, the governor relented and the reforms became law.[21]

What emerged was a streamlined system, three layers of courts: the Supreme Court at the top, district courts in seven judicial districts, and magistrate courts within those districts operating with limited jurisdiction. A number of positions, notably justices of the peace and city judges, were eliminated completely from the new system. As of the new millennium, Idaho had 39 district judges and 82 magistrates.

Cases begin in the magistrate or district courts, and may be appealed to the Supreme Court. The numbers of cases filed has risen steadily. After a steep climb in the 1980s, the increase slowed in the 1990s but continued nonetheless. District court filings in 1994 totaled 14,737 (about twice as many criminal cases as civil); the number in 2001 was 18,571. During the same period, magistrate division cases rose from 408,098 to 483,296.[22]

The courts have continued modernizing. By the mid-eighties all of the courts in the state were on a unified computer system, and the Idaho Supreme Court was among the first state court systems to set up both a computer bulletin board system and then an Internet web site. The SRBA Court has been a nationwide pacesetter in its approaches to handling massive volumes of documents and decisions, and in its advanced computer operations.

Idaho also constitutes a federal judicial district, and two federal district judges hear cases in the state. They are based in Boise. These appointments, like those to the Idaho Supreme Court, are political, but have not usually been very controversial except in the 1995 appointment of Sixth District Judge Lynn Winmill. He was not controversial. The controversial candidate was President Bill Clinton's original appointment, Lewiston Democrat John Tait. Republican United States Senator Larry Craig vowed to fight Tait's nomination; eventually it was withdrawn and Winmill was nominated and confirmed. Even though Winmill had been a county Democratic chairman, his appointment drew no opposition from Idaho Republicans, and Idaho's two Republican senators supported him.

Their support may have been influenced by the district court opening Winmill left behind: That nonpartisan state district judgeship, to be filled by new Republican Governor Phil Batt, went to Randy Smith, a Pocatello attorney who was state Republican Party chairman at the time Batt won the governorship.[23]

CRIME

Idaho is a relatively low-crime state, but in the 1990s its prison population exploded, and the state was one of the country's leading builders of new prison facilities (on a per capita basis). Beginning in the mid-1980s, mandatory minimum prison sentences became a popular cause in the Idaho Legislature, and the number of prisoners shot upward soon after.

As in much of the rest of the nation, crime in Idaho dropped in the 1990s. "Group A" offenses, which includes many non-violent as well as almost all violent felonies, were estimated by the Idaho State Police in 2001 as totaling 88,798, or about six per 1,000 people per year. There were 19,530 crimes reported against persons that year.[24] Steady declines in almost all crime categories were reported through the 1990s.

The prison population, however, more than doubled during the 1990s. In mid-1992 the prison population in Idaho totaled 2,324, but at mid-2001 it hit 5,452; most years during the decade the increase topped 10 percent annually. About half of the prisoners are incarcerated primarily because of property or drug offenses; about a quarter are classified as violent.[25]

State officials and legislators have scrambled to keep up with the rising tide. Finally, in 2000 the state contracted with a private company to open a privately-run prison facility.

Near the end of his term in office, Governor Phil Batt convened a "committee of one" to examine the problem, and concluded that sentencing in Idaho should be reviewed with an eye to reducing sentences for a number of offenses. The proposal was not followed up either by legislators or by his successor.

One reform proposal which has been adopted statewide was the system of drug courts established by District Judge Daniel Eismann, later elected to the Idaho Supreme Court. The drug courts emphasize treatment of drug offenders as opposed to incarceration. That system was extended in 2001 by the Supreme Court.

Prison numbers continue to grow, and no easy answers are in sight. Few Idaho political leaders have taken on the cause of reforming a system that seems to run so counter to Idaho values of limited government and maximum individualism.

Chapter 8 notes

1 Much of this section comes from Randy Stapilus, *Paradox Politics: People and Power in Idaho* (Boise, ID: Ridenbaugh Press, 1988), Chapter 14, "Rise and Swan Falls of Idaho Power", pp. 286-304. Key sources for that material included Hydro Era, an historical booklet published by Idaho Power; Tim Palmer, *The Snake River* (Washington: Island Press, 1991); interviews with Jim Bruce, former Idaho Power Co. chairman; state Sen. Laird Noh; state Sen. John Peavey; Perry Swisher; former Gov. John Evans; former Attorney General Jim Jones.

2 Jordan to U.S. House subcommittee on reclamation, various letters, 1952, in the Jordan papers, Idaho Historical Society.

3 For detailed description and background, see Palmer, pp. 141-145.

4 By a decade later, the court's office space had taken over most of an adjacent building as well, as Judge Hurlbutt had hired three "special masters" to assist him in processing the case.

5 Much of this material comes from the Snake River Basin Adjudication Digest, various editions early 1994, and the edition of June 26, 1995 recounting the Supreme Court decision; extensively quoted from the June 23, 1995 decision in the SRBA by Idaho Supreme Court.

6 BA Case filed as Idaho v. United States, Docket No. 21869, filed June 23, 1995.

7 Ibid.

8 Ibid.

9 Carl Bianchi, ed., Justice for the Times (Boise, ID: Idaho Law Foundation, 1990), p. 9.

10 See especially Dennis Colson, Idaho's Constitution: The Ties that Bind (Moscow, ID: University of Idaho Press, 1991), pp. 180-81.

11 I.W. Hart, ed., *Proceedings and debates of the Constitutional Convention of Idaho 1889* (Caldwell, ID: State of Idaho and Caxton Printers, 1912), p. 590.

12 Colson, Idaho's Constitution, pp. 187-88.

13 Bianchi, Justice for the Times, p. 30.

14 Ibid., p. 64.

15 Toncray v Budge (1908), 14 Idaho 621, 95 P 26.

16 Randy Stapilus, *1994 Idaho Political Almanac* (Boise, ID: Ridenbaugh Press, 1994), p. 144.

17 See Idaho Constitution, art. V, sec 9.

18 Randy Stapilus, *1992 Idaho Political Almanac* (Boise, ID: Ridenbaugh Press, 1992), p. 752.

19 Interviews with former Governor Cecil Andrus and Supreme Court Justice Allan Shepard.

20 Bianchi, p. 137.

21 Ibid., pp. 156-191.

22 2001 Idaho Supreme Court annual report

23 See Idaho Digest, January 2, 1996, p 1.

24. Idaho State Police, "Crime in Idaho 2001."

25 Idaho Legislative Budget Office, Fiscal Fact Book (September 2001).

GOVERNOR AND EXECUTIVE

T he duties and power of a governor in Idaho become most obvious when a new governor takes over, especially from the opposing party.

In 1994, for the first time in 24 years, the governorship of Idaho changed partisan hands: a Republican replaced a Democrat. (It marked a political mirror image: When Democrat Cecil Andrus had won the office in 1970 from Republican control, Republicans also had held the post for 24 years.) When Republican Phil Batt took over, a number of changes quickly occurred.

Nearly all of the Andrus cabinet-level appointees departed; most resigned, realizing that they would not be carried over. Batt, with Senate approval, named their replacements. He appointed a member of the Idaho Supreme Court almost as soon as he took office since Supreme Court Justice Stephen Bistline had announced his retirement not long before. He began appointing majority Republican memberships on state boards and commissions. The three-member state Public Utilities Commission, for example, shifted from Democratic to Republican control when the term of a Democratic commissioner expired, and Batt quickly replaced him with a Republican state senator.[1] Batt had authority to appoint several hundred positions (the number changes with legislative appropriations and the size of agencies), and he made appointments to many of them.

Batt scrambled to propose his own state budget for the 1995 Idaho Legislature, even though holdover staff in the Division of Financial Management had prepared much of it.[2] He took the state's lead role on what is in essence a legal issue: the importing of nuclear waste to the INEEL site in eastern Idaho. Andrus had for eight years vigorously opposed renewal of waste shipments there, and Batt continued that opposition until October 1995 when he and federal officials reached an agreement on some short-term import in return for long-term removal of the waste. The governor also proposed and pushed through creation of the new Department of Juvenile Corrections, and the merger of the Department of Employment and the Department of Labor. He also proposed, but saw rejected, the merger of two other departments, Insurance and Finance. Governor Batt set up a welfare reform commission which developed proposals for implementation of new federal welfare reform requirements.[3] At the beginning of his administration, Batt called for the Fish and Game commissioners to resign en masse, although they do not serve at the pleasure of the governor. The commissioners refused. Batt's call set off a storm of protest; he later reversed his stance saying it had been a mistake.

Batt's immediate and varied experiences give some sense of the broad range of duties of the governor of Idaho, a position not as powerful as in some states, but with broader authority and responsibility than in many.

In 1998, United States Senator Dirk Kempthorne was elected governor after Batt decided not to seek a second term. In the 1999 legislative session, Governor Kempthorne consolidated further gubernatorial power by transferring the Personnel Commission from the Department of Administration to the governor's office. The new legislation also provided that the governor would appoint the personnel commission director, a privilege previously reserved for the Personnel Commission. Even though this legislation seemed to give the governor unprecedented power over the hiring and firing of state employees, the Legislature easily passed the legislation with most of the dissenting comments coming from the state's media.[4] The issue hasn't been revisited since.

The power of the office of governor has encouraged Idahoans to pay plenty of attention to it at election time. Regionalism has been a big influence in electing governors, who have come from many of the regions of the state. The most recent elections have seen Batt and Kempthorne elected from southwestern Idaho, John Evans from the southeast, and Cecil Andrus and Don Samuelson from the north.

IDAHO'S GOVERNORS (SEE TABLE 2)

Idaho's first state governor, George Shoup, who was also Idaho Territory's last appointed governor, served for six months, then took a Senate term beginning in January 1891. Norman Willey, an Idaho County miner who was given the Republican nomination for lieutenant governor to fill a slot on the ballot that no one else had sought, replaced Shoup through constitutional succession. Willey was unknown, and barely taken seriously when time came to choose a new governor in 1892.[5] Willey's succession did not set a trend however, as the next century and more of statehood saw just two more governors —Arnold Williams in 1945 and John Evans in 1977—take office through succession from lieutenant governor.

The first governor of Idaho with a strong base and the ability to push an agenda was the third, William McConnell, a member of the constitutional convention who was prominent in territorial politics; he served two terms as chief executive (1893-1897). A Moscow merchant, he was the first governor to take an active role in shaping state government and setting policies, notably allowing both Mormons and women the vote, and using the state government to help build the new irrigation systems then growing rapidly in southern Idaho. But he was governor during a troubled period, the Panic of 1893, when the state's economy fell into depression, government revenues plummeted, and even McConnell's own business went bankrupt.[6] His successor, Democrat Frank Steunenberg of Caldwell (also a member of the constitutional convention), a newspaper publisher, was equally active during his governorship. Despite the efforts of McConnell and Steunenberg state government was still plagued with organizational problems as severe as defects in the state code that rendered all of the early laws of the state invalid. The code had to be fixed and the laws re-approved by the 1899 Legislature.

The 1904 gubernatorial election of Frank Gooding, a fierce, stern, Magic Valley rancher who had rebuilt the state party organization, marked a turning point. Gooding was instrumental in generating the gubernatorial election of other conservative Republicans—such as James Brady (1909-1911), John Haines (1913-1915), David Davis (1919-1923) and Charles C. Moore (1923-1927). All shared a pro-business, small-government viewpoint which both reflected and reinforced Idaho's brand of conservatism. These governors all took a limited view of government, and did not seek to expand the governor's role in the state. From 1904 to 1930 only one governor, Democrat Moses Alexander, sought to substantially change the nature of the office, by becoming much more involved than most of his predecessors in resolving mining labor and irrigation districting disputes.[7]

Idaho's first, truly activist governor (and its first governor born in what is now Idaho), elected in 1930, was Democrat C. Ben Ross.[8] He was the state's first three-term governor (serving six years), one of only three in the state's history to win the office that many times. His star rose and fell quickly, however, and he left behind few changes in policy, and proved to have little lasting impact on the power of the governor's office.

With the passage of a 1946 constitutional amendment, Idahoans
started electing governors to four-year terms, and the first governor
elected under that system, a Republican with strong Democratic backing, made the most sweeping changes in Idaho government since
statehood. Little-recalled today, Governor C. A.. Robins, a physician
from St. Maries brought Idaho government "into the twentieth century," according to Governor Robert E. Smylie.[9] Under Robins state education administration was consolidated from more than 1,200 school
districts to about 120, and state transportation efforts multiplied geo-
metrically. Robins' efforts were so substantial, for a short four-year
period, that Republican voters reacted against them in 1950, choosing
a far more conservative Republican named Len Jordan. A critic of the
Robins expansions, Jordan made moves to scale back state government, slashing the budget and even closing teacher schools in
Lewiston and Albion.[10]

Jordan's policies in turn generated another reaction among the
state's voters. Republican Attorney General Robert Smylie, a moderate who had been strongly influenced by Robins, followed Jordan, and
became Idaho's first, truly powerful chief executive.

Smylie pushed through establishment of a state port at Lewiston,
the first major expansion of state parks since early in statehood, the
establishment of a professional parks department, major expansions
of higher education including expansion of what was then Boise
Junior College to a four-year institution, the reopening of the college
at Lewiston, and massive construction and road projects statewide.
Like one of his activist predecessors, Smylie proposed and pushed
through a sales tax, and this time it stuck. But as it had with Ross,
there was a reaction, and the governor lost his next election, his bid
for a fourth term.[11]

In *Idaho's Governors*, Hope Benedict wrote that Governor Smylie's
"programs initiated the resuscitation of Idaho's economy, bringing the
state national attention . . . and he left an enduring mark on Idaho's
social, political and economic framework."[12]

Smylie was ousted in the Republican primary in 1966 by conservative state Senator Don Samuelson, whose view of state government
harkened back to a more narrow conservatism. But Samuelson did
not wind up undoing much that Smylie had put in place. In 1970 he
in turn lost to Democrat Cecil Andrus, who would become another
powerful, activist governor along the lines of Smylie.

Andrus waged his campaign philosophically on two fronts: the
need to improve and expand education in Idaho, and the need to pre-
serve "quality of life." (Andrus became one of the first successful
politicians in the nation to use that phrase as a rallying cry.) In a time

of some tumult in higher education, Samuelson had positioned himself to oppose the leaders of higher education and liberal politics no matter what issue was at hand. (He once proposed a "Kick a Beatnik in the Seatnik week".) Andrus recalled, "Don Samuelson tried to govern Idaho with a foot planted firmly in his mouth."[13] In that context, Andrus was seen as the more moderate and more articulate alternative.[14]

Andrus, through his record-breaking 14 years as governor, found a pattern for politics that served him well. While staying loyal to his fellow Democrats, he was friendly with many Republicans including many business leaders around the state. He successfully sponsored major pieces of legislation including state funding of public kindergartens and the Local Planning Act. Andrus worked diligently to stimulate economic development in the state, and the state's economic boom, that lasted to the end of the century, started soon after. Andrus also pushed for increases in education funding, an issue he had championed since his earliest days in the state senate.

In 1977, Andrus was appointed by President Jimmy Carter as his Secretary of Interior, one of the few Idahoans to serve in a presidential cabinet. (Others include Ezra Taft Benson, Terrell Bell, Bill Eberle and Phillip Habib.) He was succeeded as governor by another former state senator, Democratic Lieutenant Governor John Evans. Evans was initially seen by many Republicans as an easy mark, but he won election as governor on his own twice, in 1978 and 1982. He seemed to relish his fights with the overwhelming Republican legislature and vetoed several major pieces of legislation including attempts to repeal the Local Planning Act. He narrowly lost a 1986 run for the United States Senate.

In 1986, Andrus returned for a third term. After running for reelection and winning an unprecedented fourth term in 1990, Andrus said that he would not seek a fifth. Almost a dozen people ran, or nearly ran, for the office in 1994, but three major candidates finally emerged after the 1994 primary election. One was Democrat Larry EchoHawk, the attorney general who was elected to that post in the 1990 Andrus landslide. The Republican was Phil Batt, a veteran state senator and former chair of the Idaho Republican Party, who had narrowly lost a race for governor in 1982 against John Evans. An independent, tax activist Ron Rankin, also filed. Rankin had been a leader, both formerly and in 1996, of the One Percent property tax initiative; but in 1994, his initiative failed to obtain the petition signatures needed for ballot status, and his candidacy lacked the needed focus.[15] EchoHawk led in many polls throughout much of the campaign, but 1994 was an extremely strong Republican year, and Batt won a clear victory on election day.

In the fall of 1997 Batt surprised many Idahoans by announcing he would not seek a second term. His one-time protégé, then-Senator Dirk Kempthorne, ran instead and in 1998 swept to an easy win, garnering 68 percent of the vote.

A few elements of the executive branch changed under Kempthorne, notably the much-praised creation of a new Department of Environmental Quality (which had been a division of the state Department of Health and Welfare). Much of his staff moved with him from his Senate office, including chief of staff Phil Reberger, who was campaign manager for Kempthorne's Senate win in 1992 and his gubernatorial victories in 1998 and 2002.

Kempthorne's early legislative experience was a mixed bag as he and the Legislature—both Republican, and both similarly conservative—tried to work together. As the warden said in the movie, *Cool Hand Luke*, "What we have here is a failure to communicate." Some Republican leaders openly groused about his not consulting them on major pieces of legislation. Soon after taking office Kempthorne proposed a reduction in the supermajority for general obligation bond approval for school facilities, but legislators declined to support it, and Kempthorne backed away. Kempthorne had no legislative experience unlike the vast majority of his predecessors. In one term in the United States Senate, he had successfully sponsored two major pieces of legislation—unfunded federal mandates and safe drinking water legislation—but had trouble transferring those skills to the Idaho legislative process.

In 2001, when state government was flush with almost $300 million in surplus revenue, Kempthorne suggested dispensing with much of it in one-time expenditures such as building projects at colleges and universities, and sending much of the rest back to taxpayers in one-time tax rebates. Legislative approval for those ideas was strong at first, but as the session wore on lawmakers decided to make the tax cuts permanent instead of temporary. Kempthorne did not fight for his original idea, but simply signed the legislators' alternative into law, claiming it as his own. Later that year the state's economy took a downturn, and state revenues plummeted, forcing Kempthorne into wave after wave of budget holdbacks, through 2001 and 2002. Critics noted that most of that turmoil would have been avoided if lawmakers had adopted Kempthorne's original plan instead (and the governor had not backed down on the permanent tax cut). Kempthorne was re-elected in 2002, but with a modest 56 percent of the vote and lost his home Ada County.

The 2003 legislative session witnessed a much different, more assertive, Kempthorne. In his State of the State address, he proposed a 1.5 percent temporary sales tax increase to meet the state's projected revenue shortfall. And even though he did not get the full amount, the Legislature finally passed a temporary 1 cent increase in the longest session in its history. At least part of the reason for its passage was the leadership Kempthorne exhibited on the issue. (The sales tax increase was allowed to sunset in 2005).

TERMS OF OFFICE

According to Thad Beyle, "(h)ow long governors can serve and whether they can succeed themselves for more than one term are important factors in determining just how much power they have."[17] For the first part of the state's history, Idaho gubernatorial terms lasted two years with no limit on re-election.[18] In 1946 terms were changed by constitutional amendment to four years, with no re-election allowed—that latter provision being part of the bargaining package agreed to by both the Democrats and Republicans. Democrats were concerned that governors should not be able to succeed themselves; Republicans were more interested in having gubernatorial elections in off-presidential years (reflecting concern about the Roosevelt era coattail effect). The state Constitution was changed in 1956 to eliminate the one-term requirement as part of an elaborate complex of deals in the Idaho Legislature that involved support for two colleges and the development of the Port of Lewiston. Governor Smylie, who wanted to run for a second term in 1958, won that year —the only Republican in that Democrat dominated year to win a statewide office in Idaho—and again in 1962 before finally being defeated in his pursuit of a fourth term in 1966. There is no specific legal limit on the number of terms to which a person can be elected governor of Idaho.

GUBERNATORIAL ROLES

Governors in Idaho are the lead public agenda-setters for the state even though they only have limited formal policy-making authority. A governor can be ". . . an issue catalyst, picking the issue up from the public, focusing it, and seeking to take action on it. Some others (see) their role as that of a spectator viewing policy issues arising out of conflicts between actors on the state scene, whether they were special interest groups, the bureaucracy, or the mayor of the state's largest city. Finally, a few (see) the governor as a reactor to accidents of history and other unanticipated events. In the eyes of (other) governors, leadership (is) more a process of problem solving and conflict resolution than agenda setting."[19]

On the surface a governor's role appears to be almost entirely administrative, but in a very real sense the governor can be a major state policymaker. Even though the legislative powers of the state may be vested in the Legislature by the constitution, the governor plays a key role as legislative leader. The governor, through the state of the state, budget and other speeches, largely shapes the legislative agenda.

The governor's relationship with the Legislature is critical in determining "how successful his or her administration will be. Although the governor takes the lead, it is still the Legislature that must adopt the state budget, set or agree to basic policy directions, and, in many cases, confirm major gubernatorial appointments. A governor and Legislature at loggerheads over a tax proposal, budget, policy direction, or a major department head's confirmation can bring part or all of state government to a standstill."[20]

When the Legislature rejects the governor's legislative agenda, the governor has the prerogative to call the Legislature back into special session. These sessions can last up to 20 days (after which the governor could renew the call) and then the Legislature can consider only those matters the governor puts on their agenda.

The veto is another major power of the governor. Idaho's governors may not pocket veto legislation. They have to sign the legislation, veto it, or let it become law without their signatures. They also have line item veto authority for appropriation measures, giving them considerable clout with the Legislature. The line-item veto enhances their power over the agencies that might try an end run around the executive budget proposals. A sympathetic legislature can appropriate more dollars to a favored agency. But the governor has the final word in most cases. The threat of the veto is another important hook for a governor. "The threat of veto gives the governor an excellent means of influencing legislators to make changes in a bill before it is passed."[21] The veto is ordinarily exercised several times during each legislative session regardless of whether or not the governor and legislature are of the same party. In 2002, a series of reversals took place. That year, the Idaho Legislature repealed the voter-enacted term limits initiative, Governor Kempthorne vetoed that repealer legislation, but the Legislature overrode the veto. In 2003, Kempthorne vetoed major budget cutting legislation, virtually forcing the Legislature to pass a sales tax increase most of its members did not want.

The governor's role in the policy-making process has been demonstrated by the successes of Governors Smylie and Andrus. Each used their State of the State addresses, delivered on the first day of the legislative session, to help set the agenda for the Legislature. Smylie provided significant leadership in 1965 during, arguably, the most productive legislative session in the state's history when the Legislature enacted the state sales tax, the state parks system, and other major pieces of legislation. Andrus successfully advocated full funding for a new Department of Commerce, which has been credited with helping build a long term economic growth rate in the state. Commerce received department status as an Evans initiative, although Andrus gave it life with his successful budget request. Andrus was particularly adept at working with overwhelming Republican majorities in the Legislature and in getting the approval of most of his programs. For example, in the 14 years he served as governor, he vetoed only 120 bills (only 3 percent of the bills that were sent to him) and had only one veto overridden. All of this was done while he worked throughout his gubernatorial tenure with a Republican dominated legislature. Other governors less successful in working with the Legislature, like Don Samuelson and John Evans, relied more heavily on the actual use of the veto to try to influence the course of legislation.[22] They were generally less successful than Andrus.

"Statehouse governing," Andrus summed up in his autobiography, "is a process of making good appointments, negotiating compromises —sometimes settling for less than a full loaf—and picking times when you mount the bully pulpit."[23]

Reflecting the conservative nature of this state, Idaho's governors have been fiscal conservatives. And the governor's budget and the Legislature's appropriations have rarely been far out of line. However, that has not kept them from fighting about the details of particular budget items or revenue proposals.

The power of the governor to propose an executive budget is the culmination of administrative reforms during this century. It also signals the significant growth of the governor's power. "An executive budget in one document seeks to encompass under the chief executive's control all the agency and department requests for legislatively appropriated funds; it also reflects the governor's own policy priorities."[24] Idaho governors prepare an executive budget that includes all of the agency requests and reflects the governor's policy priorities. Through the preparation of the budget and its presentation in the budget address early in the session, the governor has a great opportunity to focus public attention on a number of fiscal issues and policy initiatives that would be affected by his budget.

The governor exercises his authority as commander-in-chief dealing with natural disasters and disorders. "How a governor responds to and handles unexpected crises greatly influences how we perceive his or her overall performance as a governor. As former governor Scott M. Matheson (D-Utah, 1977-1985) argued, '(T)he public expects the governor to take a lead. . .and a governor found wanting in a crisis situation rarely recovers politically'."[25]

As the state's leading crisis manager, the governor commands the state militia or units of the national guard unless they are called into national service. The Idaho National Guard is headquartered at Boise, with affiliated units located in 28 cities around the state. The force is part of the national armed services, and units have been sent overseas on military expeditions including Iraq. In the latter twentieth century they most often have been put to work during times of natural disaster, such as fire and flood. Only on unusual occasions, such as during a 1971 riot at the Idaho State Penitentiary, have they been deployed in conflict situations in the state.

The governor has limited authority to grant "respites or reprieves in all cases of convictions," but most of the pardoning power is vested in the state Board of Pardons and Parole.[26] The governor can veto its decision, but that has happened only rarely. Governor Phil Batt did become involved in the case of Donald Paradis, convicted of first degree murder and originally sentenced to death. Doubts about his guilt arose, and the board changed his sentence to life in prison. "The case was then put in my lap," Batt recalled in his memoir. [*The Compleat Phil Batt*, p 64] "I canceled a week of appointments and devoted my entire attention to the matter." Batt was a supporter of the death penalty and recalled he was skeptical at first, but finally decided to support the board. Later another person acknowledged guilt in the case. Batt later wrote of his role in the Paradis case, "I'm glad I didn't order his execution."[27]

The governor appoints heads of many of the state agencies; in some cases however, such as the Department of Transportation, Department of Corrections, Fish and Game Department, and Public Utilities Commission, the director is partly insulated from the governor's direction because he/she is appointed by the agency's governing board.[28] As **Figure 2** indicates, there are more state agencies whose directors are appointed by boards and commissions than those whose directors are appointed by the governor. Gubernatorial influence does eventually reach into these agencies, especially since a governor may eventually appoint a majority of the members of those boards and commissions. But, however one might look at it, the control is far more indirect than having the agency head serve at the pleasure of the governor.

In general, unless state law or the constitution provides otherwise, governors fill vacancies in public offices. On seven occasions, governors have appointed U.S. senators from Idaho. (One of those senators, John Thomas, actually reached the U.S. Senate through appointment on two separate occasions.)[29] At times, governors have filled vacancies on city councils; that happened in Lewiston in 1988 (when voters recalled most of that city's council), and again in the city of Troy in 1997 (when the council also was left with less than quorum following a recall), and in Greenleaf in 2004 (when council members resigned after the mayor had been recalled).

The governor is the titular leader of his political party. He has much to say about party organization and strategy and can have great influence, especially if he has won by a large margin and claims a mandate from the people.

Governors are typically in the middle of the intergovernmental system. They deal with both federal and local officials on a continuous basis. Their problems are increasingly expanding beyond their borders needing regional or national solutions.[30] Several Idaho governors have been highly active in national governors associations. Governor Smylie was the senior Republican governor in the nation and chair of the Republican Governors Association. Governor Evans hosted the National Governor's Association (NGA) meeting in Boise in 1986, and Governor Kempthorne did likewise in 2002. Governor Andrus chaired the NGA and the Western Governors Association, and Kempthorne was the NGA chair in 2003-2004.

Andrus also received national attention in the areas of conflict with the federal government. Governor Andrus was active and largely successful in his efforts to block the shipment of nuclear waste to the state. His successor Batt negotiated a settlement with the federal Department of Energy on the issue, calling for a total removal of nuclear waste from the state within 30 years. That deal was challenged in 1996 through a ballot issue organized by a group of anti-nuclear Idahoans, but Batt prevailed with the voters, and the terms of the agreement still are being executed.

Governors represent the state in other ways. Idaho governors have represented the state in trade missions to Europe, Asia and Canada. Kempthorne in particular was very active in representing the state before various organizations including trade groups, to the point that he drew criticism for the amount of time he spent out of state. (That criticism mirrored complaints about one of his predecessors, Robert Smylie, who also was a frequent flier.)

Last but not least is the governor's role as the state's chief administrative official. The Idaho Constitution provides that the "(s)upreme executive power of the state is vested in the Governor who shall see that the laws are faithfully executed."[31]

David Berman's description of Arizona governors fits Idaho governors closely. They may be called chief administrators "though their ability to live up to the expectations associated with these roles is conditioned by legal and political factors and by their personal inclinations and abilities."[32] To understand the day-to-day influence the governor has on the administrative process, one has to go beyond legal documents and organization charts. An effective governor mixes both formal and informal powers to take his or her rightful place at the top of the state governmental structure. Typically the governor is the most powerful figure in the state. He has influence over the decisions of the various departments and consults with their directors on a regular basis. His budget office plays a crucial role in monitoring the spending practices of these agencies and is continuously involved in either the execution or preparation of a budget. He can also issue executive orders that have the force of law. In Idaho, the governor is also a member of boards that administer state agencies. He is a member of the State Land Board and the Board of Examiners.

The role of the governor can change and sometimes does at the will of the Idaho Legislature, as in the movement to that office of signoff authority on new state administrative rules with the arrival of Republican Phil Batt and placement of the state personnel system under Republican Dirk Kempthorne.

CONSTITUTIONAL OFFICERS

Governors are at the top of the state governmental structure, but they are not alone in being elected by the voters statewide. As in other states, Idaho has a plural executive branch with administrative powers shared or fragmented among several, independently elected state officials. In Idaho, the governor shares powers with six other independently elected officials. This is significantly less than the national average of over ten elected officials in addition to the governor. In Idaho, these other officers are: lieutenant governor, controller, treasurer, secretary of state, and superintendent of public instruction. These additional executive offices are elected in the same year that the state's voters choose a governor.

The lieutenant governor has the smallest personal turf: ordinarily, just a single office and a single executive assistant. He serves as president of the Senate and as acting governor when the governor is out of state or in case of incapacitation. Idaho state history is replete with examples of the governor and lieutenant governor belonging to different parties since they do not run on a joint ticket. Usually, however, their relations have been at least cordial and sometimes better. During eight of Republican Robert Smylie's years as governor, his lieutenant governor was William Drevlow, a Democrat. But they got along. Shortly after Drevlow took office, Smylie recalled, "He came into my office and said that he knew he had been elected to be lieutenant governor and that he did not confuse himself with the governor and thought we would get along very well."[33] C. L. "Butch" Otter, elected first in 1986, occupied the office for the next 14 years, the record for longevity in the post. He worked smoothly for eight years with Democratic Governor Andrus and even more smoothly in the next six with Republican Governors Batt and Kempthorne. In 2002, Senate Majority Leader Jim Risch was elected Lieutenant Governor after having won rather easily in a crowded Republican field in the primary election.

The secretary of state is the chief elections officer and record keeper and has several other statutory functions, including membership on the state land board. Pete Cenarrusa, who held the job from 1967 through 2002, is the record holder for the most consecutive years in elective office in Idaho: he was first elected to the Idaho House in 1950 and never lost an election. He was replaced after the election of 2002 by his long-time chief deputy, Ben Ysursa.

The state controller is the state's chief financial record keeper and issues payments and warrants for the state. This incumbent, too, is noteworthy. J. D. Williams was the lone statewide Democrat to survive election night 1994, which in Idaho was a massive sweep for Republicans. In 1998, he was joined by Democrat Marilyn Howard as the only two Democrats to be elected to statewide office in Idaho. Williams resigned from the office in September 2002. Keith Johnson, his chief deputy and a Republican, replaced him when Johnson was elected to a four-year term in 2002.

The state treasurer is the money-keeper for the state and is primarily in charge of investing the state's funds. The state treasurer also administers the government investment pool which is widely used by cities, counties and other local governments. Treasurer Ron Crane was first elected in 1998 and re-elected in 2002. He is a former state representative from Canyon County.

The attorney general is chief legal counsel for the state and the various agencies. The office is chief defender of the state, and defends statutes when they are challenged. (That has sometimes become a difficult proposition for the office when the elected attorney general already has spoken out for, or against, a proposal.) The office of Attorney General represents state government in court; it is, for example, one of the most prominent participants in the Snake River Basin Adjudication. The office reviews for form and constitutionality proposed ballot initiatives. The Attorney General's office also contains a consumer protection division, that periodically takes action against businesses that violate consumer law. Former Chief Deputy Lawrence Wasden was elected attorney general in 2002, and before that served as the State Tax Commission's Deputy Attorney General.

Like many other attorneys general, Idaho's has joined in many national legal cases. Its participation in a major tobacco industry lawsuit, for example, resulted in creation of the "Millennium Fund" in Idaho state government, made up of tobacco settlement money. It has been a participant in antitrust cases (such as the Microsoft Corporation case) and others.

The sixth elected, executive official is the Superintendent of Public Instruction who administers the state department of education and serves as a member of the state board of education. The superintendent also serves as the chief spokesperson for education in Idaho. Former Moscow Principal Marilyn Howard was first elected Superintendent in 1998 and still holds that office.

These officeholders have a number of ex-officio duties. The governor, secretary of state, controller, attorney general and superintendent of public instruction, for example, constitute the state land board. The secretary of state, controller and treasurer form the state board of election canvassers, which certifies election returns. The governor, secretary of state and attorney general comprise the board of examiners that approves off-budget state spending between legislative sessions.

EXECUTIVE BRANCH DEPARTMENTS

The expansion of the executive branch through the proliferation of departments, boards and commissions has been an issue throughout state history. Idaho has gone through two major reorganizations. In 1919, there were 51 bureaus, boards and commissions. The passage of the Administration Consolidation Bill in 1920 reduced that number to nine with all of the agency directors being appointed by the governor.[34]

But governments do not operate in a vacuum. As new programs were authorized, more agencies, boards and commissions were created. In 1970, there were 269 state agencies that reported to the governor. Governor Andrus made it a priority of his administration to reduce that number. He successfully promoted a constitutional amendment in 1972 that limited the number of state agencies to 20, excluding independently elected state officials. That limitation is in effect today even though there have been some changes in departments since 1972.[35]

The governor theoretically heads the executive branch. But, while the governor does have direct control over some parts of Idaho government, he has little or no control over others. An example came in 1991 when one executive appointed by a board was accused of child abuse. (He was later acquitted of the charge.) Although the executive was a long-time ally of Andrus, the governor insisted he be fired. The governor did not get his way. The board, whose members Andrus appointed, refused to carry out that request. (Later, months after the acquittal, the executive resigned.)

The agencies have a sort of limited legislative authority of their own through the issuance of administrative rules. This once-haphazard process was consolidated in 1993 through a new Administrative Procedures Act.; a state code of rules was organized, and all rules were run through a newly established office, first in the office of the state controller, and later in the state Department of Administration. After Governor Phil Batt was elected in 1994, the Idaho Legislature gave the governor the authority to veto administrative rules before they reach the stage of public promulgation. These agencies commonly are grouped into several functional categories:

General government: Several other agencies provide services to the government, notably the Department of Administration (which operates state buildings and grounds and provides printing, parking, telephone and other services); and the Department of Revenue and Taxation (which collects taxes, under supervision of the Tax Commission). In 1999 the Idaho Legislature, at Governor Kempthorne's request, moved the Personnel Commission from within the Department of Administration to the Office of the Governor.

Economic development and regulation: One of these agencies, the Department of Commerce, is primarily concerned with boosting the state's economy. Most of the others are primarily regulators. These include the Department of Finance (banking and financial institutions), Department of Insurance, and Department of Transportation (trucking, aircraft, and roadways and construction). In 2004, the Departments of Commerce and Labor were merged into the Idaho Department of Commerce and Labor.

Human Resources: These agencies run the normal range of people-oriented services operated by state government. They include the Department of Corrections, Department of Law Enforcement, Department of Education (headed by the Superintendent of Public Instruction), the Department of Health and Welfare, and the Industrial Commission. The Department of Health and Welfare is the largest department in Idaho and several proposals have emerged to split up the massive agency. Since then a new department has been created out of one of its divisions, the new Department of Environmental Quality.

Natural Resources: Idaho's tremendous natural resource base is watched over more by the federal government than by the state, but several state agencies do play a role. These include the Department of Lands, the Department of Fish and Game, the Department of Parks and Recreation and the Department of Water Resources.

Chapter 9 notes

1 News reports in the *Idaho Statesman* and *Lewiston Morning Tribune* (December-February 1994-95).

2 State of Idaho, Division of Financial Management, Executive Budget for the State of Idaho, Fiscal Year 1996. And the budget address of Governor Philip E. Batt, January 1995. Both documents generally are available, updated by year, from the governor's office site on the World Wide Web.

3 Idaho news reports; *Idaho Digest,* issues of May-December, 1995.

4 See news reports in the *Idaho Statesman* and *Post Register* (January - March 1999).

5 Robert Sims and Hope Benedict, eds., Idaho's Governors: Historical Essays on their Administrations (Boise, ID: Boise State University, 1992), pp. 10-21.

6 Carlos Schwantes, *In Mountain Shadows* (Lincoln, NE: University of Nebraska Press, 1991), p. 150; Sims and Benedict, Idaho's Governors, pp. 22-28.

7 Stapilus, *Paradox Politics*, pp. 95-98; Sims and Benedict, Idaho's Governors, pp. 52-111; Gooding obituary, June 25, 1928, Idaho Statesman; article "W. Lloyd Adams," *Idaho Yesterdays*, by William Davis, summer 1968. Interviews with John Corlett, John Porter, Robert Smylie, Mark Ricks, Richard Egbert.

8 For background on Ross, see Michael Malone, *C. Ben Ross and the New Deal in Idaho* (Seattle: University of Washington Press, 1970); Stapilus, Paradox Politics, pp. 76-80; article "Storm Warnings," Collier's Magazine, by Walter Davenport, April 4, 1936.

9 Smylie in the *Intermountain Observer*, Sept 26, 1970; Stapilus, *Paradox Politics*, p. 100; interviews with Robert Smylie, Louise Shadduck, John Corlett.

10 Stapilus, Paradox Politics, pp. 104-106; interviews with John Corlett, John Evans, Robert Smylie; Sims and Benedict, Idaho's Governors, pp. 156-164.

11 Stapilus, *Paradox Politics*, pp. 107-109; 120-124 on his 1966 election loss to Samuelson; Sims, pp. 166-174; interviews with Smylie, Samuelson, John Corlett, Perry Swisher, Cecil Andrus.

12 Sims and Benedict, *Idaho's Governors,* p. 174.

13 Cecil D. Andrus and Joel Connelly, *Politics Western Style* (Seattle: Sasquatch Press, 1998), p. 18.

14 Sims and Benedict, *Idaho's Governors*, pp. 176-181; see also Don Samuelson (autobiography), *His Hand on my Shoulder* (Sandpoint, ID: self-published, 1993); and Perry Swisher (autobiography), The Day Before Idaho (Moscow, ID: *News Review*, 1995).

15 Office of the Secretary of State, Voting Records.

16 Thad Beyle, "Governors," *in Politics in the American States: A Comparative Analysis*, 7th ed., eds. Virginia Gray, Russell L. Hanson, Herbert Jacob (Washington, DC: Congressional Quarterly Press, 1999).

17 Thad Beyle, "Governors," p. 211.

18 See Stapilus, *Paradox Politics,* p.100; pp.108-109; Robert Sims, Idaho's Governors (Boise: Boise State University Press, 1990), p 151, 168.

19 Thad Beyle, "Governors," p. 219.

20 Thad Beyle, "Governors," p. 220-221.

21 Sydney Duncombe and Robert Weisel, "State and Local Government in Idaho," *State and Local Government in Idaho and in the Nation* (Moscow, ID: University of Idaho Press, 1984), p. 62.

22 See Randy Stapilus, Paradox Politics (Boise: Ridenbaugh Press, 1988), pp. 195-197, and 262-264.

23 Cecil Andrus and Joel Connelly, *Politics Western Style* (Seattle: Sasquatch Books, 1998), p. 20.

24 Thad Beyle, "Governors," p. 213.

25 Thad Beyle, "Governors," p. 191.

26 For a listing of the constitutional powers of the governor, see Article IV of the Idaho Constitution.

27 Phil Batt, *The Compleat Phil Batt*, Caldwell, ID, 1999.
28 Thad Beyle, "Governors," p. 212. Beyle's index of formal gubernatorial power references six agencies that are important for the governor to control: corrections, public education, health, transportation, public utilities and welfare. Idaho's governor makes executive appointments directly for the health and welfare and public utility agencies.
29 Idaho Blue Book.
30 Thad Beyle, "Governors," p. 223.
31 Idaho Constitution, Article IV, Section 5.
32 David Berman, *Arizona Politics and Government* (Lincoln, NE: University of Nebraska Press, 1999), p. 119.
33 Robert Smylie, *Governor Smylie Remembers* (Moscow, ID: University of Idaho Press, 1998), p. 111.
34 Fred E. Lukens, *The Idaho Citizen*: A Textbook in Idaho Civics (Caldwell, ID: Caxton Printers, 1937), pp. 39-40.
35 Sydney Duncombe and Robert Weisel, "State and Local Government in Idaho."

Chapter 10
Local Government

L ost River is one of Idaho's least known, most obscure cities—if "city" is the right word for it. In fact, few people even know where it is.

It was incorporated early in the state's history and then seemed to disappear, except for an "official" in Lost River who kept cashing state-shared revenue payments. The checks were stopped but the mystery remained as to where it actually was on the map. Eventually, a State Tax Commission administrator decided to find Lost River once and for all, and assigned the job to a regional representative in the Upper Snake River Valley. The staffer searched through the area from house to house and farm to farm. On the border of Butte and Custer Counties he finally found a woman who said her husband had lived in the area for most of his life and might know something about the "city" though she herself had never heard of it. She invited the staffer to come back that night and ask her husband. He did, and to his astonishment was told by her husband that, sure, he knew where Lost River was: "It's right here, and I'm the mayor!"

A bar in Lost River held a city-based liquor license. Idaho has a population-based quota system for liquor licenses, but every "city" regardless of population can issue two licenses. The liquor license may explain why the "city" was incorporated in the first place. (It would not be alone in existing for such a reason.) Lost River may still be an official city in Idaho and apparently the bar is still open under the good offices of the City of Lost River.[1]

Lost River is by no means a typical local government, to put it mildly, but it does illustrate some important characteristics of Idaho local governments. Most are small, serving rural populations. Some have been created for rather curious reasons, like liquor licenses (or, years ago, to license slot machine gambling). Many are relatively invisible. But all are intimately involved with state government—for example, state shared revenues and technical assistance.

Local governments in Idaho include cities, counties, school districts, highway districts, fire districts and about 15 various types of special purpose districts. **(See Table 3.)** "Grass roots" governments are perceived as being closest and most responsive to the people. Public opinion polls have documented Idahoan's preference for local governments over both the state and national governments. When survey respondents have been asked to rank the levels of government on measures of responsiveness, efficiency and trust, local governments have been ranked the highest on each of these measures. Idaho is a state full of small local governments—over 1,000 for 1.4 million people—a conservative state that apparently loves small, local governments. They are the mechanisms of the most direct government control over people who want as little government as possible—yet who do, especially in the case of newcomers, expect plenty of service.

FRAGMENTATION IN LOCAL SERVICE DELIVERY

Fragmentation in policymaking and service delivery has characterized Idaho's patchwork of local governments. With so many local governments, a lot of "bumping" goes on among governmental entities[2] because of duplication of services and confusion as to which entity is responsible for what service.

Even in the state's largest urban area and capital city, Boise, there is general confusion over the delivery of certain basic services, such as transportation. The City of Boise, unlike any other city of its size in the country, has no responsibility for the construction or maintenance of its streets.[3] This responsibility lies with the Ada County Highway District, which is not a county department, but a separate special purpose district with its own independently elected board of commissioners.

The delivery of fire protection services is another source of confusion among the electorate and a source of controversy among governmental officials. In Ada County, for example, seven fire protection districts in addition to the City of Boise deliver fire protection services in various areas. These examples are typical of the overlapping of jurisdictions which fosters duplication and limited accountability in the state.

A counter argument to this fragmentation critique is that the number and diversity of local governments afford more points of access, more opportunities for citizen participation, and more choice among service levels.[4] There is also great opportunity for cooperation and mutual aid agreements.

LOCAL ELECTION ADMINISTRATION

Traditionally, local governments have held elections on a wide range of days through the year. In the 1990s legislation was enacted, consolidating elections to only a few days, with some exceptions allowed. Now all local governments, except school districts and water districts (and except for emergencies involving life, health and safety), may now only hold general and special elections during one of four dates on the consolidated election calendar. Typically, cities hold "off-year" general elections, while the county, state and federal elections are held in even numbered years. Election consolidation reform was designed to promote greater visibility for some of the "invisible governments" and promote greater voter turnout by combining several different types of elections on the same date and in the same polling place.[5] So far, results have been mixed. Many of these elections attract only a small percentage of the electorate in a state that consistently ranks among the nation's leaders in turnout rates in statewide general elections.

With the exception of elections for school board members and one highway district (Ada County's), candidates run at-large. County commissioners must reside in districts but they run at-large. State law provides for the election of city council members by district or ward but no city has opted for either.

Initiative, referendum and recall are available at the local level; recalls are uncommon generally but in some strife-torn communities have become a recurring political weapon. Bond elections are common for revenue bond issues that require a simple majority approval rate for a water and sewer facility project. General obligation bonds that commit the "full faith and credit" of the governmental entity require a super majority approval rate of two-thirds for school construction and other non-revenue producing facilities. Idaho is not only a low tax state but also a low debt state.

CITIES

Idaho is either the nation's most rural state or one of its most urban, depending on who is counting and by what criteria. According to the Census Bureau definition of urban places being over 2,500 in population, Idaho qualifies as being among the most rural states in the country. An overwhelming majority of Idaho local governments have fewer than 2,500 people; only a fifth of Idaho's 201 cities have more than 1,000 residents. On the other hand, counting the number of incorporated places, cities by Idaho standards, the state is more than 60 percent urban.

Cities, as municipal corporations, are voluntarily created by the citizenry to serve their constituents. The menu of services each city provides varies by geographical location and population. No municipal services are mandated, and cities provide as many or as few services as their residents support or demand. State and federal mandates generally apply only after the city has decided to take on a particular function. Most cities in Idaho are "full service" cities and provide such basic services as police and fire protection, street maintenance, libraries, parks and recreation. Twelve cities also provide electrical services and three generate their own electrical power (though Idaho's three largest cities do neither).

Most of the significant growth in Idaho has occurred in and around cities. This growth, however, has been uneven. The growth centers have been in the five urban areas of the state, from Kootenai County in northern Idaho to Ada and Canyon counties in southwestern Idaho to south-central Twin Falls County to Idaho Falls and Bonneville County in southeastern Idaho. Another, smaller, growth area has been in the resort areas in Blaine County. There are a few small growth centers such as Teton County (next door to the resort city of Jackson, Wyoming).

This rapid growth has exacerbated urban-rural tensions. Taxation and the allocation of state revenues have been particular sources of conflict. Many smaller local governments in outlying areas have opposed local option taxation proposals which they feel would benefit the major urban retail areas and not help the rural areas. Another emerging issue centers on allocation of state revenue sharing monies among all of the cities and counties. The urban areas believe that they are the economic engines of the state. Through sales and income tax payments, their taxpayers subsidize the rest of the state. They contribute far more than the city receives in revenue sharing. Boise's Mayor Brent Coles pointed out in his 1994 "State of the City" speech that of the $131 million Boise taxpayers "generated last year, the city received just $6.3 million dollars. And of the $183 million dollars in state income taxes generated in Boise, the city received nothing to support police, fire, parks and recreation, library and other essential city services."[6] On the other hand, there are those who argue that the state returns far more money to local governments, including schools —more than $1 billion annually—than it spends on all of the other functions of state government.

Legislative proposals have been introduced to allocate some state shared revenues on a "point-of-origin" or point of collection basis, but they have not received much serious attention in the Legislature. Some of this failure can be attributed to the division within the local government associations whose membership, representative of both urban and rural localities, is seriously divided over the issue.

Although it is relatively easy for an area to incorporate in Idaho, few new cities have been created in the past 30 years. State incorporation laws provide that if at least 125 registered voters sign a petition for incorporation, they can present it to the county commissioners for their review. A simple majority vote of the county commissioners is required to incorporate a city. No vote of the people is required. Some important restrictions apply, however, such as the requirement that the proposed new city's limits cannot extend to within a certain number of miles of another city. The exact distance is determined by the population size of the existing city.

In the last third of the 20th century, just four cities were incorporated in Idaho: Carey in Blaine County, a half hour from Sun Valley; Dover, west of Sandpoint in Bonner County; and Eagle and Star, just west of Boise. In all of these cases, growth pressures finally made unincorporated status impractical, as residents in both areas sought to gain some control over growth in their communities. Still, Idahoans have proven reluctant to add new governments, and many who have moved near population centers (especially near Boise and Coeur d'Alene) have moved to unincorporated areas specifically to avoid the taxes and regulations that come with city life. There are many such people. According to the 2000 Census, of the 300,904 people living in Ada County, some 61,936 lived outside of cities—and almost all of them within 20 miles of a city. Newcomers also move inside cities, both incorporated and unincorporated areas have grown steadily in population.

Annexations do not require a vote of the annexees. In some of these areas, especially in Ada County, annexation is a hot-button issue. The City of Boise has been extending its reach westward since the early 1980s, and annexations west and south of town have drawn howls of protests, and threats by area legislators to make annexation more difficult.

All 201 incorporated places in Idaho are cities. In short, Boise with its 185,000 population or Warm River with nine citizens are both "cities" operating under the same state law provisions. There is no classification of cities into first, second, or third class, or villages, as there once was before recodification of the municipal law in 1967.

City officials believed then as now that all should be treated equally. Many of the very small cities in Idaho were created to take advantage of the state's liquor licensing law, like Lost River. In most cases, liquor licenses are granted only within incorporated areas of the state. Each city government is given two licenses regardless of population and additional authority is granted to cities on a sliding per capita scale. At least two cities (Garden City and Island Park) were created in the 1950s to take advantage of gambling law then on the books, and to bring in slot machine income. Today, the slots and the gambling income are gone, but the cities and liquor licenses remain.

Cities have both general governmental functions, such as police, fire and building regulations, and proprietary "quasi-private" functions that include the delivery of utility services, water, sewer, and sanitation. Proprietary operations are typically self-supporting and financed by user fees and service charges. They comprise approximately half of the total municipal budgets in Idaho. The amount of the charge or fee must bear some reasonable relationship to the cost of providing the service or it is considered to be a tax. As a "Dillon's Rule" state, where cities are creatures of the state, they must have explicit authority to impose a tax.[7] But there is no oversight function such as a public utilities commission to regulate rate setting as in the private sector.

In addition to user fees and service charges, other revenue sources include property tax revenues and intergovernmental aid from either the state or national government in the form of revenue sharing or grants-in-aid.

State aid includes revenues from the state sales tax, liquor profit, and highway user revenues. Of total state sales tax revenues, 3.875 percent are funneled to cities through a city-county revenue sharing program created in 1984. Allocations are distributed among the cities based upon each city's proportionate share of the state's total municipal population and market value. These state revenues are discretionary and may be used for any lawful municipal purpose. There are essentially no strings attached. Another 2.625 percent of sales tax revenues are distributed to cities under the inventory replacement program (relating to the repeal of the business inventory property tax in the 1960s). The other revenue sources are from the state highway user account, monies generated by gasoline taxes, licenses, fees, and permits. Highway user revenues are primarily earmarked for use on city streets and related transportation uses.

On the other hand, city general government functions are principally supported by property tax revenues. The percentage reliance on the property tax for general governmental revenues ranges from 35 percent to 50 percent among most cities whether they are large or small.

Given this significant reliance on the property tax, one cannot understand municipal finance in Idaho without studying the history of the property tax revolt.

In 1978, Idaho voters approved a California Proposition-style property tax limitation initiative. Idaho was one of only three states to pass such limitations during the era of "property tax revolt." This initiative was a proposed statutory change because the Idaho Constitution cannot be amended through the initiative process.[8] Consequently, Idaho legislators revised the initiative because it was written in the constitutional language of the California constitutional amendment, Proposition 13. In addition, there were provisions in this California carbon copy that would not fit within the Idaho constitutional scheme. Instead, the Legislature implemented a series of percentage caps that severely limited local governments' ability to raise local property taxes. Such restrictions had major negative effects during periods of rapid population growth and high inflation in the late 1970s and early 1980s. City services suffered accordingly. For example, in the City of Boise, "from fiscal years 1979 to 1990, the city increased in population by 25 percent and the taxable value of its property increased by over 100 percent, but the number of municipal employees essentially remained the same."[9]

Local option taxation proposals have had a long and controversial history in Idaho as city officials have sought ways to diversify their local tax bases. For over 30 years local option bills have been introduced in the Idaho Legislature but no general local option authority has been given to Idaho cities. Cities' major local revenue source continues to be the property tax. A few tourist communities like the small cities of Sun Valley and Ketchum have been given local option taxation authority to address the problems related to huge influxes of tourists. Visitors enlarge the city treasuries with local sales tax revenues but also place major strains on local services. The Idaho Legislature so far has been willing to give only a limited form of local option taxation to fund specially targeted cities. But even among resort cities, a population cap has limited this authority.

As a part of the municipal reform movement of the late 1800s and early 1900s, the council-manager form was lauded as a way to introduce efficiency and to remove politics from city government. A manager was to serve as the city's chief executive officer, analogous to the head of a private corporation. The mayor would be the chairman of the board and the council members would serve as board members. There would be a clear division between policymaking and administration. The elected officials would be the policymakers and the appointed manager would be the administrator with significant administrative authority in appointing department heads, preparing the city budget for council approval, and exercising general responsibility for enforcing city ordinances. The system is widely used in states that border Idaho.

But only three cities—McCall, Lewiston, and Twin Falls—use the council-manager form. Pocatello used it for about two decades, but voters there elected in 1985 to return to the strong-mayor form. Populist Idaho voters prefer to vote for their government officials.

All other cities in Idaho use a mayor-council form of government in which the mayor is the chief administrative officer for the city and is charged with the responsibility of seeing that city ordinances and resolutions are enforced. The mayor has authority to veto most city ordinance proposals and appoint department heads, subject to council confirmation. There are variations, however, within mayor-council cities. Several Idaho cities have recognized the need for professional administrators but have not wanted to implement a formal council-manager plan. Instead they have established a city administrator position by council ordinance or resolution. The administrator serves essentially as an administrative assistant to the mayor, not having the complete administrative responsibilities of a manager but providing professional expertise in such areas as planning, purchasing, personnel administration and grants administration.[10]

In other cities, even though the state statutes do not provide for a commission form of government, the administrative powers of the mayor are divided up among the council members so that each council member serves as a *de facto* commissioner over given city departments. This practice is mostly utilized in very small communities where the mayor does not have the time or expertise to provide all of the administration chores necessary and there are not enough resources available to pay an administrator.

The municipal reform movement never fully caught on in Idaho, though some features have been adopted. Idaho cities have at-large, non-partisan elections. Some have designated seats but the candidates still run at large.

COUNTIES

Counties in Idaho vary widely in size, population and economic base. Payette County has 408 square miles. Idaho County has 8,485, more than the state of Connecticut and eight times larger than Rhode Island. Population density is another major variant. Ada County population exceeds 300,000 whereas Clark and Camas counties each have about one thousand people. County economies range from traditional resource based economies heavily dependent on agriculture, mining or timber to metropolitan areas with expanding service and high tech sectors.

Of all of the types of local government, county government may be the least understood and most complex. County government combines traditional functions that have been extended to citizens since statehood with modern county government functions that include land use planning (setting the direction and extent of growth within the county), economic development, water quality and job training.

No other local government so straddles state and local government. Counties have historically been arms of state government, their functions mandated by state constitution or law. The constitution establishes the county government framework by limiting indebtedness, narrowing taxing powers, and authorizing optional forms of county government. State statutes are more specific about the authority and constraints on county governments in the administration of the elections, courts, health care for the medically indigent, the property tax and licensing of vehicles.

But despite the mandated nature of their existence, counties are central players in the governmental system. If counties did not provide many of these mandated functions, the state government would have to act.

Nationally, and increasingly in Idaho, counties are emerging from their traditional functions to assuming many roles as their populations grow. Citizens are demanding more and more services, which go beyond the traditional services county governments have provided. Land use planning is a growing county function (as counties deal with many nonconforming uses). Other urban services provided by larger county government include the operations of parks and other functions that traditionally were identified as urban or municipal functions.

In this evolution, county government structures have changed little despite a recent constitutional amendment and implementing state legislation that provided for optional forms of government. Both the state's most populous county and its smallest have basically the same governmental structure.

After more than 20 years of legislative attempts to give county voters optional forms of county government, the 1994 Legislature passed a constitutional amendment that was approved by the voters later that year. This amendment authorized the legislature to provide for optional forms of county government, and in response, the 1996 Legislature passed two pieces of legislation recommended by an interim legislative committee.[11] The first provides for a menu of options for county voters, ranging from a county executive to a county manager to the consolidation of county offices and consolidation of counties. Prior to the placement of any of these items on the ballot, a formal study commission must be created to analyze and advise voters of the impact the option or options would have that are being considered. The other statutory provision establishes a charter commission procedure to propose a county charter to the voters. This charter would provide for flexibility in determining the structure of a county's form of government but it would not grant additional substantive powers such as taxation.

Several counties have set up citizen study commissions. Ada County placed an optional forms proposal on the ballot in the 1996 general election; it lost by a margin of 2 percent of the vote (49-51 percent). Other measures from other parts of the state were on the 1998 ballot, and other reform proposals have followed. But at this writing, not one has passed.

The traditional county commission form (three-member commission with seven other elected officials) has raised many questions about coordination, efficiency, accountability and democracy. Reformers charge that there is no single executive authority. County commission forms combine both legislative and executive responsibilities. The commissioners share executive authority with other independently elected "constitutional" officers. Some argue that this traditional county commission form is more democratic than reformed county governments with an elected executive at the top or a county manager system that has a clearer line between legislative and executive authority. With the commission model, power is dispersed. There are checks and balances. But others argue that the commission model is flawed. No one is really in charge. No one official is answerable for county government policies and administration. That responsibility, that accountability is dispersed among many individually elected officials. Each office often accumulates its own power base independent of the commissioners. Cooperation and coordination is sometimes difficult if not impossible. To date, the clearest judgment in Idaho has been the ballot box. Idaho voters still prefer the status quo. Elected officials subject to voter approval are preferred over unelected administrators—thus no county managers in Idaho. But there are individuals in some counties who function as county administrators, quite like the city experience. County officials also run on partisan tickets, rather than the nonpartisan option reformers prefer.

As to the electoral process, county commissioners must reside in a commissioner district but are elected countywide. The terms are also staggered so that the commission is a continuing body with one commissioner being elected for a four-year term each election and one being elected for a two-year term. These terms then are rotated so that an incumbent commissioner serves a four-year term followed by a two-year term.

Without going through a formal adoption of an optional form of government, the county commissioners may appoint an administrative assistant or one of the county commissioners may serve as the county administrator.

The board of county commissioners is like a city council, acting as the legislative body for the county. Commissioners approve budgets, enact ordinances and oversee all phases of county government, from monitoring other elected officials to volunteer boards and commissions.

Other county elected officials serve four-year terms. The county clerk has five titles: clerk of the district court, auditor, recorder (deeds, marriage licenses, real estate titles, etc.), clerk of the board of county commissioners, and county chief elections officer. In addition, the clerk is also the county budget officer, gathering requests from all other county offices and submitting a proposed budget to the commissioners.

The county treasurer invests county funds, acts as ex officio tax collector, and ex officio public administrator (administration of funds from decedents with no known heirs). The treasurer also collects certain occupation license fees.

The county assessor determines valuations for taxation purposes on real and personal property. As an agent of the Idaho Department of Transportation, the assessor handles vehicle licensing and titles.

The county sheriff is responsible for the enforcement of Idaho statutes, especially in the unincorporated areas of the county. Within larger cities, the city police provide most of the law enforcement services. Some county sheriffs contract with smaller cities to provide law enforcement services. The sheriff also administers the county jail and provides drivers license examinations.

The county prosecuting attorney serves as the county's legal advisor, defends the county when necessary on such cases as land use planning decisions, medical indigency issues, and property tax valuation disputes. The prosecutor also tries criminal cases.

As with cities, the property tax is the single most important county revenue source along with intergovernmental aid, fees and charges[12] Approximately 28 percent of county revenue is property tax and 42 percent is charges and fees; both of these percentages are above the national average. State aid is 18.5 percent as compared to the national average of 33.8 percent. Federal aid is only about 2 percent, one percent below the national average.

Local option non-property taxes are seldom used in Idaho. However, there are two counties, Kootenai and Nez Perce, who have taken advantage of local option sales tax authority to fund public safety function and provide for property tax relief.

County government expenditures also diverge from national averages. Major county expenditures are health and hospital (36 percent contrasted with the national average 16.7 percent), highways (8 percent as opposed to the average of 6.1 percent) and law enforcement and corrections (18.4 percent as contrasted with 11.8 percent).[13]

County governments in a public lands state like Idaho struggle to provide services to tax exempt property. For example, the federal government owns 63 percent of Idaho land, none of which is on the property tax rolls. But obscured by this average are the number of rural counties such as Valley County, which is 90 percent federally owned. County services are still required on these lands, especially law enforcement and search and rescue missions. To address this federal impact on local services, counties working through the National Association of Counties succeeded in the 1976 passage of the Payment-in-lieu-of Taxes (PILT) federal legislation. PILT provides federal reimbursement for the impact federal tax exempt lands have on county governments. PILT is an important program to counties. In Idaho in FY 04, counties received approximately $15 million in PILT funds. The three top counties receiving funds included Elmore County ($1.3 million), Cassia County ($1 million) and Blaine County with approximately $1 million. Although in some counties, PILT funds are a significant percentage of county budgets, particularly rural counties with huge acreages of federal land, county officials assert that it is not enough to cover actual costs.

School districts

There are 114 school districts in Idaho. A board of trustees elected from trustee districts rather than at-large governs the district. Board members are non-partisan and serve without pay. Board legislative powers include the power to approve the district's budget, approve bond issues after voter approval, and appoint the district superintendent who serves at the pleasure of the board. The superintendent is the administrator for the district and plays a critical role in aiding the board in making decisions about curriculum and extra curricular activities.

Reliance of the school districts on state funding has grown. The shift from property tax dependence to more state assistance has occurred over a period of several years. But the shift was significantly accelerated when the 1995 Legislature enacted Governor Batt's proposal to move 25 percent of the schools' maintenance and operation levy off property taxes to the state's general account. The amount has grown annually. It was $40 million in FY 1996 and $73 million in FY 2004. Concerned about the increasing fiscal impact of this program on the state's general fund, the 2003 Legislature capped the amount of the relief at $75 million. The cap was reached in 2005.

Local control over public education is a major issue in Idaho, especially given the realities of school funding. It is rather difficult to maintain that local school districts control their own destiny when another level of government, a "higher" level, is providing most of the revenue to support their operations. On the other hand, equity in funding of education requires a broad based tax structure instead of a narrow, locally based property tax.

The monies for state assistance are allocated to the schools through a complicated formula that takes into account average daily attendance according to school size and categories of students. Other factors include personnel costs and the expense of transporting students to and from school.

In 1992, a school facility needs assessment identified $700 million in un-met needs in Idaho. Since that time local voters have approved more than $600 million in bonds and levies for plant facilities. But the controversy over deteriorating buildings and school safety continues.

A number of groups and agencies are involved in educational politics in the state. The State Department of Education, headed by an elected superintendent of public instruction, historically has been a significant player in helping shape public education policy and in providing technical assistance to local school districts.

The Idaho State Board of Education is composed of the superintendent of public instruction and seven members appointed by the governor. The Board is responsible for setting policy for elementary and secondary schools.

In addition, several educational associations are involved in public education policy. The Idaho Education Association has been one of the most important interest groups in the state; and the Idaho Association of School Administrators and the Idaho School Boards Association are also significant players.

In recent years there has been considerable conflict among the major educational policy players—legislature, state department of education, and the state board of education. They have clashed over the recognition of charter schools and the administration of federal education programs. In 2003 the control of federal education programs was shifted from the Department of Education to the Board, a shift directed by the legislature, reversing policy dating back to the 1960s. Differences in education perspectives and partisanship between the state board, dominated by Republican gubernatorial appointees, and the Democratic superintendent, have turned what had been a warm bi-partisan relationship into a real partisan battle.

SPECIAL PURPOSE DISTRICTS

When politicians in Idaho decry the proliferation of governments, they are usually complaining about the growth in the number of special purpose districts. Of Idaho's more than 1,000 local units of government, upwards of 800 are special purpose districts providing a variety of services primarily, but not exclusively, to the rural areas of the state.

The rationale for creation of special districts was to provide services which could not be provided by general purpose local governments. Rural unincorporated areas, for example, needing fire protection, could not go to the county government because the county did not have fire protection authority. The unincorporated area's only alternative was to create a special purpose district. The provision of this kind of service worked well until cities grew, annexed, and threatened the tax bases of these fire protection districts.

Chapter 10 notes

1 "Lost River" is not noted on every list of state and local agencies as being a city. But the Idaho Tax Commission has listed it. See Randy Stapilus, 1999 Idaho Yearbook/Directory (Boise, ID: Ridenbaugh Press, 1999).

2 Thomas Anton, *American Federalism and Public Policy: How The System Works* (Philadelphia: Temple University Press, 1989.)

3 James B. Weatherby and Stephanie L. Witt, T*he Urban West: Managing Growth and Decline* (Westport, CT: Praeger, 1994).

4 Robert L. Bish and Vincent Ostrom, *Understanding Urban Government* (Washington, D.C.: Domestic Affairs Studies, 1973).

5 Stephen Shaw and James B. Weatherby, "Election Consolidation: Reforming the Reforms" (paper presented at the annual meeting of the Pacific Northwest Political Science Association, Boise, ID, November 1989).

6 Brent H. Coles, "State of the City," City of Boise, Idaho, September 13, 1994.

7 See Michael C. Moore, "The Idaho Constitution and Local Governments - Selected Topics," Idaho Law Review 31, no. 2 (University of Idaho Law School, 1995); and Michael C. Moore, "Powers and Authorities of Idaho Cities: Home Rule or Legislative Control?" *Idaho Law Review* 14 (University of Idaho Law School, 1977).

8 James B. Weatherby and Lorna Jorgensen, The One Percent Initiative and Voter Attitudes: A Comparison of 1978 and 1992 (Boise, ID: Public Affairs Program, Boise State University, 1992).

9 Weatherby and Witt, Urban West, p. 29.

10 Sydney Duncombe, "City Administrators and City Supervisors" (Moscow, ID: Bureau of Public Affairs Research and Municipal Research and Service Center, State of Washington).

11 Idaho Legislative Council Committee on Optional Forms of County Government, "September 19, 1995 Committee Minutes," Senate Majority Caucus Room, Statehouse, Boise, ID.

12 State of Idaho, Idaho State Tax Commission, 2003 Annual Report.

13. Ibid

CHAPTER 11
STATE-LOCAL RELATIONS

Aformer Pocatello city manager often was heard to say, "our destiny is in Boise."

By this he meant that many basic local government policy decisions were made by state policymakers at the state capital. During his years as manager, he and many other city officials periodically tested the limits. In periods of tight budgets he devised a number of creative financing schemes; but all were struck down by the state Supreme Court because cities had not been granted specific legislative authority for them.[1] Dillon's Rule—powers not specifically granted to local government by the state are denied—has had much influence in Idaho. Local governments are mere creatures of the state. This rule was reaffirmed in the Pocatello cases.

Why such limited local control in a state that prefers local to state or federal government? One answer is that many of the strongest interest groups in Idaho, especially those (such as large businesses) with an especially strong interest in tax policy, would rather work with one set of policy makers at the Statehouse than with hundreds of elected boards at the local level. Another reason is that Idaho's political culture tends to view any government as a necessary evil at best, is suspicious of governmental powers at all levels, and favors constraints on government power generally. Why do Idaho legislators, who are elected by the people just as are local government officials, choose to tightly restrict local governments? Because they can and because in many cases their constituents seem to want tight restrictions.

Except for the City of Bellevue, all cities in Idaho operate under the general laws of the State of Idaho. Essentially the "charter" for Idaho local governments is in state law.

Bellevue operates under a territorial charter that was recognized when Idaho became a state, so it differs from all the other cities in its election dates and procedures and other local functions. Despite Bellevue's status as a "charter" city, it labors under an especially ironic restriction on its annexation authority. All other Idaho cities have significant annexation powers that make them the envy of their counterparts elsewhere: the power to grow, the power to annex adjacent territories by ordinance and not hold a referendum in the area to be annexed. Idaho's only "charter" city, Bellevue, cannot annex so easily, a situation that may become increasingly problematic as its high-growth area adds pressure on the city. Annexation by a charter city requires state legislative approval of a change in the territorial charter. It was because of this significant authority difference between charter cities and general law cities that both the cities of Boise and Lewiston dropped their territorial charters in the 1960s.[2] They preferred the flexibility the local charter provided but were confronted with a major limitation. Legislative approval of their charter amendment to annex new territory was a very difficult requirement.

LIMITED DISCRETIONARY AUTHORITY

Local governments operate within significant limits and the courts narrowly construe these powers. There is no recognition of an inherent right of local self-government.[3]

The United States Advisory Commission on Intergovernmental Relations conducted a nationwide survey of the discretionary authority of cities and counties. Knowledgeable professionals in each state were asked to rank their local governments by the degree of autonomy exercised in such areas as authority over their governmental structures, functions and revenue sources. Idaho's cities and counties were ranked last in this local discretionary authority index. These are the principal domains in which "home rule" local governments exercise significant control over local affairs. Control over structural arrangements and service and other functions is virtually a prerequisite for being viewed as a home rule or local control entity.[4]

The low rating for structure for counties can be attributed to the historic and uniform adherence to a three-member commission in each county and a specified number of elected officials. Cities, on the other hand, have some flexibility in choosing between a mayor-council and a council-manager form of government and variation with respect to the appointment and reporting arrangement for major city department heads.

In personnel decisions cities and counties have flexibility. Unlike local government officials in urban states, who have strong public employee unions with mandatory collective bargaining and binding arbitration, Idaho city and county officials have few restraints. There is a requirement for cities with full-time paid firefighters to collectively bargain with the officially recognized firefighter union. But, unlike states with strong public employee unions, there is no requirement for binding arbitration and other requirements that substantially tie the hands of the policymakers in a collective bargaining impasse.

Idaho cities and counties were ranked at the bottom of the national survey in their ability to exercise authority in financial matters due to their heavy reliance on a single major source of tax revenue—the local property tax that was and still is limited. There is little revenue diversification for operating budgets and most capital improvement financing requires a two-thirds voter approval.

THE HISTORY OF *HOME RULE* IN IDAHO

Obviously then, *home rule* is not a reality in Idaho even though there have been many efforts over the years to secure that authority for Idaho cities.[5] Interestingly, the fight for *home rule* has been an important part of municipal history in Idaho, even though the effort has had limited success. *Home rule* initiatives have been undertaken in Idaho since the early 1950s. In fact the efforts in the 1950s attracted so much attention that the International City Management Association noted in its publication, *Municipal Yearbook*, that the "most vigorous effort to adopt 'home rule' has apparently been that of the Idaho Municipal League (now the Association of Idaho Cities) whose 1955 proposal was defeated in the state senate by the narrow margin of a single vote."[6] Those early proposals featured a constitutional home rule provision that would have given Idaho cities charter making authority and substantial local self-government powers.

Legitimate *home rule* gives city voters and their officials considerable control over local or municipal affairs. *Home rule* is based upon the notion that one can differentiate between functions and activities of a statewide significance over which state government should have ultimate control. Local affairs should substantially be beyond the reach of legislative interference. Why, for example, should it be of statewide concern what the local tax base is in a given community? On the other hand, the state could be vitally concerned about the effects of an environmental policy in local jurisdictions, where pollution knows no political boundaries. Environmental degradation in one community typically affects others.

The last major campaign to adopt *home rule* in Idaho was in 1976 when the Association of Idaho Cities successfully sponsored a statutory home rule proposal, the Local Self-Government Act of 1976. This act is cited by some national commentators to define Idaho as a *home rule* state. The purpose of this legislation was to reverse the traditional relationship between cities and the state. The Local Self-Government Act was designed to free cities from the restrictive interpretation and to allow them to perform those services or functions that were not denied by the constitution or state laws. The act provides that any city may "exercise all powers and perform all functions of local self-government in city affairs as are not specifically prohibited by or in conflict with the general laws or the constitution of the state of Idaho."[7] Because it was not a constitutional amendment, however, the bright promise of this act of 1976 has faded as the courts have generally ignored its significance and continue to adhere to Dillon's Rule.

Some efforts were made to test this new authority, especially in the City of Pocatello. The city devised a new fire protection fee based upon a fire flow fee concept—charging property owners a fee determined by the amount of water it would take to extinguish a fire in their building. City officials claimed that they had the authority under the 1976 *home rule* legislation to charge all properties, both taxable and tax exempt, for their proportion of the total fee, and that it was not in conflict or prohibited by state law or the constitution. The Idaho Supreme Court struck the ordinance down, not because it was not well designed but, because there was no specific legislative authority to impose such a fee. Dillon's Rule again prevailed.[8]

SPECIAL LEGISLATION

The Idaho Constitution prohibits the enactment of special legislation. All cities operate under the same set of laws with few exceptions. But the Legislature has found ways to circumvent this "special" legislation limitation in order to respond to requests from various localities in the state. Boise economic development advocates promoted tax increment financing (TIF) as a way to fund capital improvements to spur the completion of the city's redevelopment plans. In response, the Legislature circumvented the constitutional prohibition by giving authority to all cities over 100,000, never mind that Boise was the only city meeting that criteria. Sponsors believed that if they limited the new authorization to just the City of Boise it would minimize opposition from legislators from other parts of the state who feared the proliferation of this authority to their local governments. Boise City officials had already received public statements of support from all of the taxing districts that would be affected by the legislation. The Boise bill passed and then later all the cities under 100,000 population successfully obtained the same authority.

Another example is that of growth impact fee legislation. In 1992, the Legislature granted the authority to local governments in counties over 200,000. Ada County and Boise area developers preferred impact fees, a more predictable system, to the development exactions local governments had imposed on a case-by-case basis. They sponsored growth impact fee legislation that would have created a uniform impact fee policy throughout the state. But city officials from outside Ada County opposed the legislation. They lobbied hard and successfully to amend the bill to make it apply only to Ada County. But again local officials changed their minds a couple of years later and a bill similar to the original proposal became law, applying to all cities and counties in the state.[9]

MANDATES

Local officials must abide by state and/or federal law that clearly prescribes what they can and cannot do. Solid waste mandates require county governments to comply with federal environmental laws and regulations that set forth how solid waste disposal sites will be maintained and specify the provisions for the hauling of solid waste to those sites. County jails are the subject of federal mandates; both legislatively and judicially imposed. The types of prisoners that can be housed together along with the dimensions and "amenities" of the cells are prescribed by judicial order or federal law.

State constitution or law mandates most county functions. Counties are, in a very real sense, administrative arms of state government. If they failed to perform their functions, the state would have to step in. For example, the property tax process is administered by county officials who are active in the appraisal of property for taxation purposes, and the collection of the property taxes, and in the allocation of those taxes to taxing districts within the county. County officials allocate most state shared revenue dollars to local taxing districts. They also play important roles in the administration of the state court system. It is the county clerk who is the ex-officio clerk of the district court. County employees undertake several district court functions. As far as state law is concerned, it is the county sheriff who is responsible for the enforcement not only of county law but also of state law. Persons who have violated state law are often arrested by deputy sheriffs and sometimes housed in county jails.

Most elections in the state are administered by county officials who administer with the assistance and guidance of the secretary of state's office.

City officials do not have to deal with as many mandates as county officials. But they still have problems with most mandates,

especially with federal mandates. Former Boise Mayor Dirk
Kempthorne said those concerns prompted him to run for the U.S.
Senate in 1992. Particularly burdensome are environmental, personnel mandates and handicapped accessibility mandates. State mandates such as legal notice publication requirements, collective bargaining with firefighters, and property tax limitations on operating
budgets are less costly and intrusive.[10]

But not all mandates are opposed by city officials. In order to
respond to the challenge of managing growth in urban fringe areas,
city officials statewide supported mandatory legislation. In 1975, the
Idaho Legislature passed the Local Planning Act that mandated planning and zoning functions for cities and counties. The act also
required cities and counties to agree to "areas of city impact".[11] The
purpose of these negotiations determines whose developmental regulations apply within the area of impact, that of the city or the county.
Compliance with this provision has been spotty. There is no direct
penalty for noncompliance. But the provision still has had an effect
especially in urban areas and also in the wake of recent state legislation that links the area of impact to annexation authority.

Though limited in many other ways, Idaho cities do possess great
power when it comes to annexation. Unlike cities in other states that
are required to go through a referendum process to obtain voter
approval in the area to be annexed, Idaho cities, under only limited
restrictions, may annex adjacent territory by council ordinance.
However a city may not annex territory outside its area of city impact,
unless requested by the property owner.

This significant annexation authority is controversial, however,
because of its impact on other governmental entities and people in
urban fringe areas who do not want to be annexed. There have been
many legislative proposals over the years to repeal this authority.
Counties, other taxing districts and directly affected citizens have
serious problems with this unilateral authority. Rural taxing districts
such as fire protection districts are concerned when their tax bases
are gobbled up in annexations. Citizens in the areas to be annexed are
concerned about having no effective say in an annexation that they
believe will force their taxes to increase. Both public and private
groups have brought their concerns to the Legislature. No outright
repealer has succeeded but the authority has been somewhat modified.

City officials have defended this unilateral annexation authority
by noting that it is necessary for the orderly growth of cities. Adjacent
parcels of property are part of the general community whether or not
they are legally or technically part of a city. Residents in existing

cities, to one degree or another, subsidize those who live outside their boundaries but who work and spend a great deal of their time in the city therefore impacting, to one extent or another, many of its services. Given this situation, people who benefit from all of these services without having to directly pay for them will invariably vote "no" on a referendum proposal that would annex them to the city and require them to pay additional taxes, mostly property taxes.[12]

STATE AGENCIES AND LOCAL GOVERNMENTS

There are a number of state agencies that regularly interact with local governments, whether it is in promulgating regulations that affect local government operations, allocating state shared revenues or providing technical assistance.

The Secretary of State's office provides technical assistance and training for county clerks in the performance of their duties as the chief elections officers in their respective counties.

The State Tax Commission provides training for county assessors in their appraisal function, promulgates regulations as they relate to property tax administration, and allocates some state shared revenues to counties who then pass some of those revenues on to other units of local government.

An investment pool is administered by the State Treasurer's Office for counties and other local governments under the intergovernmental cooperation or "joint powers" act. The Idaho Department of Transportation provides planning assistance and allocates highway user revenues to local governments. The Idaho State Police work closely with the county sheriffs and its Peace Officers Standards and Training Council provides training for city and county police forces.

The Idaho Commerce and Labor Department administers the Idaho Community Development Block Grant Program that annually allocates over $10 million of federal funds to cities and counties for infrastructure and housing needs. The Department of Public Policy and Administration at Boise State University and the Cooperative Extension Service at the University of Idaho also provide research and training services for local governments.

INTERLOCAL COOPERATION IN IDAHO AND
THE INTERGOVERNMENTAL COOPERATION ACT

Idaho's local governments have considerable authority to cooperate formally or informally. The state's Intergovernmental Cooperation Act, passed in the late 1960s, provides that a local government may enter into an agreement or contract with another government to do jointly what each could do individually. The meaning of this provision is that governmental entities cannot expand their powers but they can cooperate on a broad range of activities. Local entities share equipment such as fire trucks and fire stations. They have the authority to jointly operate regional jail and solid waste facilities.

Even though the Advisory Commission on Intergovernmental Relations' report found Idaho cities and counties to be last in local discretionary authority, there are still significant options available for these local governments as they strive to provide services to their constituents. State revenue sharing has been significant along with state technical assistance and the authority to cooperate with various types and levels of government.

On the other hand, Idaho's local governments fall far behind local governments in other western states whose constitutional framers and legislators have given them far more discretionary authority, especially in the areas of taxation and finance.

Chapter 11 notes

1 *Brewster v City of Pocatello*, 115 Idaho 502, 768 P 2d 765 (1988).

2 Michael C. Moore, *Frontier Lewiston: 1861-1890* (Lewiston, 1980).

3 Michael C. Moore, "The Idaho Constitution and Local Governments" *Idaho Law Review* 31, no. 2 (1995); and "Powers and Authorities of Idaho Cities: Home Rule or Legislative Control?" *Idaho Law Review* 14 (1977).

4 U.S. Advisory Commission on Intergovernmental Relations, *State and Local Roles in the Federal System* (Washington, DC: U.S. Government Printing Office, 1982).

5 Jean Uranga, assistant attorney general, Attorney General Opinion No. 76-3, Janaury 20, 1976.

6 American Municipal Association report quoted in Weatherby and Witt, *Urban West.*

7 See Idaho Code, Section 50-301.

8 See Brewster v City of Pocatello. Some observers say that this decision and others were understandable given the fact that the "Local Self-Government Act of 1976" was essentially "sold" to legislators by local officials as one that would not grant additional taxation powers. The courts seem to be saying that fees equal taxes. Local officials of course would disagree.

9 James B. Weatherby, Lorna Jorgensen and W. David Patton, *Idaho Cities: Growth and Mandates* (Boise, ID: Association of Idaho Cities and Boise State University, 1994).

10 Despite their concerns, a few observers note that some of the mandates local governments now complain about were once proposed by their local government associations.

11 See "area of impact" provisions in the Idaho Local Planning Act, Title 67, Chapter 65.

12 See Weatherby and Witt, *Urban West;* and Robert Lovelace, "Annexation: A Necessary Power," Tennessee Town and City, October 1977, pp. 10-11.

CHAPTER 12
FEDERALISM AND IDAHO

In 1993, only months after he was elected to the United States Senate, Idaho Republican Dirk Kempthorne sponsored legislation to prohibit most new, federal, unfunded mandates. A former mayor of Boise who had experienced federal requirements at the local level, Kempthorne had made the subject a major topic of his 1992 campaign. In 1993, the city of Boise estimated that compliance with such mandates cost the city more than $17 million annually in both capital and operating expenditures.[1] Kempthorne's effort was supported by local government officials from around the country.

In 1995, when the Republicans took control of Congress, Kempthorne's bill was featured as S1 by the new Majority Leader Bob Dole. The bill easily passed Congress with bipartisan support and was signed into law by President Bill Clinton. A delighted Kempthorne said: "To go from being told you will never get a public hearing to then being invited to the Rose Garden where the president signed the bill indicates we went the full spectrum on this."[2] He later worked on and received bi-partisan support for the passage of amendments to the Safe Drinking Water Act. It was a big year for Kempthorne even though some critics have called the unfunded mandates legislation's impact more symbolic than real in providing relief to state and local governments.[3]

Meanwhile in Idaho, the Legislature and governor struggled with some of the same issues that Idaho's new senator was confronting in Washington, D.C., except that the roles were somewhat reversed. The State of Idaho balked at limiting itself in mandating local government services and programs. In a classic demonstration of Mile's Law ("Where you sit determines where you stand"), in the same year that Congress passed Senator Kempthorne's maiden effort in Congress, the Idaho Legislature boldly rejected the same principle by killing unfunded mandates legislation.

FEDERALISM

The relationship between the national (or federal government) and state governments is established in the federal constitution and is generally understood to be one of a division of powers between the federal and state governments. This federal principle which defines the relationships between the federal and state governments is a "middle way" or compromise between a confederacy, where ultimate governmental powers reside within the constituent units in a decentralized system, and a unitary system where powers are held by the central government in a centralized system.

The powers of the federal government are both circumscribed and potentially expansive. Article I, Section 8 of the U.S. Constitution lists 17 express delegations to Congress; the 18th delegation is the "elastic" or "necessary and proper clause" which gives Congress broad, undefined powers "to make all laws which shall be necessary and proper for carrying into execution the foregoing powers, and all other powers vested by this Constitution in the government of the United States or in any department or officer thereof." All of these enumerations, explicit and ambiguous, combined with the supremacy clause of Article VI and the commerce clause seem to have given the federal government extensive powers that have been progressively expanded over the years.

There is, however, a limitation to congressional power—the tenth amendment to the U.S. Constitution. The Tenth Amendment or the "residual powers provision" states that all powers not delegated to the Congress are reserved to the states or to the people. This, along with the separation of powers doctrine, has been historically used by states and localities to limit the power of Congress by stating that it is not expressly enumerated. One affirmation of the Tenth Amendment was in the *NLC v. Usery*[4] case where the U.S. Supreme Court struck down an amendment to the federal Fair Labor Standards Act. The Court ruled that state and local government personnel policies were local matters protected by the tenth amendment. However, in a later decision in *Garcia v. San Antonio Metropolitan Transit Authority*[5] the Court reversed itself and ruled that if state and localities were aggrieved by an act of Congress they should not seek protection in the Supreme Court but should go to Congress to have the legislation amended. In short, the Court said that there was no constitutional protection for states and localities. This decision seemed to have undermined the significance of the Tenth Amendment. If congress could dictate the contents of state and local government personnel policies, what couldn't it do to state and local governments?

Scholars as well as politicians have questioned the increasing centralization of power in Washington. The subject has been an applause line in the stump speeches of Idaho candidates. Virtually every major candidate for office in Idaho has decried this steady accretion of power in Washington whether it be ultra-conservative George Hansen or liberal Frank Church.[6]

However, the trend may be changing given some recent Supreme Court decisions which often have reasserted state and local authority. In the 1995 *U.S. v. Lopez* decision, the U.S. Supreme Court utilized the Tenth Amendment to limit congressional power over interstate commerce in a gun control case. A 2000 decision also limited congressional power in the application of the federal Violence Against Women Act.

FEDERAL RELATIONS IN IDAHO

Idaho politicians need no courage to attack the federal government. Many Idaho politicians, both Democrat and Republican, have built successful careers on exactly such an appeal. In 2000 the incumbent Republican lieutenant governor, C. L. "Butch" Otter, then running for the U.S. House, campaigned against "federal bureaucrats" with a special passion. One of Otter's land developments in western Ada County had run afoul of wetlands regulations and Otter had been fined tens of thousands of dollars. In some districts, this might constitute a political problem; in Idaho's first congressional district (western and northern Idaho), it was a net plus. Otter won both his primary and general election contests in landslides.

Idahoans often express negative views about the federal government and have demonstrated their contempt in responses to statewide public opinion surveys over the past several years. In questions testing trust and confidence levels, state and local governments are more highly valued than the federal government. In fact, in some years, almost as many respondents have indicated that they have no trust in any government as those who indicate their trust in the federal government.[7]

Why such antipathy? Why do politicians routinely run against the federal government and get some of their best applause lines when they attack federal policies or an unresponsive federal bureaucrat?

Geographical distance is one obvious factor in this alienation. "Washington" is a distant, almost alien, place. It is also perceived as the place where more and more power is being accumulated and where self-serving members of Congress or unelected bureaucrats make decisions for the rest of the nation without any consideration of the unique interests and needs of each state.

Idahoans' views of the federal government have, however, under-gone some change over time.

After the territorial era, when near-colonial status resulted in strongly negative attitudes toward Washington, many Idahoans often saw the federal government in a more positive light. The Bureau of Reclamation, starting at its inception in 1902 and for the next half-century, made possible much of the state's agricultural development with its water projects. Development of the national forests provided some help for the nascent timber industry, and federal transportation projects linked Idaho economically to the rest of the nation. Cattle ranchers grazed much of their livestock on federal lands. Federal installations such as Mountain Home Air Force Base and the Idaho National Laboratory were and still are viewed generally favorably. Much of Idaho society as it now exists would not have been possible without federal intervention.

After mid-century, however, attitudes began to change. Federal agencies grew dramatically in size and, responding in part to interest groups, began to impose more regulation over federal lands and a wide range of other activities. The rise of environmental groups, which saw local and state governments as opposed to their goals, increasingly looked to (and pressured) federal agencies to restrict use of public lands. At the same time, Idaho's population and economy began, in the 1960s, to grow substantially and increasing numbers of people bumped up against the more-regulatory federal government. Much federal regulatory activity began to strike many Idahoans less as a benefit to people in the state than as a constraint on them. In more rural parts of Idaho, residents often complain, especially about regulation regarding wildlife, including protection (or introduction) of such animals as wolves or grizzly bears.

These feelings are not absolute or universal. At various times, local groups of Idahoans and federal agency employees have banded together to solve problems. Still, the political impulse to point an angry finger at Washington remains strong.

Regardless of their attitude toward the federal government and federal officials, however, members of the conservative Idaho con-gressional delegation still have to deal with the realities and com-plexities of federal-state relations. They do recognize that Idaho needs the federal government in a variety of ways, and the delegation's actions underscore this fact. For decades, members of both parties have fought to keep the programs at the INL intact and to support federal funding of the Yucca Mountain nuclear waste site in Nevada (so that Idaho will not become the *de facto* permanent repository). The delegation proudly announces awards of federal grants, consistently supports Mountain Home Air Force Base, and defends subsidization of low electric power rates in Idaho by the Bonneville Power Administration.[8]

FEDERAL LAND

Since about 63 percent of Idaho land is federally owned (only in Nevada, Alaska and Utah is the percentage higher), many activities of public and private sector groups collide with federal agencies. The Bureau of Land Management, U.S. Forest Service and Bureau of Reclamation have major administrative offices in Idaho, and play an important part in managing the resources of the state. Their more vocal critics argue that they interfere, intrude and threaten. That is not true of all federal programs; some routinely win praise from elected officials and others. A candidate who may attack the BLM or the Environmental Protection Agency (as many do) likely will praise the benefits of the INL and seek more federal dollars for that facility, or seek expansion of the Mountain Air Force Base.

Many Idahoans argue that the federal government has held onto public lands too long, and that federal regulations have frustrated economic development efforts in Idaho and in other western states. Some of the best land has been "locked-up" for wildlife and environmental considerations over the priorities and needs of the local economies. As a result federal management policies have been hotly criticized.

Federal agencies do share some funds with local governments in Idaho to compensate for the large land area they occupy. Idaho counties receive Payment in Lieu of Taxes funds as a replacement for property taxes which they cannot assess federal lands. PILT funds can be critical revenue to some counties where federal lands occupy much of the land base. Counties and schools also receive forest funds for timber cuts and mine leases on federal lands.

Support for state management of the lands is significant in Idaho among most voters and most of the state's congressional delegation.[9] Former Representative Helen Chenoweth-Hage remarked, "'(w)e're turning the lands back over to the states to sell or not to sell, depending on what the states may decide. The states can make money; I think they are better managers.'"[10] However, a 1996 study by the State Controller's Office indicated that "if the current level of management of state lands is extended to land managed by the BLM and Forest Service, the initial outlay (after current level revenues) required would be just over $90 million, or approximately seven percent of our 1996 General Fund." Controller J. D. Williams concluded that "the benefits of state management are questionable" given these and other considerations like the loss of PILT funds to the counties.[11]

Transferring land to the states is not a new idea. It first arose during the Hoover Administration and was given new impetus during the Carter Administration when efforts were made to cut back on Western water projects and place MX missiles in western states. The initial "shot" fired in the "Sagebrush Rebellion" against federal control of western lands was in Nevada where legislation was enacted requiring the transfer of 49 million acres of federal land from the national government to the state of Nevada. Several other western states followed Nevada's lead with the exception of only two states that did not pass "Sagebrush Rebellion" type legislation. One of those exceptions was Idaho. With the election of Ronald Reagan in 1980 there was great optimism in the West that President Reagan would understand the Western issues better than the easterner Carter. According to political scientist Rick Foster, the rebellion's "demise was in part due to its success. Some of the rebels became part of the establishment."[12] The rebels had a sympathetic president in Ronald Reagan and in cabinet member James Watt which helped blunt their anger. The Idaho Legislature was, after the 1980 election, certainly dominated by members sympathetic to the Rebellion, but the arrival of the Reagan Administration and of U.S. Senator James McClure, as new chair of the Energy and Natural Resources Committee, effectively ended the rebellion in Idaho as an organized force. The impulses behind it, however, have remained, and in the 1990s a new organization, called Stewards of the Range, took up the cause.

A wave of protest over federal policies on western lands has been variously known as the "wise use" or "county supremacy" movement. "Wise use" is a term taken from the definition Gifford Pinchot gave to conservation. The movement that uses the term today emphasizes the value of the multiple use of public lands. They emphasize "wise use" because they believe that the environmentalists and federal policies have emphasized preservation at the expense of local economies. This is especially a problem in rural counties where receipts on federal lands are a major part of their economies. They assert that federal policies that restrict uses also damage the local economies and are akin to a "taking" of private property that should be protected or compensated under the Fifth Amendment to the U.S. Constitution. Despite the Republican revolution of 1994, the "wise use" movement has made little headway even though many rural counties have asserted their leadership in the effort through passage of county ordinances.[13]

INL AND OTHER FEDERAL FACILITIES

One federal installation that has shaped a large portion of Idaho is the Idaho National Engineering and Environmental Laboratory, which has gone by several names since its founding in 1949 as the National Reactor Testing Station and is now called the Idaho National Laboratory. As its first name implies, it started as a nuclear reactor testing site. The City of Arco, which is near the site, was the first city in the United States powered by nuclear energy. Its activities as a national laboratory have expanded greatly over the years. It has employed as many as 13,000 people (many of them working for large contractors) though barely half that at the turn of the millennium, as much of the reactor activity phased down. Its economic impact in eastern Idaho is enormous. By some estimates, if the INL were to suddenly vanish one day, a third or more of Eastern Idaho's economy (and possibly a fourth of its population) would go with it.[14]

INL has had other kind of impacts on Idaho politics, where "nuclear waste"—referring to the radioactive material that is stored on the site—is a hot button issue.

This issue has many dimensions—economic, intergovernmental and environmental. To those in southeastern Idaho who depend upon the INL, the federal government's efforts to temporarily store more nuclear waste at INL must be understood in the context of the local and regional economies. Jobs have a higher priority than the fear of nuclear waste storage. To others in southwestern Idaho, whose jobs are not reliant on the site but whose water comes from the aquifer INL is sitting on, the threats of more nuclear waste in Idaho and making INL a permanent depository are perceived as very real .

The "site" (as it is often called in Idaho) for many years worked with the U.S. Navy on reactor development—future President Jimmy Carter worked there for a time when he was a nuclear engineer in the Navy—but its primary function never has been purely military.

The one large federal military base in Idaho is the Mountain Home Air Force Base located a few miles southeast of the city of Mountain Home. The base was started during World War II as a training range —still its major function—and was shut down several times after the war before being reactivated permanently in the mid-fifties. More than 4,000 people, civilian and military, work there. In addition, as much as half of the population of the city of Mountain Home consists of retirees from the base and people who work for support businesses.

A smaller Idaho National Guard installation exists in Boise at Gowen Field, on the south side of the city near the municipal airport. Other federal facilities exist as well. The most visible (during the summer at least) is the National Interagency Fire Center, which serves as the hub for fire fighting activity on federal lands, especially in the western states.[15]

INDIAN GAMING AND INTERGOVERNMENTAL RELATIONS

When Idaho voters decided in 1986 and 1988 to approve a state lottery system, they opened the door to a form of gaming relatively few had anticipated: Indian tribal gaming. Some critics of the lottery proposals warned that passage of the lottery proposals would open the door to all types of tribal gaming; others denounced those claims as scare tactics. History settled the matter. In the decade to come, four of Idaho's five Indian tribal groups—the Kootenai, the Coeur d'Alene, the Nez Perce and the Shoshone-Bannocks—set up casinos, which since have become important local economic engines.

The genesis of that development came in the 1988 passage of the Indian Gaming Regulatory Act (IGRA), which set the federal rules for on-reservation gaming and classification of gaming types. Nationally, gambling has become a multibillion-dollar industry among Indian tribes. The legislation, ironically, was a reaction to a 1987 U.S. Supreme Court decision, *California v. Cabazon Band of Mission Indians*,[16] that significantly restricted the authority of the states over Indian gaming. Essentially the court ruled that once a state authorizes a certain level of gaming, tribes within the state can offer the same types of games without state authorization or regulation.

The position of Indian tribes in the federal system generally is the subject of some controversy, certainly in some parts of Idaho. Interpretations of tribal sovereignty have varied (depending on the advocate) from those who hold that tribes are sovereign nations with the full rights under international law to others who believe that tribes currently have no special rights. A compromise position is that tribes have "inherent, retained powers as 'domestic, dependent nations' under the umbrella of US government protection."[17] Under that view, the states must rely upon the federal government to enforce state laws and constitutions on Indian reservations.

The intent of the 1988 federal gaming legislation[18] was to: (1) promote economic development and economic self-sufficiency; (2) provide a regulatory shield against organized crime; (3) create the National Indian Gaming Commission; (4) provide for three classes of gambling or gaming. The first class are those that are social games or relate to tribal ceremonies that the tribes should regulate, the second class such as bingo, pull tabs, lotto and others that should be authorized by state law, and the third class related to all other gambling activity that would require a tribal/state compact. States are precluded from regulating Indian gaming.

After both the state lottery and the federal gaming legislation was in place, the Nez Perce, Coeur d'Alene, Kootenai and Shoshone-Bannocks pressured the state government to negotiate a compact under the IGRA. (The fifth Idaho tribe, the Shoshone-Paiutes—whose reservation staddles the Idaho-Nevada border—never have pursued gaming activities.) Governor Cecil Andrus and Attorney General Larry EchoHawk (a member of the Shoshone-Bannocks and a former attorney for the tribe) opposed such a compact and instead sponsored a 1992 constitutional amendment to prohibit casino gambling. Interestingly, this campaign pitted Native-American Attorney General Larry EchoHawk against his fellow Native-Americans. EchoHawk, who is also a member of the Mormon church, opposed gambling on moral and religious grounds. He, like many amendment supporters, promised to help Indians find other economic development activities.

The constitutional amendment passed. But serious efforts by Andrus' successors, Phil Batt and Dirk Kempthorne, to negotiate definitive compacts on gaming, never have reached a firm conclusion.

Despite its long, controversial history in Idaho, gambling has become popular in Idaho both on and off the reservation. *Public Policy Survey* results[19] indicated strong public support for the lottery and the expansion of gaming on Indian reservations. As one commentator has suggested, gambling begets gambling. The passage of the lottery amendment opened the door. Revenues flowing into the state coffers have often exceeded expectations and so has the activity on the four Indian reservations in Idaho that operate such gaming enterprises.

Although Indian unemployment rates are still high and the per capita income is well below the statewide average, gaming revenues are being invested in their community in beneficial ways—medical clinics, job and welfare programs, education, and in other business enterprises. In Boundary County in northern Idaho, the casino is the second largest employer; the Nez Perce Tribe has been described (largely because of its casinos) as the second largest economic force in north-central Idaho after Potlatch Corporation.

INTERSTATE

Like most other states, Idaho has a number of interstate agreements, some of them overseen by the federal government.

Some of these are almost marketplace activities. For example, Idaho has no medical school, and so has joined in an interstate agreement called WAMI (Washington, Alaska, Montana, Idaho) which gives the three smaller states a prescribed number of student seats in medical school in Washington state.

Some of the more important regional organizations concern resources. Bear Lake in southeastern Idaho is split between Idaho and Utah, as is the Bear River; both are governed by interstate compact organizations. Idaho also is a member of the congressionally-established Northwest Power Planning Council, on which it has two seats alongside delegates from Washington, Oregon and Montana.

Idaho's political culture is oriented more toward local government than toward federal government on most issues except those that relate to the continuance of the federal benefits. In some respects, Idahoans want to have it both ways—attack federal programs they do not support and vigorously protect those that they do support. This love-hate relationship has led Idahoans to have the same kind of schizophrenia that many other voters in western states demonstrate.

Whether Idahoans like it or not, the federal presence in Idaho is large and will remain a big factor in the life of Idaho.

Chapter 12 notes

1   James B. Weatherby, Lorna Jorgensen and W. David Patton, *Idaho Cities: Growth and Mandates* (Boise, ID: Association of Idaho Cities and Boise State University, 1994).

2   Timothy Conlan, Riggle and Schwartz, "The Unfunded Mandates Reform Act of 1995," *Publius: The Journal of Federalism* (summer 1995): 24.

3   Conlan, Riggle and Schwartz, "The Unfunded Mandates," p. 37. However, a close reading of this new law does not conclusively show that it prohibits any new mandates. It does require analysis and impact statements. But new mandates continue to come from the federal government in spite of this law. For example, Idaho universities tried to use it to avoid new university reporting requirements under the new immigration act without success. This mandates law seems to be more about symbolism than substantive changes in federalism.

4   *National League of Cities v Usery*, 426 U.S. 833 (1976).

5   *Garcia v San Antonio Metropolitan Transit Authority*, 469 U.S. 528 (1985).

6   James B. Weatherby, "Federal-State Relations," in *State and Local Government in Idaho: A Reader*, eds. Glenn W. Nichols, Ray C. Jolly, and Boyd A. Martin (Moscow, ID: Bureau of Public Affairs Research, University of Idaho, 1970), p. 31.

7   See Idaho Public Policy Surveys 1989-1999.

8   Dan Popkey, "Pork-barrel politics are alive and well," *The Idaho Statesman*, June 13, 1995, p. 1B.

9   See Idaho Public Policy Surveys, 1989-1999.

10 Popkey, "Pork-barrel politics."

11 J.D. Williams, Idaho state controller, "Taking Control of Public Lands: A Good Deal for Idaho? - Executive Summary".

12 Richard H. Foster, "The Federal Government and the West," in *Politics and Public Policy*, ed. Clive Thomas (Albuquerque, NM: University of New Mexico Press, 1991).

13 Stephanie Witt and Leslie R. Alm, "Wise Use Movement," *International Encyclopedia of Public Policy and Administration* (New York: Henry Holt, 1996).

14 See a short essay in the *Idaho Blue Book* 1989-90, p. 278.

15 The economic impact of the National Guard activity at Gowen Field close to Boise may be roughly the same as the impact of Boise Cascade Corporation, a Fortune 500 company, on the Boise area.

16 See *California v Cabazon Band of Mission Indians*, 480 U.S. (1987).

17 Anne Merlin McCulloch, "The Politics of Indian Gaming: Tribe/State Relations and American Federalism," *Publius: Journal of Federalism* (summer 1994): 103.

18 Indian Gaming Regulatory Act, 25 U.S.C.A. 2701.

19 David Scudder, Crank, and Weatherby, *Idaho Public Policy Survey,* #8 (Boise, ID: Social Science Research Center, Boise State University, 1997).

CHAPTER 13
THE POLITICS OF
TAXING AND SPENDING

For Idaho, 1978 was a turning point in the development of taxing and spending policy.

The impulses behind tax development before the property tax revolt of 1978, and since, are quite different. According to David Brunori, the property tax revolt had a "critical effect" on local governments; since then, most candidates have "campaigned against government in general, and against taxes in particular."[1]

Idaho state and local revenue and expenditure decisions are typically made with reference to the base year of 1978; even a cursory reading of most state or local government budget materials reveals comparisons with 1978 or FY 1979. Since 1978 the state has shifted a significant share of public school funding off the local property tax and onto the state general fund. One unintended consequence of this shift has been the centralization of government decision making at the state level in Idaho and other states.[2] Increasingly, legislators have become central players not only in state government finance but in local government finance as well.

Nineteen seventy-eight was a year of property tax revolt, growth and inflation, and passage by California voters of Proposition 13. Idaho tax critics—and, ultimately, the voters—backed a similar proposal, the "One Percent initiative", the name derived from the general requirement that property taxes should not exceed one percent of the assessed valuation of the property. The Idaho and California initiatives differed in one crucial respect: Idaho's was a statutory initiative, California's a constitutional amendment. But the similarities between the Idaho and California measures were what created serious obstacles to implementation. Idaho's initiative had several technical errors, and some of its provisions conflicted with the Idaho Constitution. (That latter point led to a change in the law on

initiatives, requiring that the language of initiatives be reviewed for
constitutionality by the state attorney general's office.)

After the initiative's passage, the Legislature chose to freeze
rather than cut property taxes and then allowed up to a 5 percent
increase in most local government operating property tax budgets.
This limitation, in effect from 1981 through 1991, had wide-ranging
ripple effects across a wide range of local governments.[3] For example,
the City of Boise still maintained 1978 service levels through most of
the 1990s despite huge increases in assessed valuation and population. During the period of the "implementation of the One Percent initiative," Idaho municipal spending levels fell below population and
inflation increases.[4]

Local governments, notably schools, did receive some revenue
sharing from state general funds but this in turn cut into state agency
budgets through most of the 1980s. The percentage of the state general fund appropriated to higher education dropped from 20 percent
to 15 percent during a time of major expansion in university student
enrollment.[5]

Initiatives—sometimes the mere threat of an initiative—was what
drove much of Idaho tax policy in the 1980s and 1990s. Like her
neighbors California, Nevada, Oregon and Colorado, Idaho has been
affected by citizen-passed property tax limitations.[6] The Idaho
Legislature has enacted tax policies intended to deflect proposed initiatives such as it did in 1994 with the passage of sweeping property
tax relief legislation, coming in the wake of a survey that showed
strong public support for yet another one percent initiative.

Despite the state's prevalent "anti-government" political culture,
in terms of tax policy, Idaho is one of the most centralized states in
the nation.[7] Idahoans' preference for local over state or federal government does not translate to automatic trust of local government,
and many voters evidently prefer that governments at all levels be
constrained in taxing and spending. Granting local authorities substantial new powers, especially taxation, prompts horror stories in the
minds of both state elected officials and many citizens.

Public opinion surveys conducted during the 1990s indicated that
conservative Idahoans do not like property taxes, but they are not
necessarily preoccupied with the tax issue. When asked by pollsters
what is the major problem facing the state Idahoans have not identified "taxes and government spending" as a leading concern. The tax
issue trails behind the more visible public concerns of economic development, education, environmental protection and "rapid" growth in
importance.[8]

A Boise State University survey suggested that Idaho's most popular state tax is the same as the most hated tax overall: the personal income tax. Idahoans historically have ranked the federal income tax as the worst tax while the state income tax—based and "piggybacked" on the federal tax—is judged to be the fairest. (Such results speak more to Idahoans' view of the federal government than the nature of the two taxes.) Income taxes account for slightly less than half of the state general fund.

PROPERTY TAXES

Ever since the 1970s, the property tax has been controversial, particularly in the West.[9] Recent surveys have indicated that the hostility towards the property tax is again festering.[10] People dislike the property tax because it is the most complex, least understood, and perceived to be the most unfair. Although it once bore a direct relationship to taxpayers' ability to pay, it no longer does. Today's property tax is in many respects a tax more on debt than on what individuals actually own outright, especially for residential property tax payers. In Idaho, the scheduling of the first half property tax collection just before Christmas, on December 20, is a classic case of bad timing. It is a visible tax and most threatening to those in growth areas where market values and assessment levels are rising without a received-corresponding increase in the volume or quality of public services.

There is an emotional dimension to the property tax. It is a tax on people's homes, often their most valuable asset. As one taxpayer wrote in a guest opinion in the Boise *Idaho Statesman*, ". . .it is convenient to classify a home as an asset, no amount of sterile evaluation can even remotely take into consideration that a home is where we put our heart and soul, not some book. Our castle, no matter how humble, if you will. Something is fundamentally wrong to penalize people by taxing them more for acting responsibly and maintaining their home in a pleasing manner, i.e., higher assessed value and conversely regarding those who let their property develop into an eyesore."[11]

All of the above is part of the folklore of public finance literature and rhetoric. The property tax is typically called the "worst tax." Rarely is the tax defended for its stability, certainty, relationship to services provided, or aid to local autonomy. The potential of taking people's homes is the ugly flipside of the certainty/stability dimension. This ugly side is emphasized far more than the safeguards built into the tax that can provide for substantial relief—circuit breaker (property tax relief to low income elderly, widowed and disabled) homeowners exemption, and the hardship exemption. The role the tax plays in funding local services and the future of local government autonomy is tied to the use of the property much more clearly than either the sales or income taxes.

SALES TAX

The sales tax is relatively popular with citizens. It is perceived as a tax that everyone pays regardless of income or residence, even though there are many substantial exemptions to the payment of the state sales tax such as production and service exemptions. The transformation of Idaho's economy from a manufacturing to service-based economy has meant that the sales tax accounts for only about 40 percent of the state general fund, though it also funds local revenue sharing programs. More than 60 percent of retail sales are not subject to the tax, and Internet sales have further eroded the base.

Despite these concerns, there have been a series of both temporary and permanent sales tax increases beginning in the 1980s. These increases did not result in any major political bloodshed or loss of manufacturing plants or businesses to the non-sales tax states of Oregon or Montana. But the concern that such flight might happen remains a concern for lawmakers. The border areas of Payette and Washington counties, which lie across the Snake River from Oregon, which has no sales tax, have reported serious damage to their retail communities.

Controversy over the sales tax lingers. One debate centers on the many exemptions, which have drawn criticism from, among others, Governor Andrus in 1993. The idea of revising the exemption structure arose again in the 1998 and 2002 statewide campaigns. A legislative task force in the summer of 2003 looked at the sales tax structure yet again but could not support removing any of the exemptions.

Others question sales tax allocation formulas. When the sales tax was passed in the mid-1960s, it was touted as a measure to "save our schools." The assumption was that the revenues would be dedicated for public schools. Now 13.75 percent of sales tax revenues go to local governments. Five million dollars each go to the permanent building fund and to the water pollution control account. Schools do not get all of the sales tax revenues but, on the other hand, the total general fund allocation to public education exceeds the total sales tax collections.

The future of the sales tax as a major revenue producer for state and local governments is in doubt. A system that will capture remote sales revenues requires a simplified tax structure that seems to preclude the growth of local option sales taxes. A single tax rate in each state makes taxing Internet based commerce far more efficient and effective. In addition, the continued discussion of a federal sales tax makes preemption of the state and local tax bases far more likely.

CHANGING THE TAX STRUCTURE

Conservative Idahoans are slow to adopt changes, particularly radical departures in tax structure. Just twice since statehood has the tax structure been substantially changed, with adoption of the Property Tax Relief Act of 1931 (the state income tax) and adoption of the state sales tax in 1965 by the Legislature (with voter approval of a referendum in 1966). Idaho was the last state in the West to adopt a sales tax among those that have done so at all.[12]

Idaho policymakers take great pride in the fact that their tax structure is among the most balanced in the country.[13] Idaho's reliance on three major taxes—income, property and sales, the "three-legged stool"—has been noted for balance and stability and, to a degree, progressivity (wealthier taxpayers pay a greater percentage of their income than do low income people) even though progressivity or regressivity are rarely considered in Idaho tax policy debates.[14] The stability of the tax structure and its impact on the business sector are far more important considerations. The dominant economic groups help set the parameters of most debates. One of the important criteria of an effective tax system is that it should be composed of a variety of taxes—both elastic and inelastic. Taxes should tap various types of wealth and have a variety of responses to the growth or decline in the economy. Taxes that are responsive to economic growth and taxes that are stable help cushion the blow of an economic downturn.

Idaho's tax structure is similar to that of Utah but distinctive from most other nearby states. Of the five states without sales taxes, two (Oregon and Montana) border Idaho. Of the nine states with no income tax, three (Nevada, Washington and Wyoming) are Gem State neighbors.

The continued utility of the "three-legged stool" in an economy shifting toward service industry and the Internet has been seriously questioned. In addition, the proliferation of user fees has raised major questions about the direction, balance, adequacy, and equity of public funding in Idaho. Moreover, while the taxes are balanced in the state as a whole, various governments tend to rely heavily on specific taxes. Local government officials are quick to point out that their revenues, overwhelmingly reliant on property taxes, are far from balanced or diversified. Unlike local governments in 33 other states, Idaho cities and counties generally have no significant local option non-property tax authority.[15]

Partly for that reason, fees, service charges and other miscellaneous revenue charges have become a growing source of revenue since the late 1970s. The passage of the One Percent Initiative has had a major impact in shifting the costs of government. Rather than increase property taxes, Idahoans have shown a preference to increase user fees if additional revenues are needed. This trend accelerated in the 1990s. Idaho's three-legged stool appears to be turning into a four-legged stool, as total fees and charges approach one billion dollars annually statewide. Some regressivity is changing the progressive tax structure. Nevertheless, Idaho is ranked nationally by some experts as having one of the most progressive tax systems in the country.

Even though, according to Brunori, user fees "have a limited base,"[16] they add to the efficiency of local governments. They are "a better gauge of demand for services" and the true costs of government are exposed in the imposition of a comprehensive user fee system. Their primary drawback is that they are regressive. The poor pay a greater share of their income for these public services as opposed to the wealthy that pay far less in percentage terms.

Tax burdens are relatively low in Idaho, though higher than might be expected in a state renowned for its conservatism. Idaho per capita tax burden generally has ranked lower than the national average and 44th among the states in 2002. Part of the reason for this lower ranking is Idaho's per capita income is 18.3 percent lower than the national average. An analysis by the Idaho State Tax Commission indicated that Idaho property taxes, based upon income, placed the state 31st on a national basis; the sales tax rank also was 27th and the income tax ranking was 22nd.[17] Curiously, Idahoans themselves have described the state income tax as being among the fairest and the property tax as being among the least fair.

TAX POLICY IN THE 1990S

When in 1991 the last remnants of the One Percent Initiative—the 5 percent cap on local government revenue growth—were removed, property tax protesters generated a new One Percent petition. Public opinion surveys in December 1991, showed the public closely split on the issue.[18] But by a two to one majority, it was defeated in November 1992.That happened in part because of an extraordinarily broad coalition mobilized against the initiative, including the Idaho Association of Commerce and Industry, the Idaho Hospital Association, Idaho Association of Realtors, the Idaho Education Association, and a combination of business groups, public entities and many others, which spent more than $400,000 on their campaign. Coalition president and

IACI President Steve Ahrens noted, ". . .Idahoans have seen 13 years of demonstrated impact from the 1978 initiative. . .It resulted in tax shifts more than tax reductions. It resulted in a loss of services and hampered economic development activities all the way through the '80s as we were recovering from the recession."[19]

No statewide property tax limitation measure has passed since 1978 (another initiative in 1996 also was defeated), but the threat of a new initiative has made governors and the Legislature sit up and take notice.[20]

Among his proposals to the 1993 Legislature, Governor Andrus proposed a sweeping series of tax changes. He proposed doubling the grocery tax credit, expanding the homeowners' property tax exemption, expanding the "circuit breaker" (a property tax break for senior citizens), and cutting some property taxes. The Legislature quickly rejected almost all of his proposals.

The next year, however, the legislators became the visionaries. The lawmakers, saying "growth" in the current tax structure would make it possible, voted to shift most of the costs of public education from the property tax to state general account revenues. Governor Andrus vetoed that plan, saying he wanted to protect the state's "revenue stream." Replacement revenues had to be part of the package.

In the months that followed, both leading candidates for governor in 1994, Phil Batt and Larry EchoHawk, offered similar though less radical tax relief proposals during their campaigns. After the election, Governor Batt's property tax relief plan easily passed in the 1995 legislative session. It effectively reduced about 25 percent of the public school operating budget levy and replaced those revenues with state revenues. It also imposed a 3 percent cap on property tax increases for all non-school local units of government (cities, counties, etc.).

The relative share of the total that each revenue source represents of the state general fund has not changed significantly in recent years, even though there has been a noticeable increase in personal income tax revenues. In the past few years, Idaho has been among the top 20 states in the amount of individual and corporate income taxes.[21] This income tax liability led to the income tax cut legislation of 200 when both the individual and corporate rates were cut by .4 percent.

STATE BUDGET PROCESS AND TRENDS

Idaho's general stability in revenue sources has made budgeting less dramatic and contentious than it has been in neighboring states where reliance on less balanced tax structures has led to legislative stalemate. An understanding of the budget process is critical to understanding how tax policies evolve and how policies are made. The budget is the most important policy document in state government.

The governor plays a major role in shaping major state policies and budget priorities. As in most states, the governor's role in setting priorities in the budget process is critical regardless of whether or not the governor's party controls the Legislature. This can be a very powerful agenda-setting exercise.

The degree to which a governor can influence the budget and state policymaking in general is illustrated in the record of the Andrus administration. During most of his administration, especially his last two terms (1987-1995), Governor Andrus emphasized at least three major policy goals: environmental protection, public education funding, and economic development. These priorities were reflected in his budget recommendations, and not coincidentally, were priorities clearly supported by the general public in Idaho as documented in several public policy surveys.

Reacting to the governor's speeches, the opposition typically finds fault with certain items in the speeches. The majority party, even when in the opposition to the governor, usually begins the session by attacking the governor's proposals, but ends it by enacting appropriations bills similar to the governor's recommendations..

During a 20-year period of divided government, the governors' recommendations and subsequent legislative appropriation were very close.[22] In his last two years in office, Governor Andrus' recommended budget exceeded the legislative appropriations that followed but there were also years in which the Republican legislature outbid the Democratic governor's recommendations.

There can be serious challenges to the governor's leadership role. In 1994, the Republican legislative leadership dramatically announced in a press conference immediately following Andrus' budget address that his major proposals were DOA (dead on arrival)— and they were.

Each spring, the budget preparation stage begins. About 15 months before the start of a new fiscal year, the governor's and Legislature's budget offices send request forms to state agencies. Typically, a statement accompanies these forms indicating the governors spending priorities. Agencies fashion their requests to conform with these priorities, to fit executive budget themes. For example, a gubernatorial priority that emphasizes economic development or public education can be used by agencies to claim that their new programs or spending will assist the governor in achieving his economic development priorities.

Sometimes the governor's directives have angered legislative leaders and staff. In 1991, Governor Andrus' budget director sent instructions that most state agencies should "present a FY 93 base budget calculated on 97 percent of FY 1992 estimated operating expense and zero capital outlay. Expansion decision units may be added to this modified maintenance of current operation base, but they will not exceed five percent of that FY 1993 base amount with" only certain exceptions.[23] This approach angered John Andreason, the then director of the Legislative Budget Office, who viewed the gubernatorial directive as a direct challenge to the budgetary authority of the Legislature, by limiting the information available to the lawmakers. Andreason called the dispute "a major policy issue between the Governor (Executive Branch) and Joint Finance and Appropriations Committee (JFAC) (The Legislative Branch)."[24] Some observers believe that view was overblown, but it does suggest the conflict potential.

This issue of control over agency budget requests is a sensitive issue in the budget process, and is not a partisan issue. It surfaced again in the second year of the Kempthorne administration, in which a "preliminary" budget request was to be reviewed by the governor's office only, prior to the the submission of the formal agency request. Jeff Youtz, the Legislature's budget director, rejected that approach as a loss of legislative control and oversight. He was supported by JFAC and the attempted change in the budget process has not been attempted since.

This preparation of the executive budget recommendation has been primarily a behind-the-scenes process but it has been opened from time to time. From 1984 to 1986, the Evans Administration held budget hearings throughout Idaho as the executive budget was prepared—the only instance of public input into the budget being actively pursued. In recent years, the governor's and legislative budget staffs have coordinated much of their budget work and budget guidelines are now developed jointly.

While the governor's budget recommendation is being prepared, the governor's economic unit develops revenue projections for the upcoming fiscal year. It uses econometrics models to anticipate economic changes that may positively or negatively impact revenues for the upcoming fiscal year. The accuracy of their projections has been at times the subject of some controversy. Since Idaho is a state with a constitutionally-mandated balanced budget, revenue projections set the parameters of the debate, and these estimates play an important role in determining ultimate spending parameters and/or the need for a tax increase.

In November and December, as the beginning of a new legislative session approaches, the proposed budget recommendations and budget address are finalized. The budget address is given in the opening days of the legislative session.

PRESENTATION AND ADOPTION STAGES

Early in January, a joint revenue projection committee (Economic Outlook and Revenue Committee) takes testimony from economic experts about the future of the economy. Economists from banks and utilities, representatives of taxpayer organizations and others, all weigh in on the state of the economy. Settlement on revenue numbers can become highly political, and in some legislative sessions no figures ever are formally adopted.

The committee vote and subsequent legislative adoption of the revenue projection sets the available revenue anticipated for the upcoming fiscal year. Sometimes, these revenue projections are low, based on legislative fear of creating shortfalls that may cause increased pressure for a revenue increase. There are considerable calculations, politically and economically, involved in setting the revenue amount, depending upon whether the goal is to deny dollars to agencies that will spend them or to force a tax increase to fund existing or expanded service levels.

The key legislative committee in the budget process, and perhaps, in the entire legislative process, is the Joint Finance and Appropriations Committee. JFAC is the only committee with a permanent staff, even though the staff since 1993 is formally housed under the auspices of the Legislative Services Office. Just as the Division of Financial Management staff (in the governor's office) specializes so does the Legislative Services staff; its analysts too have developed expertise in assigned areas. They assist legislators by preparing their own analysis. They are non-partisan staff responsible for providing objective analyses of state programs, both financially and funchionally. This staff capacity gives the committee the expertise and independence to objectively analyze the governor's budget recommendations. This independence is particularly important when different parties control the Legislature and governor's office.

JFAC holds about six weeks of hearings prior to making final budget decisions, which are formalized into about 100 appropriation bills. A key indicator of JFAC power is that approximately 98 percent of the JFAC bills become law without amendment.

Two other committees critical to the budgeting process are the House and Senate tax committees. The state constitution provides that revenue-raising measures must originate in the House of

Representatives, giving a decided advantage to the House Revenue and Taxation Committee. Senators are largely forced into a reactive role. Over the years, the House committee often proposes tax law changes, but its Senate counterpart is renowned in the Statehouse for "disposing" of many of those ideas.

BUDGET IMPLEMENTATION

Budgeting implementation is a less visible, less understood part of the process, but still vital.

Regular appropriations are for the upcoming fiscal year that begins in July. Supplemental appropriations are often passed to provide additional moneys for agencies during the current fiscal year.

As the fiscal year progresses, revenues may match expectations, exceed them or fall below. The constitutional requirement of maintaining a balanced budget is taken seriously. In the case of a shortfall, the governor may have to impose a holdback to help assure that, at the end of the current fiscal year, expenditures will match revenues, that the "budget will be in balance" as required by the state constitution. A holdback is typically imposed as an "across the board" percentage amount applied to all agencies, except for some agencies deemed to be "essential" such as public education. Education may experience a holdback but full spending authority usually is restored. (The 2001 permanent public school holdbacks were an exception.) If the funding is not restored, property tax increases are automatically triggered to make up for the shortfall and to guarantee funding school districts so they can fulfill their contracts. As the fiscal year progresses and revenues pick up or exceed adjusted expectations, the holdback amounts may be restored or supplemental appropriation provided in the next legislative session.

There can be audits for both financial compliance and performance. The state controller performs the pre-audit function. The post-audit function has been transferred to legislative staff. The Legislature created a legislative performance audit function in 1993 where non-fiscal, performance issues are scrutinized. This audit is intended to answer questions about the effectiveness of certain programs and how well they conform to legislative intent.

The Idaho Constitution contemplated the audit function as occurring in the office of the state auditor. Over a period of decades, the Idaho Legislature assumed that authority, eventually prompting the long-time state auditor, Joe Williams, to sue to reclaim the authority. He won in court, but the issue was not over. Eventually his successor, J. D. Williams, resolved the debate, with the Legislature taking over the post-audit functions and the auditor's office renamed as the state controller's office.

BUDGET AND SPENDING TRENDS

Though state expenditures have grown over the last couple of decades, Idaho—compared to its western neighbors or with states of similar size and service levels elsewhere—is relatively conservative in several expenditure patterns, though the numbers have been increasing in recent years. **Table 4** shows the patterns of expenditures and their rankings with other states. It shows that Idaho ranks 47th on a per capita basis in direct general expenditures, 40th in elementary and secondary education, and 39th in welfare. But one can also take a closer look at some of these categories on an income basis per $1,000 of income. The numbers indicate a more significant effort: direct general expenditures 29th, public education 18th, and welfare 31st. The tax effort made by Idaho state and local governments in a number of areas puts Idaho above most of the states in a number of categories, especially in the personal income tax 22nd on an income basis and fees and special assessments 9th.[25]

Funding for public education is a top priority in the state, or at least so claim legislators and other state politicians. Public opinion surveys by Boise State University support this contention. However, the public school lobby and other public education advocates do not agree that public education is the state's top priority. It is really a matter of perspective. Expenditure levels are not impressive on an interstate comparison but on a statewide comparison among state agencies in Idaho, public education is clearly the highest priority. Though education funding has slightly declined, it is still about 46 percent of the state general fund (See **Table 4)**. The table shows that higher education appropriations have steadily declined. In 2002, however, **Table 4** shows that Idahoans have made a fairly significant effort in higher education support with Idaho being ranked 33rd nationally on a per capita basis and 24th on an income basis. [26]

The past decade has had considerable impact on many of the major functional areas in the state budget. (See state government organizational chart in **Figure 2** illustrating these functional arrangements.) Public schools' portion of the state general fund has declined. Even though the public expresses support for public education as the major priority and legislators seem to agree, the percentage increase for this "top priority" somewhat pales in comparison to other categories such as "Law and Public Safety" and "Health and Human Services."[27]

In 1987, corrections was 2.5 percent of the general fund. In 2005, it is 5.5 percent. Medicaid was 3.9 percent in 1987. In 2005, it is 15 percent. Since 1987, schools and higher education have dropped four percentage points which means a loss of approximately 80 million dollars as a share of the general fund. In 2005 dollars, each percentage is worth 20 million dollars.[28]

Population and economic growth have played a major role in generating new revenues and in increasing the costs of government. Growth has contributed to significant increases in state general fund expenditures. Growth also has contributed to substantial property tax valuation increases that fueled two major property tax limitation campaigns during the 1990s.

It does not in most respects of taxing or spending run to the extremes among the 50 states. Rather, as in so many other ways, Idaho's brand of conservatism connotes more a sense of cautiousness and status quo than it does reaction.

Chapter 13 notes

1 David Brunori, *Local Tax Policy: A Federalist Perspective*, (Washington, DC: Urban Institute), 2004, p. 40.

2 Alvin Sokolow, "The Changing Property Tax and State-Local Relations," *Publius: The Journal of Federalism,* 28 (Winter 1998): 165-187.

3 Jim Kempton, state representative, and James B. Weatherby, Interface 'of the People': An Overview of Growth Funding, Revolving Debt, and Representative Government. Idaho State House of Representatives, State of Idaho, 1997.

4 James B. Weatherby and Lorna Jorgensen, *The One Percent Intiative and Voter Attitudes: A Comparison of 1978 and 1992* (Boise, ID: Public Affairs Program, Boise State University, 1992).

5 State of Idaho, Legislative Services Office, Budget and Policy Analysis, Idaho Fiscal Facts, various years.

6 Donald J. Stabrowski, "Oregon," in Proceedings Roundtable: State Budgeting in the 13 Western States, by Robert Huefner, F. Ted Hebert, and Carl Mott (Western Political Science Association, 1998).

7 U.S. Advisory Commission on Intergovernmental Relations, "State and Local Roles."

8 Idaho Public Policy Surveys 1989-99.

9 James B. Weatherby and Stephanie L. Witt, *The Urban West: Managing Growth and Decline* (Westport, CT: Praeger, 1994).

10 Idaho Public Policy Surveys 1989-2002.

11 Hinckle, Letter to the Editor.

12 Richard F. Winters, "The Politics of Taxing and Spending," in *Politics in the American States: A Comparative Analysis*, eds. Virginia Gray, Russell Hanson and Herbert Jacob (Washington, DC: Congressional Quarterly Press).

13 Robert J. Kleine, US State-Local Tax Systems: How Do They Rate? (Lansing, MI: Public Sector Consultants, 1992).

14 Ibid.

15 Winters, "The Politics of Taxing and Spending."

16 Brunori, *Local Tax Policy*, p. 11.

17 Idaho State Tax Commission, "Comparative Tax Burden Study" (Boise, ID: State of Idaho and Associated Taxpayers of Idaho, 2004). How Does Idaho Compare? 2002 (Boise, ID: September 2004)

18 Gregory A. Raymond, *Idaho Public Policy Survey,* #2 (Boise, ID: Survey Research Center, Boise State University, 1991).

19 Steve Ahrens, "Commerce Comes Out Against 1 Percent," *The Idaho Statesman*, June 19, 1992.

20 Idaho Universities Policy Research Group, "Continuing the Dialogue on Idaho's Tax Policy: Report to the Legislative Council Committee on Taxation" (Boise State University, University of Idaho, Idaho State University, 1994).

21 Associated Taxpayers of Idaho, How Does Idaho Compare? (2004).

22 Please note that sometimes they are "apples to oranges" comparisons. There have been many instances where the books have been "cooked" so that the two figures have appeared closer than they might otherwise have been.

23 Charles Moss Memorandum, Director, Division of Financial Management, April 23, 1991.

24 John Andreason, Director, Legislative Budget Office, 1991.

25 Associated Taxpayers of Idaho, How Does Idaho Compare?.

26 2004 Idaho Legislative Budget Book, Legislative Services Office, State of Idaho.

27 Ibid.

28 Ibid.

CONTEMPORARY PUBLIC POLICY ISSUES

S ome policy preferences are so ingrained in Idaho political culture that they need almost no discussion—and rarely generate
meaningful debate. Gun control? Agin it. Water rights? Protect
'em. The dominant economic groups help guarantee that a narrow
range of issues will be considered.

Other topics are less easily settled. Sometimes subjects come
unsettled when the interests that bring people to Idaho—the use of
the vast unpopulated spaces, the conflict between liberty and morali-
ty—bump into each other. If for many newcomers Idaho is a place of
escape, they still differ on what they intended to leave behind, and
what they intend to find. Some of them confront these questions as
soon as they arrive in Idaho, for their very presence creates some conflicts automatically.

Public policies are often discussed but seldom defined clearly. As
used here, public policy is what government does, or in some cases
what it does not. Both the active and inactive dimensions are critical.
Inaction can be as important as action. When a governing body refuses to act, it narrows the focus of policymaking and favors one side over
another. A decision not to raise taxes may hugely benefit wealthy taxpayers, at least superficially, and damage those who are dependent
upon the under funded services.

Agenda setting is a test of openness and access. Some topics make
the agenda—become the focus of attention. The right to bear arms
and water rights are easy attention-getters in Idaho. Other issues
may struggle for years to surface, and proposals requiring changes in
existing policies are often brushed aside. Those who challenge the
establishment or the status quo have to generate a lot of energy and
exhibit considerable group solidarity. Citizen activists have a mixed
record in this regard. Some have succeeded, with the passage of the
1974 Sunshine Initiative and the 1982 homeowner exemption, but

others have failed—property tax limitations and term limits initiatives.

Timing is also critical in facilitating change. For years, migrant farm workers sought minimum wage and worker compensation benefits to match those enjoyed by most other workers in Idaho; for years they dashed themselves against the buttress of Idaho farm interests. But the workers persisted and, over time, gained allies in extending workers compensation insurance to agricultural employment. Finally, extensive news media coverage gave them the clout they needed. The clout came in the form of statewide news about a terrible farm machinery accident in the Magic Valley that maimed a farm worker. Farm workers also won assistance from a conservative governor, Phil Batt, who was a farmer himself and who expended great political capital to pressure his conservative, agriculturally oriented legislative friends to pass a bill they were not convinced was in their best interests. According to journalist Charles Mahtesian, "those who stood to benefit from (the existing work compensation coverage). . .were not part of (Batt's) constituency. . .It was Idaho's version of Nixon going to China, an act of heresy so traitorous that only a farmer could get away with it."[1]

PROPERTY RIGHTS

Private property rights and individualism, key elements of Idaho conservatism, remain hallmarks in this state. In Idaho, policymakers generally prefer limited government so that it does not encroach on those rights. The 1975 passage of a major land use-planning law, that included bold, new, extraterritorial planning and zoning powers ran afoul of that preference, and remains controversial in some places. "Takings" legislation, of the type which has passed in other western states, has not yet passed in Idaho, though such efforts have been made repeatedly. The Speaker of the House, a former justice of the Idaho Supreme Court, and the Idaho Cattle Association strongly lobbied for a far reaching constitutional amendment protecting private property rights. Instead, a watered down version passed in 2003 that is notable more for its symbolic value than substantive import.

A corollary to Idahoans' passionate support of property rights is an emphasis upon water rights. Idahoans realize how dependant they are on water, especially for irrigation of the vast arid spaces in southern Idaho. A major and unique feature of the Idaho Constitution is the water rights article. Protection of water rights remains a "third rail" of Idaho politics.

Idaho operates on the "prior appropriation" doctrine, which gives priority to those who first claim "beneficial" use of the water. A beneficial use can mean anything from using water for drinking or for industry—in the case of most of the water used in the state—crop irrigation. The system works smoothly if enough water is flowing to meet al the beneficial needs. If the needs outstrip the water, thinks turn tense, quickly.

Determination of water rights became a front-burner issue in the 1980s with the establishment of the Snake River Basin Adjudication, but the subject became superheated in late 2004 and 2005. A long succession of drought years hit southern Idaho, and several major water users with earlier priority dates issued a "call." A call is a demand that those with newer priority dates—especially many groundwater pumpers—stop water use until the older users have drunk their fill. That, coupled with a controversial agreement between the Nez Perce Tribe, the state and other parties over the tribe's Snake River water right claims, made water the keystone issue of the 2005 legislative session.

MEDICAID

Medicaid is a state-federal health insurance program (formerly called the Medical Assistance Program) that provides services to the poor and disabled. (It is often confused with Medicare, which is a federal program administered through the Health Care Financing Administration.) Medicaid is a matching program—the states contribute 30 percent and the federal government contributes 70 percent. As in most other states, Medicaid continues to demand a growing share of the state general fund. In the recent zero-sum budgeting games, this rise in costs crowds out other general fund expenditures. Cost containment has been investigated by lawmakers but has proven elusive, even in cutback years or in times of revenue shortfall (such as Idaho experienced in 2002 and 2003). From 1982 to 2004 the average annual growth in medicaid was 7.6 percent. Medicaid expenses have nearly doubled every seven years. Medicaid now accounts for 13 percent of the state general fund expenditures; it was only 4 percent in 1982.[2]

The intergovernmental context of Medicaid has rendered cost containment a tricky issue; cost shifting to another level of government, as opposed to cost reduction, is often the effect. But whether the money is state or federal, it is a taxpayer expense.

Even a savings to the state Medicaid program may result in a greater burden on local governments. Hospital charges and tax rates go up when patients cannot pay their hospital bills. Indigent costs are absorbed by the hospital or passed on to other patients in the form of higher hospital bills. The county taxpayers also pick up a higher property tax bill when indigent medical care bills are added to the rolls.

Addressing the issues of spiraling Medicaid costs was a top priority of the National Governors Association in their July 2002 meeting in Boise. The governors called for an 18-month federal bailout for states suffering from budget shortfalls and a weakening economy. Bush administration officials replied that shifting dollars does not solve problems, and such federal help was not forthcoming. The Idaho Legislature responded by commissioning a study to find ways to cut Medicaid costs. It concluded few savings could be made without major service reductions. This is clearly an issue that has no readily apparent cost effective solution, despite a presence on the national as well as the state agenda.

Gambling and tribal relations

As in so many other places, there have been disputes over the amount and location of tribal lands in Idaho. In the 1980s and 1990s jurisdictional questions arose in northern Idaho. The Coeur d'Alene Tribe won, and the Nez Perce Tribe lost federal cases in which they was seeking jurisdiction in areas claimed also by non-tribal governments. Disputes have occurred over the years in southern Idaho, too. The Shoshone-Bannock Fort Hall Reservation was said, at one time, to include virtually the entire city of Pocatello.

The treaty-making process that began almost 40 years before statehood "reduced their once vast domain to a few widely scattered reservations." Reservation life forced a transition to an agrarian way of life from "a hunting and a gathering way of life."[3] Other intrusions on Indian property and lifestyle included land rushes (especially on the Nez Perce Reservation in northern Idaho) that further reduced the size of the reservations.

Along with jurisdictional disputes and land rushes, issues have included fishing rights, taxation policies, and more recently, reservation gambling. Gambling has become a significant issue. The tribes, whose reservations have a poverty-ridden history, point out that their reservation casinos have brought additional revenues to the tribes; they have used the money to upgrade tribal schools and medical and social services, and to seed a variety of other economic ventures, turning the tribes into substantial and broad-based economic entities. Four of the five Indian tribal organizations in Idaho—the Coeur d'Alenes, the Nez Perce, the Kootenai and the Shoshone-Bannocks—established casinos on their reservations in the 1990s. In the Idaho Panhandle, Indian gaming has been one of the major employers in the area.[4]

The history of gambling in Idaho is very complex. The original Idaho Constitution is sternly anti-gambling, completely banning nearly all forms of gaming. The decades that followed statehood saw repeated attempts at finding loopholes in the constitutional language. In the 1940s and 1950s, slot machines appeared in many Idaho cities, which had an incentive to allow them as major contributors (by way of licensing fees) to infrastructure funding. The Idaho Legislature passed laws regulating the machines, but to no avail. It was not until slot machines were declared unconstitutional by an Idaho Supreme Court decision in 1953 that their use was generally discontinued. The legality of gambling remained a hot political topic, and Democratic nominees for governor supported major pro-gambling planks in 1958 and 1962. In 1958, Democrat and pro-gambling candidate, Al Derr came within 5,000 votes of defeating the Republican incumbent Robert E. Smylie, but—maybe indicatively—he was the only Democrat to lose a bid for statewide office that year. Most other Democratic candidates in that era (such as Senator Frank Church) declared themselves anti-gambling, and Republicans were almost all anti-gambling.

Idaho voters have been fickle on gaming. "In 1953 they voted for anti-gambling candidates, the Legislature outlawed slot machines, and the Supreme Court declared the acts unconstitutional. A generation later, in 1988, they voted for a state lottery."[5]

Actually, the voters supported lotteries twice in the 1980s. In 1986 they backed a lottery initiative aimed at setting up a state lottery, only to see it thrown out by the Idaho Supreme Court as violating the constitution. This statutory initiative clashed with two Idaho Constitutional prohibitions. Two years later, the voters passed a constitutional amendment to allow for a lottery, and the games began a year later. The legislative measures were intended to allow certain types of gambling, bingo and the statewide lottery by specifying the exceptions to prohibition,while the amendment specifically was intended to deny casino type authority to Native Americans and anyone else. But it did not work out that way. The enactment in 1988 of the federal Indian Gaming Regulatory Act gave Indians the authority to use the same class of gaming as the state government authorized. The tribes said their electronic gaming devices were the same as some of the state's "green machines" authorized under the lottery.

Tribal relations with the rest of Idaho were again tense in the 1990s. The Nez Perce Tribe was involved with several jurisdictional court cases, not the least of which was a claim to a large amount of Snake River water for fish protection. (That water was critical to farmers and others for irrigation and other purposes upstream.) The

Coeur d'Alene Tribe in the Panhandle had for years sought control of Lake Coeur d'Alene; a 1998 federal court case decided in Boise, and reaffirmed by the United States Supreme Court, gave the Tribe control of the southern third of the lake. The Tribe and other regional interests then began sifting through possibilities for how the lake will be governed in the years ahead.

In the late 1990s , the Idaho Legislature, at Governor Batt's urging, passed legislation creating a new Indian Affairs Council. The purpose of the Council is to establish a permanent framework for ongoing discussions between the tribes and the State of Idaho. Under the Batt administration, the tribes were given more access to the governor and his top administrators than in previous administrations. Batt, the father of the Idaho Human Rights Commission, made communications with the tribe a top priority and met with tribal representatives on a monthly basis.[6]

Batt opposed tribal gaming when he first became governor, but came to the view that controlled gambling on Indian reservations was preferable to wide open casino type gambling. He also recognized that the state had provided the tribes no economic alternative to gaming, as many elected officials had promised when they supported a 1992 constitutional amendment aimed at prohibiting most tribal gaming.

A 2000 compact negotiated between the Sho-Ban tribe and Governor Dirk Kempthorne included an agreement that each would waive its sovereign immunity in order to arrive at a final judicial determination of the legal status of the games and devices. The state and the tribes waived their sovereign immunity in order to allow a federal judge to determine whether, under Idaho state law, the Sho-Bans could use the gaming machines being played on other reservations in the state. Fearing an adverse decision, the northern tribes opposed the compact. Lewiston state Senator Joe Stegner said he opposed it because "the state has evolved to a level of gaming not through any conscious decision-making process, but through a series of federal law and federal court cases."[7]

The northern tribes, much more heavily invested in gaming than the Shoshone-Bannocks, went back to the table. Over 14 months, they and Kempthorne's office hammered out a new compact. Legislation sponsored by Governor Andrus in 1993 had authorized the governor to negotiate without legislative approval. (The 2001 Legislature would eliminate that authority.) The agreement set limits on the number and type of tribal gambling machines, required that five percent of profits would be dedicated for social and educational purposes, waived sovereign immunity, and banned expansion of gaming off reservation land. Andrus and Batt supported the compact as a containment strategy to slow the proliferation of gaming. Sectional differences were evident in this issue, not only from the standpoint of the general population, but also the tribes. In expressing his support for the compact, Senate Pro Tempore Bob Geddes, from southeastern Idaho, emphasized the need to get gaming under control and thought the compact was the best vehicle available. But Geddes also made it clear that his conservative constituents would like to prohibit all types of gaming.

This second compact passed the House but was killed in the Senate largely due to the efforts of then Senate Majority Leader Jim Risch who said the Senate should defeat the "harlotry of casino gambling." He strongly maintained that there was no difference between the "tribal gaming devices" and slot machines. He was convinced that the state would have the superior position as it had four other times in court, and boasted that "we are 4 and 0 against the Indians." Senator Judi Danielson, who had supported the compact, said that the senators needed to recognize that they were dealing with sovereign nations and that should make a difference.[8] However, the compact died in the Senate, 16-19. Generally, legislators from northern and southwestern Idaho were in support and legislators from southeastern Idaho were opposed.

In 2002, the tribes and their supporters gathered over 40,000 signatures to place on the ballot an initiative which mirrored most of the compact provisions. The base date for tribal gaming machines was set at January 1, 2002, when about 3,000 machines were operated by the tribes. That number could increase by 25 percent annually for the next 10 years. (The failed compact set the number at 15 percent growth annually over 10 years.) The initiative passed with a 58 percent majority vote in November 2002.

Idahoans appear to support the state lottery, not only with their dollars but also with their votes.[9] Efforts to stop gambling operations on reservations have not been successful. With the growth of revenues on the reservation have come funds for the tribes to hire some of the state's most effective lobbyists to protect their interests in the Legislature. Tribes have become a major political force in the state.

INL AND NUCLEAR WASTE:
ENVIRONMENT AND ECONOMIC DEVELOPMENT

Economic development and environmental protection have alternated as major priorities in public opinion polls. Idahoans have often listed as a major concern the protection of the environment. They voted out of office an incumbent governor in 1970, Don Samuelson, because he supported open pit mining in the White Clouds and his opponent Cecil Andrus did not. Environmental protection was clearly a major factor in the race.

Environmental discussion has remained a hot topic in Idaho, but it has changed focus over the years with the future of one of its major installations in doubt.

In July 2002, Energy Secretary Spencer Abraham announced in Idaho Falls that the Idaho National Engineering and Environmental Laboratory (recently renamed the Idaho National Laboratory) would become the center for nuclear research in the United States. The Abraham plan proposed a Generation IV nuclear reactor to be built by 2030, an Idaho Advanced Fuel Cycle Technology Initiative—cutting the nuclear waste stream—and a nuclear fuel transportation upgrade. The plan also addressed environmental concerns such as the threats of nuclear accidents and terrorism, and the need for improved storage of long-term waste.

This was a major announcement in Idaho because of uncertainty surrounding the role and mission of the installation. The Idaho National Laboratory is one of the major employers in the state and one of the dominant forces in the region, and the future of INL has been a major concern for many years, especially since the employment base has sharply declined in recent years (it fell by about half in the 1990s). In the early part of the 21st century both residents and site administrators asked what would be its next mission, and whether it would even survive.

Despite the positive tone of Abraham's announcement, many Idahoans were skeptical. Abraham had not been the first cabinet official to make such a positive declaration. Former Energy Secretary Bill Richardson had declared that the site would become the national lead nuclear lab, but there was no financial backing or other follow-through. The Labratory has been the site of significant nuclear reactor technology development in the U.S., but it has some credibility problems given the location of its waste over the aquifer that serves much of South Central and Southwestern Idaho. An effective program for the removal of buried waste has been the subject of extensive debate over the years. Both Andrus and Batt negotiated agreements to get the waste out. Both agreements were unique in the United States.

The handling of the nuclear waste storage issue got Governor Phil Batt into hot political water in the first week of his administration in 1995; in fact, the subject of nuclear waste dominated his first two years in office.

For almost seven years, Batt's predecessor, Governor Cecil Andrus, vigorously opposed federal government demands to ship more nuclear waste to Idaho. He took the federal government to court and succeeded in imposing a ban of shipments to Idaho. But Batt concluded that Idaho could not continue to stop shipments into the state, especially when the Navy raised the issue that a continued ban would jeopardize national security. He also was concerned about the impact stopping nuclear shipments might have on the future of the installation. When he negotiated on this issue controversy erupted in Idaho, and Batt had to make clear that he did not want Idaho to become a nuclear waste dump. Then he re-started negotiations, and finally in 1995 reached an agreement with the Department of Energy, in which Idaho would accept some more shipments temporarily, but all of the nuclear waste would have to be removed from Idaho over a 30-year period. That agreement was not universally accepted around Idaho. One activist group mounted an initiative campaign aimed at voicing opposition. The voters, however, supported Batt, giving his agreement a 62.5 percent vote of approval.

The landmark 1995 agreement between the Department of Energy and the State of Idaho is predicated on locating a permanent site. That has made Idaho an active player in the national debate over funding a permanent nuclear waste repository.

Yucca Mountain in Nevada has been targeted as that permanent site. The passage of the federal legislation over the veto of Nevada Governor Kenny Guinn has provided the authority for a single permanent repository for high level nuclear waste. Nevadans remain strongly opposed, however, and may continue to try to block the Yucca Mountain activity.[10]

Nationally, no nuclear reactors have been started since 1979, the year of the disaster at Three Mile Island. In Idaho, attitudes toward nuclear energy depend on state geography. Eastern Idaho sees it as a major economic development factor; Southwestern and Magic Valley Idahoans are concerned about the storage of waste over the Snake River Plain Aquifer. But national attitudes may dictate, and even if the administration follows through on its promise to make the INL the nation's center for nuclear research, it is unclear how much it will mean.

SOCIAL ISSUES—ABORTION

Idahoans support individual freedom when it comes to economic endeavors, but are less consistent about governmental intervention into private lives. Idaho's most publicized venture into the social issue arena was over anti-abortion legislation.

House Bill 625, passed by the Idaho Legislature in 1990, would have been the most restrictive abortion statute in the country. At the time, national debate on abortion was at a peak. Changes in membership on the United States Supreme Court had resulted in limiting the effect of the 1973 *Roe v. Wade* decision and encouraging pro-life, anti-abortion forces nationally and in Idaho, especially in the case of *Webster v. Reproductive Health Services.* The 1990 legislative session opened with expectations that abortion would be a dominant issue, and it was. The national "right to life" organization had targeted Idaho as one of the most likely states to enact a restrictive anti-abortion law.[11]

An extensive list of legislation across the philosophical spectrum was considered, often at crowded, emotional and heavily packed committee hearings. The interest level was so high that two hearings were moved from the Statehouse to a large auditorium at Boise State University. Some measures would have weakened the state's existing laws against abortion (which held that if *Roe v. Wade* were overturned, harsh penalties would be exacted against most of the participants in an abortion). But most attention went to proposals aimed at toughening Idaho's law even under *Roe v. Wade,*[12] a move which seemed possible under then-recent U.S. Supreme Court decisions.

The measure that gained majority support in the House State Affairs Committee, House Bill 625, would have represented the cutting edge of the anti-abortion movement; legal tests on it almost certainly would have gone to the United States Supreme Court. (That was precisely why the national right to life proponents were so interested in finding a state like Idaho: to test the extent to which attitudes on the Court had changed.) House Bill 625 passed both houses, following bitter and emotional debates.

Attention then focused on Democratic Governor Cecil Andrus, who faced re-election that year. His office was promptly deluged with phone calls and written messages—and who, while declaring himself pro-life, said he had some concerns with the bill. Rallies on both sides of the issue were held outside the Statehouse and national representatives from pro-choice and pro-life organizations promised nationwide boycotts of Idaho commodities depending on what action Andrus took on the bill. Finally, Andrus pounded his veto stamp.

A widely held perception at that time was that pro-life attitudes held a strong majority in Idaho, and pro-choice was in the minority. That turned out not to be so. Self-selecting telephone surveys showed more than 90 percent of respondents calling for a veto, and public opinion surveys indicated the voters preferred the issue be decided by a referendum vote rather than by the Legislature. More scientific surveys showed smaller but still substantial anti-bill sentiment. That fall, Andrus coasted to a landslide win, and Democrats (most of whom had supported the veto) had their best election year in Idaho in three decades. In contrast, the lead sponsor of the bill, Republican Senator Roger Madsen of Boise, lost his seat to a Democrat in an overwhelmingly Republican district; and several other key backers of the bill either lost their seats or barely won re-election.

This massive debate over abortion, and the split results on the subject in the Legislature and in the voting booth, point out the conflict between the individualistic and moralistic elements in Idaho's political culture—a characteristic of the divided state. Idahoans tend to be more economically oriented conservatives rather than social conservatives. The libertarian strain in Idaho politics tends to influence citizens to support measures that promote less governmental intervention in the economy and in people's lives. The abortion debate highlighted the importance of religion and sectionalism in Idaho's political culture, and showed why neither the moralistic nor the individualistic political cultures have predominated. It also pointed out some deep fissures in the Republican party where the religious right has tried to make the abortion votes litmus tests in Republican primaries. In the 2004 primary, the issues were Republican moderate legislator votes against anti-gay marriage legislation and support of a sales tax increase. All of the moderates won.

Chapter14 notes

1   Charles Mahtesian, Phil Batt: Unlikely Crusader," *Governing* (June 1996), p.88.

2   2004 Idaho Legislative Budget Book.

3   Carlos Schwantes, *In Mountain Shadows* (Lincoln, NE: University of Nebraska Press, 1991), p. 14

4   Betsy Z. Russell, "Tribes disappointed, but they won't give up," The *Idaho Spokesman Review*, February 28, 2001, pp. 1-2 (The Handle).

5   Carlos Schwantes, *In Mountain Shadows*, p. 16.

6   Betsy Z. Russell, "Senate moves to have a say on tribal compacts," The *Idaho Spokesman Review*, March 1, 2001, pp. 1-2 (The Handle).

7   Brian Peters, "Idaho lawmakers scotched the gaming compact that the governor and three state tribes had pieced together," Lewiston Morning Tribune, April 21, 2001, p. 1.

8   Randy Stapilus, "Senate Rejects Indian Gaming Pact; Agreement between governor, three tribes falls on Senate floor," Lewiston Morning Tribune, March 27, 2001, p. 6.

9   Idaho Public Policy Survey, 1998, p. 52.

10 "Move ahead on Yucca Mountain," Chicago Tribune editorial reprinted in The *Times-News* (Twin Falls, ID), March 8, 2002, p. 8.

11 Stephanie L. Witt and Gary Moncrief, "Religion and Roll-Call Voting in Idaho: *The 1990 Abortion Controversy,*" in *Understanding the New Politics of Abortion*, ed. Malcolm L. Goggin (Newbury Park: Sage Publications, 1998), pp. 123-133.

12 *Roe v. Wade,* 410 U.S. 113 (1973)

EPILOGUE

I daho's general election of 2002 arrived under conditions most incumbents would dread—and ordinarily with good reason.

The economy had tanked. The "dot-com" collapse at the opening of the millennium combined with continued losses in the resource industries to generate almost daily reports of layoffs and business closures. Starting in the spring of 2001, some of Idaho's largest employers in both public and private sectors either shuttered their doors or scaled back, and the bad news continued month after month. Unemployment shot up to levels Idaho had not seen since the early 1990s.

The state revenue picture was gloomy, and it became clear that either massive spending cuts or major tax increases lay ahead—a situation complicated by a $111 million tax cut passed by the 2001 Idaho Legislature. Now the incumbent Republican legislators and statewide elected officials, including Governor Dirk Kempthorne, were on the hot seat, defending the tax cut while attempting to come to grips with the state's economic quandary. (Only after the election did Kempthorne release his proposal: an increase of 1.5 cents in the sales tax, and a massive increase in the state tobacco tax.)

Elected officials were being criticized on other grounds as well. Party caucuses in the Idaho Legislature historically had been closed, but now Republicans so dominated the Legislature that a closed-door Republican caucus in either chamber was tantamount to the whole chamber meeting behind closed doors. Kempthorne's actions in late 2001 to step up security around the Statehouse—actions mostly reversed over the course of the next year—were highly unpopular. Lawmakers explicitly overturned a voter initiative on term limits, and a ballot issue to reinstate the initiative was on the 2002 general election ballot. So was a proposal to set in place a state policy allowing some gambling on Indian reservations in the state, a proposal which closely matched a state-tribal agreement negotiated earlier by the tribes and Governor Kempthorne—but rejected by the Idaho Senate in 2001. That new 2002 initiative proved to be extremely popular.

Critics of the incumbency had more material to work with than they had in a generation fashioning an argument for the voters to reject their leaders. And the opponents of the Republican incumbents, Democrats and in some cases others as well, pointed out the need for change, loudly and repeatedly, through 2002. In many states, and in earlier years in Idaho, conditions milder than these would lead to sweeping changes.

On election day, however, very little changed.

Kempthorne was re-elected, but with only 56 percent of the vote, far less than the 68 percent he received in 1998 and without the support of his home county, populous Ada County.

Republicans retained unanimous control of the congressional delegation and all the statewide elected offices save one; and almost all of those Republicans won in landslides.

Perhaps the most interesting races in Idaho in 2002 were the two ballot measures. Neither outcome fits the typical stereotype of this conservative state. Proposition 1 was intended to ratify current gaming on Indian lands. It passed by a 58 percent margin rolling up majorities in southwestern and northern Idaho counties, while conservative southeastern Idaho opposed it.

With a razor-thin majority, Idaho voters did the unexpected—they threw out term limits by voting yes on Proposition 2. Idaho's term limits law, passed as an initiative in 1994, was radical, the most far-reaching measure of its kind in the United States, capping gubernatorial terms all the way down to local school board members. In early 2002, the Idaho Legislature became the first in the country to repeal a term limits initiative. Angry term limit backers successfully placed the repeal proposition on the November ballot. This was the first Idaho referendum that proposed to repeal a repeal of a state law. That created the double-negative ballot question—do you support the repeal of term limits? Yes meant no to term limits. No meant yes. Were the voters confused? Term limit opponents say no. Proponents, who had extolled the wisdom of voters say yes.

And while Democrats did pick up seats in the Idaho Legislature, it remained overwhelmingly Republican, and little changed from the year before on taxes and other issues.

Most of the preceding suggests Idaho government and politics, in general, is unlikely to change dramatically in the years immediately ahead. If voters had any interest in swapping horses, they had a case for doing so in 2002—and opted not to make that switch.

Idaho has gone through periods of turmoil, and other periods of relative stasis. In the new millennium, the Gem State seems firmly ensconced in the latter.

Moreover, some of the factors that led to cupheaval in the past have diminished in significance. Labor and other constituencies that have periodically worked against conservative incumbents have diminished in size, and the state's regions, historically so important a component and roiling factor in the state's politics, have become somewhat less important as they become more alike. Even so, differences still remain as evidenced in the vote on Indian gaming.

To be sure, this lack of change is in many ways a reflection of much of what Idaho is and has been: a conservative state. Most major office holders now, as in the past, are conservative, especially in fiscal matters, whether Democrat or Republican. Over the last several decades taxing and spending patterns have reflected a preference for a balanced, stable tax structure and the maintenance of relatively low governmental spending levels with only incremental changes in either. Idaho rarely sticks out as being the most stingy in the spending categories or lowest in the tax categories. Reflecting an individualistic political culture and appreciation for the individualism that characterized the frontier, Idahoans still prefer to avoid many regulatory controls that are present in other states. (Ironic, in fact, since local governments in Idaho have less local control than seen in most other states.)

Public opinion polls seem to document that Idaho is one of the most, if not the most, conservative state in the country—though what that conservatism means is a matter of ongoing debate. It is not the most conservative on taxes (the 2001 legislative actions notwithstanding). Idaho-style conservatism seems better reflected in the strong emphasis among elected officials on property rights, especially water rights, and in the absence of legislative activism. Idaho legislators and most of their constituents usually resist major change from either the left or the right. As far as policy is concerned, even though there are moralistic strains in Idaho politics, the reluctance of legislators to impose mandates on the private sector is evident. Conservatism shows up in the very strong influence of the corporate sector, but is periodically countered by a budding populism that arises from time to time. It also shows up in the constraints on government action repeatedly imposed by the state's electorate. Constraints that make Idaho government, especially local government, one of the the most tightly controlled in the country.

A special case can be made for the conservatism of Idaho governors regardless of political predisposition. Idaho governors over the last 50 years have generally governed from the center of the political spectrum. The vocal, extra-conservatives in Idaho politics have served in the Congress or in the Legislature but not in the governor's office, whether they are Democrats or Republicans.

Idaho, last of the 48 contiguous states to be seen by European-Americans and one of the last settled, ever-remote and still a misunderstood enigma to many, is today one of the nation's fastest-growing states. It has seen massive in-migration, largely from politically, culturally and socially conservative people seeking "their own kind."

The composition of the population will change as Idaho is projected to gray more quickly than the rest of the country and as it increases its percentage of Hispanic citizens above the national average.

This last frontier has been the safe haven for disaffected coastal conservatives. But what will these conservatives want? What will their priorities suggest about Idaho's future, and how might those priorities differ from those of the natives?

The new residents migrating in search of a tranquil "quality of life" in Idaho also bring with them high public service expectations which may conflict with their conservative inclinations. Their homes either strain general-purpose government services or give rise to more special purpose governments.

When all these pressures, and others currently unforeseen, eventually force change in Idaho politics and government, as eventually they will, Idaho will take another dramatic turn.

The Idahoans of that day will be able to reflect that their state has had plenty of such experience.

C. W. Cornell

This statue of Governor Frank Steunenberg stands in a park, facing the Idaho Statehouse. Steunenberg was killed by an assassin's bomb outside his Caldwell home, in December 1905.

BIBLIOGRAPHICAL ESSAY

In 1988, one of the authors of this book wrote a general history of Idaho government and politics over the previous half-century. The book is titled *Paradox Politics* (Stapilus, 1988). Part of the reason the book was written was that no one had done such a thing, at least not for many years. The student of Idaho politics had little recourse except (as the author did) to go to the original source materials, and the memories of the many people interviewed. The most recent Idaho political biographies are about Governor C. Ben Ross (Malone, 1970) and former Senator Glen Taylor (Peterson, 1974), figures whose active years were nearly a half-century in the past.

The situation has changed drastically in recent years. Biographies or autobiographies about many of Idaho's major political leaders have emerged in the last decade. Books by or about the careers of Governor Cecil Andrus (Andrus, 1998), Governor Robert Smylie (Smylie, 1998) Governor Don Samuelson (Samuelson, 1995), Senator Frank Church (Ashby and Gramer, 1994), veteran public official Perry Swisher (Swisher, 1995) and others have appeared at a steady pace.

Idaho's 1990 centennial celebration resulted in publication of a wide range of books about the state, ranging from oral history (Stacy, 1990) to a history of the state's court system (Bianchi, 1990) to a study of the formation of the state's constitution (Colson, 1991) and Idaho's governors (1992).

There are several useful general-purpose histories of Idaho. One of those recommended is Carlos Schwante's *In Mountain Shadows: A History of Idaho* (University of Nebraska Press, 1991), a brief but thoughtful (and well-illustrated) overview of the state's development.

General public affairs research has also expanded in recent years. The University of Idaho for many years has developed reports on Idaho elections, political trends and related subjects. Boyd Martin's *Idaho Voting Trends: Party Realignment and Percentage of Votes for*

Candidates, Parties and Elections 1890-1974, is the essential standard reference for voting trends up to the mid-seventies. The University's Bureau of Public Affairs Research has also published many biennial voting trend reports.

The Department of Public Policy and Administration at Boise State University has in more recent years also become highly active in public affairs areas. The Department has produced handbooks that are widely used by officials throughout Idaho: the *Idaho Municipal Source Book* and the *Handbook for Elected County Officials*. It also publishes the *Idaho Legislative Manual*. Boise State's Social Science Research Center publishes the *Idaho Public Policy Survey*.

Some private organizations conduct research or produce reference materials on Idaho government. The Associated Taxpayers of Idaho produces reports on taxes and budgets in Idaho that often are used as reference materials by governmental entities. The state associations of cities and counties also produce reports of use to their members and the public.

State documents generally are open for public access under the state's public records law. Students of politics and government can find a wealth of materials at the Idaho Historical Society, where the papers of former governors and many other officials are located. The Idaho State Library also has an extensive collection of state documents, many going back several decades. The papers of some prominent Idaho politicians (notably those of Senator Frank Church and Governor Cecil Andrus) can be found at the Albertson Library at Boise State University. Official state election records can be found at the Idaho Secretary of State's office; election returns from recent years are available on the website of that office.

The state's university libraries at the University of Idaho, Boise State University and Idaho State University contain collections of master's and doctoral theses on political and governmental matters in Idaho.

The Idaho Historical Society is the best source for back issues of Idaho newspapers. All but a few of Idaho's newspapers, from statehood and even earlier, are available there on microfilm. The Society publishes a quarterly magazine, *Idaho Yesterdays*, which contains articles on Idaho history.

There are numerous state documents that provide excellent source material for political research. The Idaho Supreme Court and Court of Appeals decisions are contained in the *Idaho Reports*. Current opinions are included in the judiciary's web site.

A number of executive branch agencies produce important governmental documents. The Department of Commerce annually publishes the *County Profiles of Idaho* that contain social, economic and natural resource data on Idaho's 44 counties. The Secretary of State's office biennially publishes the *Idaho Blue Book*. This is an excellent guide to the history and contemporary structure of state and local governments in Idaho. Information is also provided on all the agencies, boards and commissions.

The governor's office produces several related budget documents that provide a wealth of information on state government. There is considerable information on revenue sources and expenditure history as well as information on the organizational structure of each agency. *Attorney General's Opinions* are annually published; they include both formal opinions and informal guidelines.

There are several sources for information related to the lawmaking process. The *Idaho Code* is a comprehensive collection of Idaho laws and is annually updated with a pocket supplement. The *Code* is published by the Michie Company of Charlottesville, Virginia. The laws enacted by each session prior to codification are published in the *Session Laws*. These laws are also available on the website as are the legislative rules and journals of proceedings. The journals are a record of the daily proceedings.

An excellent reference on the state fiscal operation is the *Fiscal Facts*. It contains historical as well as current data on revenue and expenditure patterns. *Fiscal Facts* also includes a good deal of information on state and local revenue formulas.

A good overall reference on state and local government is contained in *The Idaho Citizens Guide*. In addition to a glossary, it contains discussion of the structure and operations of state government. The political aspects of state government, as well as an exploration of the political aspects of state government.

BIBLIOGRAPHY

Alm, Leslie R., Ross E. Burkhart, W. David Patton, and James B.
  Weatherby, "Intra-state Regional Differences in Political Culture: A
  Case Study of Idaho." State and Local Government Review 33, no. 2
  (spring 2001): 109-119.

Andrus, Cecil, and Joel Connelly. *Politics Western Style*. Seattle: Sasquatch
  Books, 1998.

Anton, Thomas. *American Federalism and Public Policy: How the System
  Works*. Philadelphia: Temple University Press, 1999.

Arrandale, Tom. "Can Polluters Police Themselves." Governing (June 1997):
  36-39.

Arrington, Leonard J. *History of Idaho*. Vol. 2. Moscow, ID: University of
  Idaho Press, 1994.

Ashby, Leroy, and Rod Gramer. *Against All Odds: The Life of Senator
  Frank Church,* Pullman, WA: Washington State University Press,
  1994.

Association of Idaho Cities. "Results: The Cities and the 1997 Legislature,"
  Idaho Cities (1997).

Barone, Michael. "Divide and Rule." *National Journal*, no. 28 (12 July
  1997): 1411.

Barrett, Glen. *Idaho Banking: 1863-1976*. Boise, ID: Boise State University,
  1976.

Batt, Phillip E., Governor of Idaho. State of the State Address. Boise, 1995.

Benedict, Robert C., and Ronald J. Hrebenar. "Political Parties, Elections
  and Campaigns, I: The Legal and Political Setting." *Politics and
  Public Policy in the Contemporary American West*. Albuquerque, N.M.:
  University of New Mexico Press, 1991.

Berman, David R. *Arizona Politics and Government: The Quest for
  Autonomy, Democracy, and Development*. Lincoln, NE: University of
  Nebraska Press, 1998.

Bianchi, Carl F., ed. *Justice for the Times*. Boise, ID: Idaho Law Foundation,
  1990.

Bish, Robert L., and Vincent Ostrom. *Understanding Urban Government*.
  Washington, D.C.: Domestic Affairs Studies, 1973.

Blank, Robert H. *Regional Diversity of Political Values: Idaho Political
  Cultures*.Washington, D.C.: University Press of America, 1978.

Bowman, Ann O'M., and Richard C. Kearney. *State and Local Government*.
  Boston: Houghton Mifflin, Co., 2002.

Brunori, David. *Local Tax Policy: A Federalist Perspective*. Washington,
  DC: The Urban Institute Press, 2004.

Bunderson, Harold R. *Idaho Entrepreneurs Profiles in Business*. Boise, ID: Boise State University, 1992.

Burgess, Philip M., and Richard F. O'Donnell. *Western Political Outlook*. Denver: Center for the New West, 1998.

Coles, H. Brent, Mayor of Boise. "State of the City." September 13, 1994.

Colson, Dennis C. *Idaho's Constitution: The Ties That Bind*. Moscow, ID: University of Idaho Press, 1991.

Conlan, Timothy, James D. Riggle, and Donna E. Schwartz, "The Unfunded Mandates Reform Act of 1995," Publius: The Journal of Federalism (summer 1995).

Conley, Cort. *Idaho for The Curious*. Cambridge, ID: Backeddy Books, 1982.

------. *Idaho Loners*. Cambridge, ID: Backeddy Books, 1994.

Crowley, Donald, and Florence Heffron. *The Idaho State Constitution: A Reference Guide*. Westport, CT: Greenwood Press, 1994.

Davis, William. "W. Lloyd Adams." *Idaho Yesterdays* (summer 1968).

Duncan, Dayton. *Miles from Nowhere*. New York: Viking, 1993.

Duncombe, Sydney. "City Administrators and City Supervisors." Moscow, Idaho: Bureau of Public Affairs Research and Municipal Research and Service Center, State of Washington.

------. "The Idaho Legislature." In *State and Local Government in Idaho: A Reader*, edited by Glenn Nichols, Ray C. Jolly, and Boyd A. Martin. Moscow, ID: University of Idaho, Bureau of Public Affairs Research, 1970.

Duncombe, Sydney, and Robert Weisel. *State and Local Government in Idaho and in the Nation*. Moscow, ID: University of Idaho Press, 1984.

Dye, Thomas. *Politics in States and Communities*. 8th ed. Englewood Cliffs, NJ: Prentice Hall, 994.

------. *Politics, Economics, and the Public: Policy Outcomes in the American States*. Chicago: Rand McNally, 1996.

Elazar, Daniel J. *American Federalism: A View from the States*. 2nd ed. New York: Harper & Row, 1984.

Erikson, Robert S., Gerald C. Wright, and John P. McIver. *Statehouse Democracy: Public Opinion and Policy in the American States*. New York: Cambridge University Press, 1993.

Foster, Richard H. "The Federal Government and the West." *In Politics and Public Policy*, edited by Clive Thomas. Albuquerque, NM: University of New Mexico Press, 1991.

Gilder, George. *The Spirit of Enterprise*. New York: Simon and Shuster, 1984.

Gray, Virginia, and Peter Eisinger. *American States and Cities*. New York: Longman, 1997.

Gray, Virginia, Russell L. Hanson, and Herbert Jacob, eds. *Politics in the American States: A Comparative Analysis*. 7th ed. Washington, DC: Congressional Quarterly Press, 1999.

Hall, Bill. *Frank Church and Me*. Pullman, WA: Washington State University Press, 1995.

Hrebenar, Ronald J., and Clive S. Thomas, eds. *Interest Groups in the American West*. Salt Lake City: University of Utah Press, 1987.

Harrigan, John J. *Politics and Policy in States and Communities.* New York: Harper Collins Publishers, 1991.

Hart, I.W. *Proceedings and Debates of the Constitutional Convention of Idaho.* Caldwell, ID: State of Idaho, Caxton Printers, 1913.

Idaho Universities Policy Research Group. *Idaho Tax Facts and Principles.* Boise State University, University of Idaho, Idaho State University. 1996.

Jochum, Linda. "The Changing Face of Idaho." Idaho Issues. Boise, ID: College of Social Sciences and Public Affairs, Boise State University, 1977.

Josephy, Alvin. *The Nez Perce Indians and the Opening of the Northwest.* New Haven, 1965.

Kempton, Jim (State Representative), and James B. Weatherby. *Interface 'of the people': An Overview of Growth Funding, Revolving Debt, and Representative Government.* Idaho State House of Representatives, State of Idaho, 1997.

Kincaid, John. "Developments in Federal-State Relations, 1990-91." The Book of the States,1992-93. Lexington, Kentucky.: Council of State Governments, 1992.

------ "The New Judicial Federalism: The States' Lead in Rights Protection." The Journal of State Government (April-June 1992): 50-52.

------"The State of U.S. Federalism, 2000-2001: Continuity in Crisis." Publius: The Journal of Federalism 31, no. 3 (summer 2001): 1-69.

Kleine, Robert J. *US State-Local Tax Systems: How Do They Rate?* Lansing, MI: Public Sector Consultants, 1992.

Lavender, David. *Let Me Be Free: The Nez Perce Tragedy.* New York: Harper Collins, 1992.

Limbaugh, Ronald H. *Rocky Mountain Carpetbaggers: Idaho's Territorial Governors.* Moscow, Idaho: University of Idaho Press, 1982.

Lovin, Hugh. "The Nonpartisan League and the Progressive Renascence in Idaho, 1919-24," *Idaho Yesterdays* (Fall 1988).

Lowery, David, and Lee Sigelman. "Understanding the Tax Revolt: An assessment of Eight Explanations." American Political Science Review 75 (1981): 963-974.

Lukas, J. Anthony. *Big Trouble.* New York: Simon & Shuster, 1997.

Lukens, Fred E. *The Idaho Citizen: A Textbook in Idaho Civics.* Caldwell, Idaho: The Caxton Printers, 1937.

Madsen, Brigham. *The Bannock of Idaho.* Caxton, 1958.

Malone, Michael. *C. Ben Ross and the New Deal in Idaho.* Seattle: University of Washington Press, 1970.

Martin, Boyd A. *The Direct Primary in Idaho.* Stanford: Stanford University Press, 1947.

------ "The Sectional State." *In Politics in the American West,* edited by Frank H. Jonas. Salt Lake City: University of Utah Press, 1969.

McCulloch, Anne Merlin. "The Politics of Indian Gaming: Tribe/State Relations and American Federalism," Publius: Journal of Federalism (summer 1994): 103.

McCulloch, Ann and J. Reinward. "The Mormon Influence in Idaho's
    Politics: A Rethinking of Elazar's Political Culture Model." Paper pre-
    sented at the 1988 Pacific Northwest Political Science Association
    Annual Meeting, Portland, Oregon, November 1988.
McKenna, Marian C. *Borah*. Ann Arbor, Michigan: University of Michigan
    Press.
Moncrief, Gary F. "Idaho: The Interests of Sectionalism." In *Interest Group
    Politics in the American West*, edited by Ronald Hrebenar and Clive
    Thomas. Salt Lake City: University of Utah Press, 1987.
------ "Idaho." Redistricting in the 1980's. Idaho Policy Survey, #5. Boise,
    Idaho: Survey Research Center, Boise State University, 1994.
Moore, Michael C. "Powers and Authorities of Idaho Cities: Home Rule or
    Legislative Control?" *Idaho Law Review* 14 (1977).
------ *Frontier Lewiston: 1861-1890* (Lewiston, Idaho: 1980).
------ "The Idaho Constitution and Local Governments - Selected Topics."
    Idaho Law Review 31, no. 2 (1995).
Morehouse, Sarah M. State Politics, *Party and Policy*. New York: Host,
    Rinehart and Winston, 1981.
Palmer, Tim. *The Snake River*. Washington, DC: Island Press, 1991.
Peirce, Neal R., and Jerry Hagstrom. *The Book of America: Inside Fifty
    States Today*. New York: Warner Books, 1984.
Peavey, John. "Government - Let the Sunshine." Idaho Cities. Boise, ID:
    Association of Idaho Cities, October 1974.
Peterson, Harold. *The Last of the Mountain Men*. Cambridge, ID: Backeddy
    Books, 1969.
Peterson, Keith. *Company Town: Potlatch Idaho and the Potlatch Lumber
    Company*. Pullman, Washington: Washington State University Press,
    1987.
Peterson, Ross. *Prophet Without Honor*. University Press of Kentucky, 1974.
Plastino, Ben. *Coming of Age: Idaho Falls and the Idaho National
    Engineering Laboratory*.Boise, Idaho: n.p., 1998.
Raymond, Gregory A. Idaho Policy Survey, #1. Boise, Idaho: Survey
    Research Center, Boise State University, 1990.
------ Idaho Policy Survey, #2. Boise, ID: Survey Research Center, Boise
    State University, 1991.
------ Idaho Policy Survey, #3. Boise, ID: Survey Research Center, Boise
    State University, 1992.
------ Idaho Policy Survey, #4. Boise, ID: Survey Research Center, Boise
    State University, 1993.
Ripley, Rich. *The Ridgerunner*. Cambridge, Idaho: Backeddy Books, 1987.
Saffell, David C., and Harry Basehart. Governing States and Cities. New
    York: The McGraw-Hill Companies, 1997.
Samuelson, Don. *His Hand on My Shoulder*. Sandpoint, Idaho: ParBest &
    Dickoens, 1995.
Schwantes, Carlos A. *In Mountain Shadows: A History of Idaho*. Lincoln,
    Nebraska: University of Nebraska Press, 1991.
Scudder, David R. Idaho Public Policy Survey, #8. Boise, Idaho: Social
    Science Research Center, Boise State University, 1997.

Scudder, David R., John Crank, and James B. Weatherby. Idaho Public
    Policy Survey #9. Boise, Idaho: Social Science Research Center, Boise
    State University, 1998.
Shaw, Stephen. "Harassment, Hate, and Human Rights in Idaho." In
    Politics in the Postwar American West, edited by Richard Lowitt.
    Norman, OK: University of Oklahoma Press, 1995.
Shaw, Stephen and James B. Weatherby. "Election Consolidation:
    Reforming the Reforms." Paper presented at the annual meeting of the
    Pacific Northwest Political Science Association, Boise, ID, November
    1989.
Shuler, Marilyn. "An Analysis of Legislative Role Behavior As An
    Alignment of Role, Reference Sources and Issue Definition in the Idaho
    Legislature: A Case Study of the 1975 Public School Kindergarten
    Law." Master of Public Administration Thesis, Boise State
    University, 1977.
Sims, Robert C., and Hope A. Benedict, eds. Idaho's Governors: Historical
    Essays on Their Administrations. Boise, ID: Boise State University,
    1992.
Smylie, Robert E. *Governor Smylie Remembers*. Moscow, ID: University of
    Idaho Press, 1998.
Sommers, Paul. "Consensus Report Denies Economy's Complexity."
    Northwest Region Watch. Newsletter of the Northwest Policy Center.
    Seattle, WA: University of Washington, 1996.
Stabrowski, Donald J. "Oregon," in Proceedings Roundtable: State
    Budgeting in the 13 Western States, by Robert Huefner, F. Ted
    Hebert, and Carl Mott (Western Political Science Association, 1998).
Stacy, Susan, ed. Conversations. Boise, ID: Idaho Public Television
    Broadcasting Foundation, 1990.
Stapilus, Randy. *Paradox Politics: People and Power in Idaho*. Boise, ID:
    Ridenbaugh Press, 1988.
------. "Lobbyists." *Boise Magazine*. (December 1990/Janaury 1991): 38-41.
------. *The Idaho Political Almanac*. Boise, ID: Ridenbaugh Press, 1992.
------. *The Idaho Political Almanac*. Boise, ID: Ridenbaugh Press, 1994.
------. *The Idaho Yearbook/Directory* 1998. Boise, ID: Ridenbaugh Press,
    1998.
State of Idaho, Division of Financial Management. "Idaho Economic
    Forecast." Vol. XVIII, no. 4. October 1996.
State of Idaho, Governor's Committee on Taxation. Idaho Taxes:
    Comparative Analysis, Evaluation and Recommendations. 1978.
State of Idaho, Idaho State Tax Commission. "Comparative Tax Burden
    Study." How Does Idaho Compare? Boise, ID: State of Idaho and
    Associated Taxpayers of Idaho, 1998.
State of Idaho, Legislative Services Office. "1998 Legislative Session
    Summary." April 1998.
State of Idaho, Legislative Services Office, Budget and Policy Analysis.
    Idaho Fiscal Facts 1997.
------. Idaho Fiscal Facts 2001.
------. Idaho Fiscal Facts 2002.

State of Idaho, Office of the Secretary of State. *Idaho Blue Book*: 1989-1990. Boise, ID, 1990.

------. *Idaho Blue Book*: 1993-1994. Boise, ID, 1994.

------. *Idaho Blue Book*: 1995-1996. Boise, ID, 1996.

------. *Idaho Blue Book*: 2003-2004. Boise, ID, 2004.

Swisher, Perry. *The Day Before Idaho*. Moscow, ID: News Review Publishing Co., 1995.

Taylor, Glen. *The Way It Was With Me*. Secauscus, NJ: Lyle Stuart, 1979.

Thomas, Clive. *Politics and Public Policy in the Contemporary American West*. Albuquerque, NM: University of New Mexico Press, 1991.

Thomas, Clive S., and Ronald J. Hrebenar. "Interest Groups in the States." In *Politics in the American States: A Comparative Analysis*, 5th ed., edited by Virginia Gray, Herbert Jacob, and Robert B. Albritton. Glenview, IL: Scott, Foresman/Little, Brown, 1990.

Tilove, Jonathan. "The New Map of American Politics." *The American Prospect* (May 1999).

U.S. Advisory Commission on Intergovernmental Relations. Measuring Local Discretionary Authority. Washington, D.C.: U.S. Government Printing Office, 1981.

------. State and Local Roles in the Federal System. Washington, D.C.: U.S. Government Printing Office, 1982.

------. Changing Public Attitudes on Governments and Taxes. Washington, D.C.:U.S. Government Printing Office, 1994.

University of Idaho, College of Agriculture. You and Your Community: Summary   Report of Impact of Older Immigrants on Idaho Small towns and Rural Communities. 1997.

Uranga, Jean R., Assistant Attorney General. "Attorney General Opinion No. 76-3." 20 January 1976.

Walker, Deward. *Indians of Idaho*. Moscow, ID: University of Idaho Press, 1978.

Walter, Jess. *Every Knee Shall Bow*. New York: Regan Books, 1995.

Watson, Sheilah, and Morgan, David R. "Political Culture, Political System Characteristics, and Public Policies Among the American States." Publius: *The Journal of Federalism* (spring 1991): 31-48.

Weatherby, James B. "Federal-State Relations." In State and Local Government in Idaho: A Reader, edited by Glenn W. Nichols, Ray C. Jolly, and Boyd A. Martin. Moscow, ID: Bureau of Public Affairs Research, University of Idaho, 1970.

------. "Idaho: Growth and Change in A Conservative State." Paper prepared for delivery at the American Political Science Association Annual Meeting, Washington, D.C., August 1997.

Weatherby, James B., ed. Idaho Legislative Manual 1998. Boise, ID: Center for Public Policy and Administration, Boise State University, 1998.

Weatherby, James B. and Glenn W. Nichols. "Interest Groups in Idaho Politics." In State and Local Government in Idaho: A Reader, edited by Glenn W. Nichols, Ray C. Jolly, and Boyd A. Martin. Moscow, ID: Bureau of Public Affairs Research, University of Idaho, 1970.

Weatherby, James B., and Lorna Jorgensen. The One Percent Initiative and Voter Attitutdes: A Comparison of 1978 and 1992. Boise, ID: Public Affairs Program, Boise State University, 1992.

------. Implementing California's Proposition 13 in Idaho: Is It Possible? Boise, ID: Public Affairs Program, Boise State University, 1992.

Weatherby, James B., and Stephanie L. Witt. Urban West: Managing Growth and Decline. Westport, CT: Praeger, 1994.

Weatherby, James B., Lorna Jorgensen, and W. David Patton. Idaho Cities: Funding Growth and Mandates. Boise, ID: Association of Idaho Cities and Boise State University, 1994.

Willmorth, Michael, Patricia Hyle, and David F. Scudder. Idaho Policy Survey, #7. Boise, ID: Social Science Research Center, Boise State University, 1996.

Witt, Stephanie L., "Idaho." In State Party Profiles: A 50-State Guide to Development, Organization, and Resources, edited by Andrew Appleton and Daniel S. Ward. Washington, D.C.: Congressional Quarterly, Inc., 1998.

Witt, Stephanie, and Gary Moncrief. "Abortion and the Idaho Legislature: The Vote on H625." Paper prepared for delivery at the 1990 annual meeting of the Pacific Northwest Political Science Association, Portland, Oregon, 8-10 November 1990.

------. "Religion and Roll-Call Voting in Idaho: The 1990 Abortion Controversy." In Understanding the New Politics of Abortion. Edited by Malcolm L. Goggin. Newbury Park: Sage Publications, 1993.

Witt, Stephanie, and Leslie R Alm. "Wise Use Movement." International Encyclopedia of Public Policy and Administration. New York: Henry Holt, 1996.

Zeigler, L. Harmon, and Michael Baer. Lobbying: Interaction and Influence in American State Legislatures. Belmont, CA: Wadsworth, 1969.

APPENDICES

Figure 1

Idaho

Idaho Blue Book
2003-2004 edition

Figure 2

2003 Organization Chart
Idaho State Government
State agencies based on gubernatorial appointment authority

Prepared by the Division of Financial Management

Legislative Branch

Senate - House of Representatives

Budget & Policy Analysis
Legislative Audits
Performance Evaluations
Research & Legislation

Executive Branch

Statewide Elected Officers

| Controller | Lieutenant Governor | Treasurer | Office of the Governor / Governor | Attorney General | Superintendent of Public Instruction | Secretary of State |

Agencies with Executive Appointed by the Governor

Education	Natural Resources	General Government	Health and Human Services	Economic Development	Transportation and Public Safety
Board of Education	Department of Fish and Game	Department of Administration	Dept. of Health & Welfare	Athletic Commission	Dept. of Juvenile Corrections
	Department of Water Resources	Division of Financial Management	Commission on Aging	Bureau of Occup. Licenses	Idaho State Police
	Department of Lands	Liquor Dispensary	Comm on Women's Programs	Department of Agriculture	Military Division
	Department of Parks and Recreation	Lottery Commission	Veterans Services	Dept of Commerce/Labor	State Appellate Public Defender
	Office of Species Conservation	Tax Commission		Department of Finance	
	Lava Hot Springs Foundation	Div. of Human Resources		Department of Insurance	
				Division of Building Safety	
				Public Utilities Commission	

Agencies with Executive Appointed by a Board

Education		General Government	Health and Human Services	Economic Development	Transportation and Public Safety
Boise State University		Board of Tax Appeals	Comm on Hispanic Affairs	Board of: Accountancy,	Correctional Industries
Commission on the Arts		Commission on Idaho Code	Comm on Human Rights	Dentistry, Engineers,	Dept. of Correction
Eastern Idaho Technical College		Commission on State Uniform Laws	Public Health Districts	Geologists, Optometry,	Transportation Dept.
Historical Society		Endowment Fund Investment Board	Commission for the Blind	Medicine, Nursing, Pharmacy,	
Idaho State University		Public Employee Retirement System	Vocational Rehabilitation	and Veterinary Medicine.	
Lewis-Clark State College				Brand Inspector	
Public Broadcasting				Certified Shorthand Reporters	
School for the Deaf and the Blind				State Insurance Fund	
State Library				Industrial Commission	
University of Idaho				Outfitters and Guides	
				Public Works Contractor's License	
				Racing Commission	
				Real Estate Commission	

Judicial Branch

Supreme Court

Court of Appeals
District Court
Guardian Ad Litem
Judges Retirement
Judicial Council
Law Library
Magistrate Court
Supreme court

TABLE 1 - LEGISLATIVE POLITICAL PARTY BREAKDOWN 1931–2005

Year	Senate Total	Republican	Democrat	House Total	Republican	Democrat
1931	44	23	21	70	43	27
1933	44	9	35	63	4	59
1935	44	8	36	59	6	53
1937	44	11	33	59	9	50
1939	44	27	17	59	39	20
1941	44	21	23	64	36	28
1943	44	31	13	59	32	27
1945	44	24	20	59	30	29
1947	44	31	13	59	42	17
1949	44	20	24	59	35	24
1951	44	29	15	59	36	23
1953	44	33	11	59	45	14
1955	44	24	20	59	36	23
1957	44	19	25	59	32	27
1959	44	17	27	59	24	35
1961	44	23	21	59	31	28
1963	44	23	21	63	34	29
1965	44	25	19	79	42	37
1967	35	22	13	70	38	32
1969	35	20	15	70	38	32
1971	35	19	16	70	41	29
1973	35	23	12	70	51	19
1975	35	21	14	70	43	27
1977	35	20	15	70	48	22
1979	35	19	16	70	50	20
1981	35	23	12	70	56	14
1983	35	21	14	70	51	19
1985	42	28	14	84	67	17
1987	42	26	16	84	64	20
1989	42	23	19	84	64	20
1991	42	21	21	84	56	28
1993	35	23	12	70	50	20
1995	35	27	8	70	57	13
1997	35	30	5	70	59	11
1999	35	31	4	70	58	12
2001	35	32	3	70	61	9
2003	35	28	7	70	54	16
2005	35	28	7	70	57	13

Source: *Idaho Blue Book 2003-2004, Idaho Secretary of State*

Table 2

GOVERNORS (1890 THROUGH PRESENT)
Party designations: ® Republican; (D) Democrat; (S.R.) Silver Republican; (P) Populist

Name/Party	Term of Office	Remarks
Shoup, George L. (R)	1890 to12/1890	Elected 1890, resigned to become U.S. Senator
Willey, N.B.(R)	12/1890 to 01/1893	Succeeded to office
McConnell, William J. (R)	01/1893 to 01/04/1897	Elected 1892; re-elected 1894
Steunenberg, Frank (P-D)	01/04/1897 to 01/07/1901	Elected 1896; re-elected 1898
Hunt, Frank W. (D)	01/07/1901 to 01/05/1903	Elected 1900
Morrison, John T. (R)	01/05/1903 to 01/02/1905	Elected 1902
Gooding, Frank R. (R)	01/03/1905 to 01/04/1909	Elected 1904; re-elected 1906
Brady, James H. (R)	01/04/1909 to 01/02/1911	Elected 1908
Hawley, James H. (D)	01/02/1911 to 01/06/1913	Elected 1910
Haines, John M. (R)	01/06/1913 to 01/04/1915	Elected 1912
Alexander, Moses (D)	01/04/1915 to 01/06/1919	Elected 1914; re-elected 1916
Davis, D.W. (R)	01/06/1919 to 01/01/1923	Elected 1918; re-elected 1920
Moore, Charles C. (R)	01/03/1923 to 01/03/1927	Elected 1922; re-elected 1924
Baldridge, H.C. (R)	01/03/1927 to 01/05/1931	Elected 1926; re-elected 1928
Ross, C. Ben (D)	01/05/1931 to 01/04/1937	Elected 1930; re-elected 1932, 1934
Clark, Barzilla W. (D)	01/04/1937 to 01/02/1939	Elected 1936
Bottolfsen, C.A. (R)	01/01/1939 to 01/06/1941	Elected 1938
Clark, Chase A. (D)	01/06/1941 to 01/04/1943	Elected 1940
Bottolfsen, C.A. (R)	01/04/1943 to 01/01/1945	Elected 1942
Gossett, Chas. C. (D)	01/01/1945 to 11/17/1945	Elected 1944; resigned 11/17/1945
Williams, Arnold (D)	11/17/1945 to 01/06/1947	Succeeded to office
Robins, Dr. C.A. (R)	01/06/1947 to 01/01/1951	Elected 1946
Jordan, Len B. (R)	01/01/1951 to 01/03/1955	Elected 1950
Smylie, Robert E. (R)	01/03/1955 to01/02/1967	Elected 1954; re-elected 1958, 1962
Samuelson, Don (R)	01/02/1967 to 01/04/1971	Elected 1966
Andrus, Cecil D. (D)	01/04/1971 to 01/24/1977	Elected 1970; re-elected 1974, resigned 01/24/1977
Evans, John V. (D)	01/24/1977 to 01/05/1987	Succeeded to office; elected 1978; re-elected 1982
Andrus, Cecil D. (D)	01/05/1987 to 01/02/1995	Elected 1986; re-elected 1990
Batt, Phil (R)	01/02/1995 to 01/04/1999	Elected 1994
Kempthorne, Dirk (R)	01/04/1999	Elected 1998; re-elected 2002

Source: *Idaho Blue Book 2003-2004*, Idaho Secretary of State

Table 3
LOCAL TAXING DISTRICTS

Taxing District or Authority	Total Statewide	Taxing District or Authority	Total Statewide
Ambulance	18	Levee	1
Auditorium	3	Library	56
Cemetery	180	Mosquito Abatement	12
City	201	Museum	0
Community College	2	Port	1
County	44	Recreation	30
Drainage	1	Regional Airport	0
Pest Control	5	School	114
Fire	147	Sewer	32
Flood Control	14	Sewer & Water	53
Highway – Country Road & Bridge	101	Water	26
Hospital	20	Watershed Improvement	10
		Total	1,071

Source: Idaho State Tax Commission 2003 Annual Report

Table 4

Idaho Ranked with Other States - Expenditures
(1+ Highest and 51+Lowest)

Exp. Comparisons	Per Capita	Per $1,000 Income
Direct General Expenditures	47	29
Elementary and Sec. Educ.	40	18
Higher Education	33	24
Public Welfare	39	31
Health and Hospitals	24	16
Highways	21	18
Police	33	21
Fire	39	35
Corrections	25	15
Sewerage	18	10
Natural Resources/Parks	16	9

Other Comparisons	Rank	Amount
State Population	39	1,343,000
Per Capita	44	24,962
Income Remaining After Taxes	14	90.18%

Source: 2002 – *How Does Idaho Compare?*, Associated Taxpayers of Idaho, 2004. (Expenditure data compiled from *2002 State and Local Government Finance* Report from the US Census Bureau. 2002 personal income data obtained from Bureau of Economic Analysis).

THE AUTHORS

James B. Weatherby is Chair and Associate Professor in the Department of Public Policy and Administration at Boise State University. He is a co-author of the book *The Urban West: Managing Growth and Decline*. He is co-editor of the *Idaho Municipal Sourcebook*. He is a former executive director of the Association of Idaho Cities and was a member of the Board of Directors of the National League of Cities. He has served on the faculty at the University of Idaho and Northwest Nazarene College.

Randy Stapilus has been a journalist, analyst and author in the region since 1974. An award-winning reporter and editor for daily newspapers in Boise, Pocatello, Nampa, Lewiston and Coeur d'Alene, Stapilus is also the author of a number of books, including *Paradox Politics*.

INDEX

Other books about Idaho
From CAXTON PRESS

Idaho's Historic Trails
ISBN 0-87004-432-x
6x9, 308 pages, paper, $13.95

J. R. Simplot
A Billion the Hard Way
ISBN 0-87004-399-4
6x9, 288 pages, cloth, $24.95

Cool North Wind
Morley Nelson's Life With Birds of Prey
ISBN 0-87004-426-5
6x9, 50 photographs, 458 pages, hardcover
$24.95

The Idanha
Guests and Ghosts of an Historic Idaho Inn
ISBN 0-87004-414-1
6x9, 222 pages, paper, $14.95

River Tales of Idaho
ISBN 0-87004-378-1
6x9, 344 pages, paper, $17.95

For a free catalog of Caxton books write to:

CAXTON PRESS
312 Main Street
Caldwell, ID 83605-3299

or

Visit our Internet Website:

www.caxtonpress.com

Caxton Press is a division of The CAXTON PRINTERS, Ltd.